MW01132233

THE STORY OF FRENCH NEW ORLEANS

THE STORY OF

FRENCH
New Orleans

History of a Creole City

Dianne Guenin-Lelle

University Press of Mississippi   Jackson

www.upress.state.ms.us

The University Press of Mississippi is a member
of the Association of American University Presses.

Artwork on p. 48 is by Michael Dixon.

First printing 2016

∞

Library of Congress Cataloging-in-Publication Data

Guenin-Lelle, Dianne.
  The story of French New Orleans : history of a creole city / Dianne Guenin-Lelle.
    pages cm
  Includes index.
    ISBN 978-1-4968-0486-0 (hardback : alkaline paper) — ISBN 978-1-4968-0487-7
  (e-book) 1. New Orleans (La.) — History. 2. New Orleans (La.) — Civilization. 3.
  New Orleans (La.) — Social life and customs. 4. France — Colonies — America — History. 5. French — America — History. 6. United States — Civilization — French influences. I. Title.
  F379.N557G84 2016
  976.3'35 — dc23
                    2015020151

British Library Cataloging-in-Publication Data available

TO MARK, HANNAH,
AND AUSTIN

CONTENTS

ACKNOWLEDGMENTS

Craig Gill in many ways began this project by his interest in my research and his invitation to begin a conversation with him about my work. His support has been invaluable. I will be forever grateful.

I would like to thank Julia Medina for getting me to rethink New Orleans as part of the Caribbean Basin and for being always generous with her time, thoughts, resources, and editing skills. This book took shape through our many conversations in Albion, New Orleans, Spain, Nicaragua, and, of course, San Diego.

To Emmanuel Yewah, my dear colleague for over twenty-seven years, I owe debts that can never be repaid. His understanding, generous and open heart, sharp intellect, and sense of humor have supported me for all these years. In particular I want to thank him for his proofreading much of this manuscript. His introducing me to Cameroon and allowing me to live the connections between New Orleans and West Africa transformed me in profound ways and inspired me in the writing of this book. I am also grateful to the village of Batchingou, Cameroon, and Chief André Flaubert Nana and his family for their warm welcome over the years, the honor they have bestowed on me, and the lessons they have taught me.

Albion College has provided financial support through the Hewlett-Melon Faculty Development fund and through the Howard L. McGregor Jr. Endowed Professorship in the Humanities. Colleagues at Albion College offered advice, support, and encouragement. I wish to thank Catalina Perez Abreu for her generous sharing of materials on the Canary Islands, as well as Perry Myers, Kalen Oswald, Susanne Myers, Marcie Noble, and Linda Clawson for their support and patience during this project. I also deeply appreciate all of the dinners spent talking over these ideas with my "gang" at Albion College — you know who you are. Thank you, too, Ronney Mourad for past collaborations that informed my approach to this work, and to Judith Lockyer, who so willingly introduced new aspects of nineteenth-century American literature and helped edit parts of this book. Brandon Hill while doing his undergraduate student research on Alexandre Latil opened up the door to Éditions Tintamarre for me. The librarians at Albion College have been tireless in tracking interlibrary loan items over these last years and have made acquiring materials a smooth process. To each of my dear friends in Albion who have nurtured me and nourished me—thank you all.

The staff at the Bibliothèque Nationale de France offered invaluable support, especially Mme Claude Collard for her assistance in organizing my research and M. Jacques Petillat for his painstaking help in locating resources in the library. I would like to thank the staff at the Bibliothèque de l'Arsenal in Paris for assistance in locating and duplicating some of their holdings that are real New Orleans treasures.

I am grateful to the staff of the Historic New Orleans Collection for their help and in particular would like to offer special thanks to Erin Greenwald for her interest in the Pellerin manuscript and her generous advice about early New Orleans research. Also, Russell Desmond of Arcadian Books and Prints helped me obtain materials and clarify some of my ideas as he offered rich insights into New Orleans history and its connection to France.

My dear friends in Noisy-le-Roi and Bailly, France, have supported this project in so many ways by offering advice, support, and networking connections, as well as taking such care of me during my research visits to France. In particular I want to thank my French sister, Marie-Noëlle Dupuy, and her family, for being amazing hosts over the years, as well as Annick Theis-Viémont, François Amet, and other members of the *Comité de Jumelage de Noisy-le-Roi/Bailly.*

I will never be able to thank my New Orleans friends enough for keeping me grounded in the life and culture of the city since I moved away. Jennyse Paz has been my best friend, my guide, and my tireless cultural informant, and R. Alexis De Bram and Keven Lovetro have been there whenever I've needed their help or advice over the years. Mae Ola Dunklin, along with her husband, Robert, have been my Louisiana lifeline for the last three decades in Albion, Michigan, where we share ex-pat status.

Writing this book has made me more proud and grateful for my family's Francophone Louisiana heritage. To my late parents, Carmen Prevost Guenin and Gustave Guenin, who nurtured me in so many ways and instilled in me a profound sense of place, as well as to other members of my family who taught me about being Creole, Lucille McNeil, Constance Prevost, William Pellerin, and Lucille D'Amico, I thank you. I am grateful to my siblings Connie Whitener, Bruce Guenin, and Janet Guenin-Oliva for their love and for the memories of childhood that became once again vivid through writing the book. To my sister-in-law Anita Guenin goes special thanks for generously sharing her expertise and offering important advice on genealogical research. To my cousin and former colleague at Albion College, Mark Soileau, thank you for teaching me a lesson in how small this world really is. To the Lelle family, especially Clark and Mary, thank you for the love and support over all these years.

To my dear children, Hannah and Austin Lelle, thank you for all that you are and all that you give, especially the love, joy, and the lessons you have taught me. I hope this book helps you to understand your heritage, and opens up New Orleans even more for you. To my partner in life, Mark Lelle, there are no words for how much you mean to me and how grateful I am to share this journey with you. Your encouragement, engagement, and love hold this book together just as much as the words in each sentence do. Mark, Hannah, and Austin, this is dedicated to you.

Unless otherwise indicated, all translations from the French are my own.

PREFACE

New Orleans is a city like no other in North America. The city rejoices in its longstanding traditions. Its multicultural population enjoys a shared sense of identity. New Orleans serves as an incubator for music, art, and new ways of living. Sitting on the edge of North America, the city has been destroyed and rebuilt. It celebrates the sensual, the religious, the mundane, and the fantastic simultaneously. Its food, music, and Mardi Gras represent its most valued commodities, produced as well as consumed by its people. Its sounds, words, sights, smells, lands, and waters form a unique amalgam.

This urban space lies at the crossroads where North America's Deep South meets the north coast of the Caribbean. Over the centuries, this intersection constituted a place where different cultures met and interacted. The cultural fusion occurring in this robust contact zone helped produce New Orleans' unique culture. The city stands as the only one of its kind in the United States, a melding of American, French, African, Spanish, and Caribbean influences. New Orleans' distinctive cultural blend often seems exceptional, with the city's culture not quite fitting into the contours of what it considered a "truly American" city. Popular culture generally depicts New Orleans as an exotic place, romanticizing its history and people. Recent publications have named New Orleans "the least American place in America" and "America's most foreign city."[1] Just as the rest of the United States does not treat the city as a completely American space, neither does the city itself identify as such. As a primary example, the bustling tourist industry in New Orleans promotes the city as an exotic destination for US travelers, a place offering American tourists a "foreign" experience without needing a passport.

New Orleans does not offer easy answers to the questions it raises about its history, culture, and people; instead its answers remain complex and nuanced. Life just seems somehow different there. Perhaps this can be explained by how New Orleans appears to have resisted the forces of Americanization and has not made the same kind of shift assimilating into Anglo-America as other cities founded by the French. For example, the French founded Detroit, St. Louis, and New Orleans in the early eighteenth century.[2] Yet, as opposed to New Orleans, the other two cities eventually blended into the American melting pot and became spaces where Anglo-Saxon Protestant culture took firm root. In addition, they developed into economic hubs crucial to the growth of the United States economy, especially relative to industry. New Orleans, however, never blended into that same melting pot, as the city never completely shifted from being a French to an American urban space. In spite of the city's economic worth to the United States, with its location on the most important waterway in North America, New Orleans remains distinct and set apart from its surroundings. So while it serves as the southern gateway to the United States and functions as the primary port city of the Mississippi delta, New Orleans still does not appear to be an actual US city.

By not easily fitting into the American melting-pot narrative, there exists a play of presence and absence, where New Orleans although geographically a part of North America seems not to fit into what constitutes an American locale. Because the city remains a cultural outlier for Anglo-America, it seems as if the city exists simultaneously here in the United States and elsewhere—occupying an in-between hybrid space, both exoticized and localized. This in-between space calls out to the imagination, the far-off, and the mystical to write its story, to create its narrative. So just as the Mississippi River shifts course and casts off bayous as it seeks new routes, the city born by the river has a history that shifts, falls back on itself, and is continuously being rewritten.

Mythmaking and illusion have been part and parcel of New Orleans' history since John Law relied on propaganda to lure the earliest colonists to settle in the territory by his painting a picture of the idyllic, serene, and cultured life awaiting future settlers. Since Louisiana was at the time anything but orderly and civilized, Law understood the need to weave an imagined tale of the value and opportunities to be found in Louisiana, through commissioning fictional travel narratives, in order to promote the colony and ensure its success. Colonists themselves followed suit and through slippages and mythologizing were also able to reinvent themselves, taking on new identities, even noble titles, that suited them in this new world built on collective relation. Cultural slippages, mythologizing, and tendencies toward self-fashioning have been a part of New Orleans ever since.

This study seeks to answer the question "Why is New Orleans considered a French city?" What is it about the city's history, location, and culture that continue to link it to France while distancing it culturally and symbolically from the United States? The situation, as we will see, seems motivated by a fundamental and persistent resistance to considering the city as an American space. Representing the city as a "foreign" place underscores the uncertainty about New Orleans' geographical location, situated both on this southern edge of North America and the north coast of the Caribbean, as well as its history and identity. Moreover, in this study I explore some of the reasons why this might be so, as this work seeks out the traces of French language, history, and artistic expression that have been present in New Orleans' cultural landscape over the last three hundred years. The historical scope of the volume includes the French, Spanish, and early American periods in order to understand the imprint that French sociocultural systems left in the collective memory and imaginary in New Orleans' culture during and after French colonial rule. Furthermore, I examine the creolization processes occurring throughout these colonial times, long after the city was no longer an official French space, both to uncover the persistent play of presence versus absence relating to French New Orleans cultural history, as well as to gain a deeper understanding of why French figures so prominently throughout New Orleans' history.

THE STORY OF FRENCH NEW ORLEANS

Introduction

New Orleans began as a French project and the city remains a tangible reminder of the legacy of French colonialism in North America. Shortly after its founding it became the capital of *la Louisiane,* an expanse covering roughly one-third of the United States. In spite of the composite nature of New Orleans' culture, that includes Creole[1] elements as well as those from Mexico, Central America, and South America, in what was suggested earlier as the play of presence and absence, the assumed home to that culture has historically been associated with France. Although the vast majority of the buildings in the French Quarter were built after New Orleans became a part of the United States, tourists nonetheless continue to flock there to experience "the least American place in America" and "America's most foreign city," lured by its supposedly French architecture and its urban design.

In considering its colonial history and what traces of French culture might have been transposed onto the city's cultural landscape, we are faced with a serious dilemma because a considerable gap exists between the "official" historical record linking New Orleans to France and the affective imagery tying New Orleans to its Mother Country. Founded in 1718, the city lost its territorial status a mere forty-four years later when King Louis XV secretly gave it to Spain (1762), and then Spain returned the territory to Napoleon, who held it for just a few weeks, before selling it to the United States (1803) through the Louisiana Purchase. Thus, the territory was a Spanish colony virtually for as long as it was French and has been a part of the United States for over two hundred years. This begs the question of why New Orleans is still considered a French space, while Detroit or St. Louis are not, although all three were French colonial cities sharing much of the same colonial history. The challenge in reconciling these very different perceptions of place and resultant perceptions of demographics and geographical association exists in part because these elements alone do not explain the cultural transmission — real or imagined — that occurred in New Orleans and not throughout the larger Louisiana territory. These elements also do not fully explain how the French legacy persists when for over one hundred fifty years the lingua franca in New Orleans has been English and the only surviving structure in the French Quarter from the French period is the Ursuline convent, hardly an icon of the city.

While the French harbor a desire to sustain a privileged connection with New Orleans, given the unique cultural ties that continue to bind the two places[2] in the areas of diplomatic, economic, and educational initiatives, when we consider what the French perspective might be on the issue of just how "French" New Orleans actually is, we can assume the answer to be "not much," at best. There lacks a connection between the official historic record linking France to New Orleans and the actual social, cultural, and linguistic composition of the city and its people. The French notion of the history of *la Nouvelle France* with its southern component known as *l'Amérique septentrionale*, privileges the association between New Orleans and Quebec, reflecting the chronology of French colony building in North America. In this French way of thinking, they associate New Orleans with Quebec rather than the Caribbean or even the American South because the history of French colonialism in North America started with Quebec and continued to Louisiana, which became the southern flank of *la Nouvelle France*.[3] The operative assumption within this French perspective seems to be that most aspects of the colonial process followed an order and a logic originating in France and transplanted directly on the colonial landscape, first to Quebec, and then to Louisiana. By extension the French would expect New Orleans to bear a significant resemblance to Quebec culturally, socially, and linguistically.

The reality that New Orleans shares few qualities with Quebec problematizes this French paradigm and its legacy in the New World. Furthermore that New Orleans' history depends largely on north-south movements from the Caribbean islands, and Haiti in particular, as well as Mexico, Central America, and South America rightly opposes the notion of New Orleans as a "French" place. The language and culture in New Orleans differ significantly from Quebec, as well as France. The city's culture and geography, as well as the remaining linguistic vestiges of French, such as *Laissez les bons temps rouler*, are quite distinct from standard French language usage and current cultural forms of expression.[4] Typically in New Orleans, just as in Quebec and other places that identify as Francophone, when a French person is confronted with a gap between standard French cultural and linguistic practices and the varieties of cultural and linguistic expression found in its former colonies, the initial reaction is to say, *Ce n'est pas français, ça.*[5] This speech act serves to problematize the genuine historical connections between France and its former colonies as it is embedded in the metropole's notion of its own universalism and this universalism's resistance to engage in a negotiated relationship with other Francophone areas, especially its former colonies. From this universalist perspective, what counts as French should operate within contemporary French norms as established by the *Académie Française*, with their assumed timelessness, rather than traces of norms dating from the French colonial period that differ from these current standards. In other words, there is a resistance to accept as "French" vestiges of French culture and language from France's past when the historical cultural norms are not properly in alignment with French standards today.

So if New Orleans should not be considered "French" from this assumed French perspective, we are left to ponder the persistent presence of the French in New Orleans cultural history. This appears especially vexing given that the city and the larger Louisiana territory seemed of so little importance to the French that they willingly gave it up on two different occasions, going so far as to treat it as a commodity to be sold in 1803. Looking at the social construction of early New Orleans history, it becomes clear that in its earliest iteration, rather than being built by the French, the city emerged as a product of French Canadians' efforts, instrumental in the building of the city. Although technically a French enterprise, the founder of the city and its biggest advocate is the French Canadian Jean-Baptiste Le Moyne de Bienville. Bienville served as the visionary, indeed functioning as the father of the city. His extended family represented the earliest cohort of settlers, standing to gain financially by developing their settlement. In part because of the disengagement of aristocrats and the monarchy in France, New Orleans during the early 1720s seemed more like a Canadian outpost than a French colonial urban area. For most, it represented a frontier town comprised of a motley, disorganized—if not downright dishonest—crew of Canadian and French colonists. These settlers coexisted, enslaved, and battled with the local Quinipissas, Bayougoulas, and Natchez Indian Nations.[6] In spite of New Orleans' literally being developed over older autochthon settlements on high ground and close to portages, and the colonists needing to rely on native practices, knowledge, and cooperation for their survival, the relations between the Francophone colonists and local Amerindians were constantly strained; the French ideal of *mission civilisatrice* would not allow it to acknowledge its debt to the local Indian Nations.

The thought of being sent to *la Louisiane*, especially when it served as a penal colony in the early eighteenth century, terrified the French. Given their advanced class sensibilities, and Manichean concept of the world in which they saw themselves as the civilized on a mission to civilize others, is it any wonder that the French, in spite of Law's propaganda, viewed Louisiana primarily as a savage wilderness? The colony lacked needed infrastructure stemming from its weak economy, one that did not turn a profit for France, although pirating and privateering did indeed flourish. Trade to

Saint-Domingue, Havana, Veracruz, and elsewhere in the Caribbean far outweighed trade to France (Dawdy 102). Unlike the Spanish counterpart, no newspapers, theater, or literature appeared during the French period, except for the travel narratives written by early settlers and administrators. It was only later after the French period ended that an a posteriori flowering of newspapers, theater, and most importantly for our purpose here, literature written in French, appeared.

During the French period, following preexisting patterns of colony building by the French crown in Canada, the early management of the Louisiana territory was given over to a private company, John Law's Company of the Indies. The company did not offer the support to colonists that it had promised them relative to their basic needs. At the same time, its primary concern was turning its own profit. Given the French crown's habit of not investing in its North American colonies, decisions made about how to build the colony more often than not reflected a Eurocentric mindset. This resulted in ineffective settlement strategies and conflicted management of the colony throughout the French territory.

Simultaneously the French Crown considered any agency on the part of colonists, whose precarious lives and livelihoods called them to action in order to fight for their survival, as a serious transgression. The colonists would become liable when engaging in any trade, transfer, barter, or action not officially sanctioned by France or its company, with such acts considered a punishable crime. Although these policies were largely unenforceable, they had negative consequences for the colonists who were victims of the corrupt management of the colony. Colonial administrators spuriously enforced these policies, while they failed to provide colonists with basic essentials for life that the Crown and the Company had promised to give them. Colonists had to fend for themselves, and this need for survival operated as a great social equalizer in early New Orleans, just as throughout the French Caribbean, requiring the forming of new social ordering and relationships among those who elsewhere would have been considered as belonging to disparate racial, cultural, or class groups.

In New Orleans, immigrants created new identities for themselves, resulting in a society very different from that intended by the French *mission civilisatrice*. Those French settlers quickly understood the need to "go native," at least to some degree, in order to avoid starvation, disease, and certain death, following the model of the French Canadians *voyageurs* and *coureurs de bois*, trappers and fur traders who served as their (perhaps unwitting) guides. Settlers to Louisiana also relied on the local autochthon Nations whose footprint early colonists quite literally followed. Shannon

Dawdy, in her outstanding analysis of early New Orleans development, explains the swift transformation of French settlers into seasoned Creoles as follows, "If they survived the long seasoning period of disease, hunger, and coerced labor, immigrants found themselves in a place where they could experience a great range of physical and social mobility. In their movement, they picked up nicknames like souvenirs. And enslaved immigrants used alternate names to facilitate psychological, if not physical, distance from their enslavers . . . Bienville is the first local resident known to have used the term *creole*."[7]

Mobility and freedom allowed for the birth of a new kind of social order that included a racially mixed creolized population. The new social order reflected the creolization process that occurred throughout the former French colonies, including the Caribbean; a process that "dissolves the opposition of self and other, here and elsewhere,"[8] thus providing ferment for an original society to develop. The emergence of Creole populations represents new peoples with a new social order resulting in a new hemispheric genealogy. While in the Spanish colonies, Creole referred to whiteness and the highest rung of social hierarchy, in the French colonies, including New Orleans, the term referred to and foregrounded cultural, linguistic, and religious bonds over racial associations. The enormous sociocultural upsurge that occurred during the colonial enterprise throughout the greater Caribbean Basin resulted in divergent cultures and peoples being thrown together in a relatively short period of time. These people found themselves in situations of forced dependency and collaboration and the creolized societies that emerged built on shared cultural and linguistic connections. French policies and (mis)management in its colonies intensified creolization with their disorderly, even chaotic, process of colonization. Newly arrived peoples had to rely on themselves more than any "mother country" for their survival. From the very moment that these settlers—free, indentured, and enslaved—arrived, intense cultural, linguistic, and economic fusion began, a creolization fueled by necessity and the exigencies of colony building.

The notion that "French" New Orleans might be understood as a trope for this unscripted "original" Creole social and cultural constructs found in New Orleans can be seen as stemming from the hegemony that France had historically enjoyed in Europe and by extension in the Americas. Association with France, self-fashioned or historically grounded, would serve to add value to a Creole space that would otherwise have been a cultural outlier by virtue of its geographic situation and its sociopolitical marginalization as a colony. Early settlers from France needed to quickly adapt to New World ways of living and to abandon notions of a strict, codified social hierarchy. This meant, for example, accepting that the vestiges of their material existence in France relating to food, shelter, and other matters necessary for their personal lives and material culture were largely absent in the colony. Settlers needed to hastily adapt to their new environment, and jettison attachment to those aspects of material culture that they could no longer access.

For the settlers' basic survival, as well as for the colony's sustainability, they needed to build on the material culture and social practices that were local and common to the Amerindians as well as those of the *voyageurs* and *coureurs de bois*. The necessary adaptations by French colonists existed in tension with France's *mission civilisatrice*. That French colonists made families with Native and African peoples, creating a hybrid population, was a further transgression of the French sense of order and exceptionalism. This put the metropole in a reactionary position as we will see regarding how it attempted to regulate interactions, especially of a sexual nature, between Africans and Europeans through its *Codes Noirs*.

The slave economy built on the backs of Africans and their descendents operated according to colonial laws seeking to control all important aspects of a slave's life. Through its *Code Noir* of 1685 and 1724, the French Crown also sought to impose limits on the control that slaveholders could have over their slaves in its colonies. Dawdy explains the relatively small impact of the *Code Noir* in New Orleans as follows, "Saint Domingue's *Code Noir* of 1685 already used the terms *blancs* and *noirs*. Louisiana's version of this code, created by French ministers in 1724, reiterated this color binary, corresponding to the directions given to colonial engineers, to separate white and black spaces. On the colonial ground, however, these terms appear to have been little used. One Louisianan explicitly challenged the idea that skin color was the most important difference between *nègres* and Europeans; rather, the difference lay in culture" (155). Both the *mission civilisatrice* and the attempt at codifying interactions between the French and the Africans were at best impractical and at the least completely irrelevant to how these populations lived or were forced to live their lives.

Settlers needed to live in "Relation" to one another, to use Glissant's term, and "Relation" existed among Amerindians, French, Canadians, *voyageurs/coureurs de bois*, Africans, as well as others of European descent who populated New Orleans (i.e., Germans, Swiss, Spanish, British, etc.). This Relation was the "contact zone" of creolization.[9] In the earliest years of New Orleans, the "presence" of the French was most often characterized by its "absence" at providing social structures and support for the colony it purported to build, and this absence engendered all the more intense creolization at the local level. The new settlements were only sustainable when relational coexistence flourished. Borrowing from Glissant, in *The Poetics of Relation*, the different cohorts can be understood to exist in relation to one another within a context of being "there and elsewhere, rooted and open" (33). Given the apathy and absence of the colonizer, in New Orleans' early years, cohorts needed to be evermore "there and open" in their coexistence and codependence than otherwise would have been the case. Thus, the society that emerged under French and later Spanish colonial rule was all the more creolized due to the hesitancy and inconsistency characterizing French and Spanish colonial governance. This continued under American rule due in part to the traumatic way in which the city became part of the United States, as a commodity liquidated by Napoleon.

Over the centuries what emerged in this area grew into a unique and distinctive culture unlike any other in North America. Nick Spitzer offers the following description of south Louisiana today: "South Louisiana—and to some extent contiguous areas of the Gulf Coast into Texas, Mississippi, and Alabama—is distinguished from the rest of the South by languages such as French Creole, Cajun French, and Isleño Spanish; folk Catholicism, including Vodou (or locally, voodoo) home altars, and a ritual/festival complex that includes Toussaint (All Saints Day) and Mardi Gras; foodways such as *gumbo* and *congrís* that blend African culinary ideas and ingredients (gumbo is the word for okra in several west African languages and also a term used to name the deeper form of Louisiana Creole French). We also have Spanish, French, and Native American ingredients, seasonings, and cooking methods; and, of course, Creole music genres such as zydeco and New Orleans jazz" (Spitzer 38). In ways of speaking, eating, living, and worshiping, New Orleans has come to be a particular kind of place, distinct from other American cities while connected to cultures and peoples from Europe, Africa, and perhaps most of all the Caribbean.

Regarding the organization of the chapters in this study, chapter 1 begins by situating Louisiana within the context of French colonial history, and examines how the French generally lacked interest in the development and well-being of their colonies. Their half-hearted engagement in colony building stands in contrast to the privileged position that France holds in New Orleans history. I explore the disconnect between official administrative policies governing the colony and colonists' actual needs to survive in this very challenging environment. The study incorporates early French travel narratives into its analysis, including one important early eighteenth-century manuscript written by the early colonist Gérard Pellerin, forgotten for over a century.

The second chapter presents an original interpretation of the urbanization of New Orleans as an attempt at transposing a "French space" onto the colonial wilderness through studying the design and construction of early New Orleans, today's French Quarter. This interpretation extends the imagined connections between New Orleans and France to the spatial realm. Beginning with the colonial desire to construct a French imprint in the New World, building on the metropole's values of logic and order, the argument then treats the symbolic and historical connections of early eighteenth-century France as represented in this space. This analysis also demonstrates ways in which the locals contested and negotiated their relationship to the colonizer through time as imprinted on the urban design of eighteenth-century New Orleans.

In chapter 3 I extend the theory of *créolité* as posited by Edouard Glissant and other Antillean Francophone theorists to the context of New Orleans in order to understand the social construction of its colonial society. New Orleans and the Caribbean share numerous historical, cultural, and linguistic connections. These connections reveal a shared process of creolization that occurred throughout New Orleans' colonial period. The current volume theorizes that "French" New Orleans might be understood as a trope for the unscripted "original" Creole social and cultural constructs found in New Orleans. This work compares "French" and "Creole" identities relative to New Orleans and how these identities also differed in important ways from the Francophone islands in the Caribbean. Furthermore, it contends that "France" and "French" operated in the collective imaginary as cultural tropes for uniting or distancing the disparate, competing Creole elements of this society, especially concerning issues of race.

In the fourth chapter I examine the Spanish colonial period and how it was arguably the period of the most intense creolization in New Orleans history because, on the one hand, Spain was not interested in being given Louisiana by Louis XV and therefore was generally deferential to the local population in administering the colony. On the other hand, the manumission practices allowing slaves to buy their freedom, as well as Spain's renewing the slave trade, made New Orleans the most African of North America cities in the late eighteenth century. Spain's King Carlos III awarded exceptional status to his *Luisiana* as it was the only colony to be associated with the Ministry of State, who received instructions directly from him. This sense of exceptionalism fed creolization, the chapter maintains, as it also emboldened the local elite who resisted Spanish rule.

Chapter 5 explores New Orleans at the time of the Louisiana Purchase when it became a part of the United States. Particular attention is paid to the arrival of refugees from the Haitian Revolution to New Orleans. Arguably the most important historical moment during the early American period that reinvigorated the notion of New Orleans as a "French" space was these Francophone refugees doubling the size of the French-speaking population in New Orleans right at the moment it became part of the United States. Not only did their arrival add to the Francophone presence of the city, but this cohort of free people of color and whites brought with them the first true "high" culture to be found in New Orleans. Newspapers, theater, and literature flourished in French, especially in the period just before the Civil War. They also brought the notion of plaçage, the practice of Quadroon balls, and economic stimulus to the city, as well as new forms of political activism.

The sixth and final chapter of this volume takes a look at selected texts of nineteenth-century literature, primarily reissued texts by Éditions Tintamarre. The publications treated in this chapter represent the earliest African American works of fiction, including those of Victor Séjour, as well as the earliest African American newspapers, representing an antislavery network that triangulated from New Orleans to France and Haiti. The chapter addresses the representation of nineteenth-century multicultural Creole realities especially as they relate to the self-fashioning of Francophone identities in North America. These texts give voice to the Francophone Creoles of New Orleans as they allow for an understanding of the fluidity and plurality of Francophone perspectives in the decades after New Orleans became an American city. This chapter treats what can be considered as the endpoint of the French colonial process because by the end of the nineteenth century, French was no longer a common language of communication in New Orleans.

CHAPTER ONE

Building a French Colony

Introduction

Early historical texts and travel narratives give insight into the complex connections between New Orleans and France, especially the troubled governance of the colony and local agency of the colonists. The Crown desired to maximize its control of the colony, resisting any delegation of authority to those not directly affiliated with the Crown. While minimally investing in the building up of the colony, the Crown hoped to profit from the colony's natural resources and to enjoy prestige in the European arena the role of colonizer brought. Given the lack of interest and understanding of the needs of the colony, French colonizers were transformed through the creolization process that operated in and around them, and going so far as to take on "local" identities as they came to identify affectively with the local culture and way of life, negotiating challenges presented in the colonial environment. The conflicted affective connections to France contributed to the sense that New Orleans occupied an in-between space—one that was not quite "French" although it was a French colony, with a French colonial administration, a French army, and settlers from France.

Founding of Louisiana

When compared to the Spanish, the Portuguese, and the Dutch, France's primary political focus remained continental, within the European arena, rather than with an aim toward colonial expansionism in the New World. While Spain and Portugal ushered in the Age of Exploration in the early 1400s, official French efforts came a full century later. Despite this lack of interest on the part of the French Crown, fishermen from Normandy and Brittany sailed to Newfoundland as early as 1504 and made settlements there as well as further inland along the Saint Lawrence, in what is now Quebec Province (Durand 10). France's official colonial efforts began with Jacques Cartier, who explored the Saint Lawrence River and in 1536 established *la Nouvelle-France* there, with its capital Quebec City founded eighty years later in 1608 by Samuel de Champlain.

Much further south, French settlements in the Caribbean began with the creation of colonies in French Guyana in 1624, in Guadeloupe and Martinique in 1635, and in Saint-Domingue, later known as Haiti, in the mid-seventeenth century, although it was not made official until the Treaty of Ryswick in 1697 (Dessens 6). Elsewhere during the early seventeenth century the French established trading posts along the coast of West Africa and later founded Pondicherry in India in 1674. Ile Bourbon, which became Réunion, was founded in 1664 and Ile de France, which became Mauritius, in 1718. It was not until the nineteenth and twentieth centuries that France launched a second wave of colonization, claiming lands and developing colonies in North and West Africa, Indonesia, and the South Pacific.

Louisiana was founded late in the first wave of French exploration.[1] The French Crown agreed to explore the area primarily as a way of keeping the British and the Spanish from taking control of the Mississippi River. In 1682 the tenacious Norman René-Robert Cavelier, Sieur de La Salle, was given a commission by King Louis XIV to claim new areas of North America in the hope of finding an overland route to the Pacific and China. His best-known journey in 1682 began with him and his party traveling south along the Illinois River, then down the Mississippi River. Although not arriving at the actual mouth of the Mississippi, but near it, La Salle claimed all the lands, waters, people, and natural resources that were connected to this great waterway in the name of King Louis XIV of France on April 9, 1682, at a spot along the Mississippi near present-day Venice, Louisiana.[2] He called these vast lands *la Louisiane* after Louis XIV and the great river the Colbert, after Louis XIV's finance minister Jean-Baptiste Colbert, although it was more consistently called by its Ojibwa name, the Mississippi. The official proclamation made by La Salle on that day reads as follows:

> By the very high, very powerful, very invincible and victorious Prince Louis the Great, by the grace of God king of France and Navarre, the fourteenth of this name, today on the ninth day of April 1682, I, by virtue of His Majesty's commission that I hold in my hand, ready to show whomever to whom it belongs, have taken and am taking possession in the name of His Majesty and the successors to the crown, of this country Louisiana, adjacent seas, harbors, ports, bays, straits, and all nations, peoples, provinces, cities, towns, villages, mines, mining, fishing, rivers, streams that make up the said Louisiana, from the mouth of the great Saint Louis River from the east coast, formerly called the Ohio, Olighinsipou or Chukagoua, and this from the agreement with the Chaouesnons, Chicachas and other people living there with whom we have created alliances, as well the length of the Colbert River, or Mississippi, and

streams that empty into it, from its source beyond the Sioux or Nadoue-sioux country, as by the Ototantas, Islinois, Matsigamea, Akansas, Natchez, Koroas, who are the most considerable nations living here, with whom we or people representing us, have been accorded their consent through alliances.

Additionally, he adds,

This from the river's mouth in the sea or the Gulf of Mexico, approximately 27 degrees of elevation from the North Pole to the mouth of the Palms, hav-ing been assured by all these nations that we are the first Europeans ever to have descended the said Colbert River. Protesting against all who might in the future undertake to seize all or any of the said countries, peoples, lands, as specified, by prejudice to the right that His Majesty acquires here, from the consent of the aforementioned nations, of what and of all needs there may be, take as witnesses those who hear me and ask for an act of the present notary to serve as proof.

Signed by La Salle, F. Zénobe, Recollect Missionary, Henry de Tonti, Fran-çois de Boisrondet, Jean Bourdon, sieur d'Autray, Jacques Cauchois, Gilles Meneret, Jean Michel, surgeon, Jean Mas, Jean du Lignon, Nicolas de La Salle, and La Métairie, notary. (Margry 190–93)

This grandiloquent proclamation, typical of seventeenth-century French prose, claims for France a remarkably vast area that includes Minnesota, Wisconsin, Michigan, Ohio, Indiana, Illinois, Iowa, North Dakota, South Dakota, Nebraska, Kansas, Wyoming, Oklahoma, Colorado, Montana, Kentucky, Missouri, Arkansas, Tennessee, Mississippi, Alabama, and of course, Louisiana.[3] La Salle was, nonetheless, not the first European to explore the Missis-sippi River. The Spaniard Hernando de Soto generally receives credit for "discovering" it in 1541, although other Italians, Portuguese, and Spanish conquistadors preceded him (*Time and Place in New Orleans: Past Geographies in the Present Day* 18–19). In fact, Cabeza de Vaca had already discovered the mouth of the Mississippi in the early sixteenth century while traveling along the Gulf Coast. The first French team to chart the river included Fa-ther Jacques Marquette, a Jesuit, and the French Canadian Louis Joliet, who explored the river from the Great Lakes to the mouth of the Arkansas River in 1673. It was, however, La Salle who was the primary advocate for creating this colony of *la Louisiane*, and when his subsequent efforts to locate the mouth of the Mississippi River failed leading to his being assassinated by his own men in the "Texas wilderness" (Mann 237), this project came to a halt. An Italian priest, Henri de Tonti, a longtime associate of La Salle who had participated in several of La Salle's explorations, eventually convinced Louis XIV of the strategic and political advantages that Louisiana provided in countering British and Spanish expansionism (Giraud, Vol. 1 10–17).

The Founding of the Colony

It took seventeen years before the French Canadian Pierre Le Moyne d'Iberville, at the behest of the French Crown concerned about English and Spanish threats to French holdings in North America, successfully located the river's mouth in 1699 and established Louisiana as a French settlement, making him the "father" of Louisiana. Born near Montreal, Iberville "was the third of fourteen children of Charles Le Moyne, who had come to Nouvelle-France at the age of fifteen, beginning as an indentured servant to the Jesuits. Le Moyne *pére* learned the languages of the Huron and the Iroquois—Iberville grew up speaking them—and with time became a wealthy fur trader. Iberville was considered a hero for his bravery during King William's War" (Sublette 36). Riding on the tails of this success, Iberville, his younger brother Jean-Baptiste Le Moyne de Bienville, and their party set sail from Brest. It was a motley crew of "pirates, and Spanish deserters, Spanish-speaking Frenchmen and several Canadians, the latter to be left behind after the landing to maintain a garrison" (*The Accidental City: Improvising New Orleans* 12). This multicultural, multilingual cohort represented the first colonists France sent to build its colony in *L'Amérique septentrionale*, better known as *la Louisiane.*

Iberville's exploration built on La Salle's 1684 trip, making port in Saint-Domingue, which became standard sailing protocol for tall ships, before heading north.[4] Relying on the assistance of his crew plus buccaneers, trappers, both licensed *voyageurs* and illegal *coureurs de bois*, and Native Americans, they first attempted to land in Pensacola, but found it had just been claimed as a Spanish territory by Spaniards from Vera Cruz.[5] Making landfall instead on the island Iberville named Massacre, so named due to bones found on the site from a previous battle between Native Americans,[6] he continued exploring the Gulf Coast for nearly one month before locating the mouth of the Mississippi River. According to Iberville's own account, this long-sought prize was found by accident during a storm. In Iberville's entry for March 2, 1699, he explains how due to heavy seas in the Gulf of Mexico, he was forced to seek out shelter before dusk to save his crew from drowning.[7] His plan was to run ashore in spite of the very rocky area that stood in his way. To his surprise, he explains:

> I became aware that there was a river. I passed between two of the rocks, in 12 feet of water, the seas quite heavy. When I got close to the rocks, I found fresh water with a very strong current. These rocks are logs petrified by the mud, changed into black rocks, which withstand the sea. They are countless, above water, some big, others small, separated from one another by distances of 20 yards, 100 yards, 300 yards, 500 yards, more or less, running south-west. This made me know that here was the Palisade River,[8] which appears to me to have been rightly named; for, when I was at its mouth, which is 1 ½ leagues in from these rocks, it appeared to be entirely obstructed by the rocks. (51–52)

What he thought were rocks were mud lumps found in the bird-foot delta of the Mississippi River, a geographical formation he had never seen before and which was thus unrecognizable to him. With Iberville's having located the mouth of the Mississippi River, the process of colony building began in earnest; the first fort, known as Fort Maurepas, was built on Biloxi Bay.

Iberville was given much latitude by Louis XIV, via the minister of the marine, Pontchartrain, to establish settlements as he saw fit (Langlois 185). So from the very founding of the colony, there was local agency accorded to the colonists within the structure of the colonial administration, which stands in contrast to the absolutism of Louis XIV, and supports the notion that, while the colony was an extension of the sociopolitical norms in France, with the king being the ultimate authority, the king was not much vested in colony building or in creating new ambitious "utopias" such as Versailles (Langlois 185). It was enough to send administrators deemed competent for a few key posts to do the tasks that the king prescribed. This design of colonial government belies a tension between the absolutism of the French Crown with its official colonial policies in Louisiana, on the one hand, and the Crown's lack of engagement or investment in the success of the colony, on the other. As opposed to Saint-Domingue, whose value to the French stemmed from the sugarcane that supplied the country with sugar, there appeared to be no clear natural resources or agricultural crops in Louisiana that could compare. Therefore, the French did not recognize the new colony as having significant value for them and consequently treated the colony with general disinterest. Beginning with Iberville, important decisions about building and managing the colony were made locally, a tendency that only grew during the French colonial period, as we shall see shortly.

John Law and the Company of the Indies

Although the French colonial enterprise was primarily political to strategically enhance France's standing in Europe, relative to England and Spain in particular, it was also economic, aiming to furnish France with raw materials and agricultural products for French markets. The strategic benefits of colonizing *la Nouvelle France* added to French prestige and bargaining clout in the European theater, while the Caribbean, especially Saint-Domingue, provided France with sugar. However, when it came to the end of the first wave of French colonialism in the eighteenth century, given French indifference in the colony's welfare, an irreconcilable tension played out in the French Court. Louis XIV "was frankly indifferent to overseas adventures unless they produced quick returns . . . It is true that Louis was averse to giving up a colony once he owned it, but he was equally loath to pour resources into it. For that reason, French colonial policy in North America was largely one of aimlessness and drift" (*The Accidental City: Improvising New Orleans* 18). Given the French hesitancy to fully invest in developing its colonies, the French tended to turn the job of colony building over to independent companies, engaged to explore and settle the colonies in order to make a profit. As such, the Crown remained vested in the colony's political structures and administration, but the actual promotion and daily workings of the colony occurred through private companies. For example, in eastern Canada, the East India Company followed the Company of One Hundred Associates, also known as the Company of Canada, in 1664, all of which played an exclusively economic role in developing that French colony (Durand 19).

In Louisiana, France handed the responsibility for establishing its settlement from an appointed military governor over to a private individual, Antoine Crozat, and then to a private company, John Law's Company of the West (later renamed the Company of the Indies). Antoine Crozat was given a fifteen-year exclusive concession by Louis XIV in 1712, which he promptly returned to the Crown in 1717. He saw no chance of further enriching himself through mining precious metals in the colony, in addition he could not manage the quagmire of colonial administration. "The lack of mineral riches and scarcity of settlers for agriculture, coupled with mismanagement, feuding among the governors, and increased tensions with the

Indians, forced Crozat out of business in five years" (*Time and Place in New Orleans* 23). The Crown understood that it was no longer a viable option to offer a vast concession to one single individual to develop (De Villiers du Terrage, *Histoire de la Fondation de la Nouvelle-Orléans* 4). However, even if the Crown had wanted to change the structure of government, it would not have been possible to do so because the French economy found itself in ruins at Louis XIV's death (1715), in the wake of his opulent and militaristic reign. Powell offers the following summary of the transition of proprietorship of Louisiana from Crozat to Law:

> But when Louisiana failed to become the "French Peru" or to serve as a siphon for the silver and gold of New Spain, Crozat began to lose interest in his exclusive monopoly. And in 1716, when Paris, in its never-ending quest to find new revenue, assessed him and other wealthy bankers and merchants a mammoth retrospective wartime profits tax, he decided to relinquish Louisiana altogether. Crozat's exclusive trading monopoly was transferred to the Company of the West in 1717. His proprietary successor was also interested in profiting from the charter, but with a difference. Instead of empty rhetoric, the new proprietor would pour real resources into Louisiana. In fact, he committed to accomplish nothing less than the transformation of Louisiana into a Chesapeake on the Mississippi, the tobacco supplier of an entire kingdom. (25)

This new proprietor, John Law, controlled the Louisiana Territory between 1715 and 1720 and during that period he became arguably the most important person in France. With the country on the brink of bankruptcy when Philippe duc d'Orléans became the French regent for Louis XV in 1715, the financial system needed to be overhauled, and the ambitious Scottish financier John Law did not hesitate to offer his ideas for rescuing the entire French economy. The regent was quick to accept "[t]he beguiling inclusiveness of Law's plan—its promise to retire the national debt, revive the French domestic and overseas economy, and establish an autarkic source of tobacco—is what drew the Regent to Law's theories" (*The Accidental City: Improvising New Orleans* 28).

Just nine months after King Louis XIV's death, the *Banque Générale* was formed headed by Law and his Company of the West. The regent and Parliament accorded the bank the right to print bank notes and quickly the "notes, and not the current coinage, became the medium of exchange, and soon acquired a value in excess of the specie they normally represented" (Wiston-Glynn 44). Just as the regency had given Law and his company the responsibility for running the French economy, making him the financial savior of France, it gave him the privilege of administering *la Louisiane* undoubtedly with the same lofty hopes of financial success in this colonial endeavor. It might be more accurate to say that just as Law had designs on running the French economy, he also had designs on running the new colony in Louisiana, with the promise of vast new markets in the Americas, Africa, and Asia, and the regent had no choice but to abide by his wishes. In "May, 1719, a decree was published which conferred upon the Company the new and more pretentious title of the Company of the Indies; permission was given to increase the capital; and to the rights already possessed was added the monopoly of trade 'from Guinea to the Japanese Archipelago, of colonizing especially the Cape of Good Hope, the East Coast of Africa, that which is washed by the Red Sea, all the known islands on the Pacific, Persia, China, Japan, and South America'"(Wiston-Glynn 75). The height of the Company of the Indies' influence and power (1719–1720) coincides with the founding of New Orleans. However, Law's financial empire was not sustainable and the boom quickly turned to bust when the confidence in the notes issued by the *Banque Générale* evaporated. In December 1720, the run began on Law's bank leading to Law's swift and irrevocable downfall and to the bursting of his Mississippi bubble, resulting in the French Crown having to assume sole responsibility for running the colony.

During Law's tenure, New Orleans was still a colonial outpost and not yet the capital of the territory. The building of the city, just as with colony building throughout the Louisiana territory, happened very slowly in part because of the unimaginable challenges it posed to the French and Canadians, and in part because of the conflicted colonial administration of the colony that exacerbated local resistance to control by the metropole. The colonial administration that developed in the 1720s consisted of a governor, who at the founding of the colony had ruled single-handedly, a *commissaire-ordonnateur* (modeled after the *intendant* of the French provinces) and a Superior Council, overseen by the *commissaire-ordonnateur*. Originally the military governor wielded control over most of the workings of the colony, and a *commissaire-ordonnateur* was responsible for finances. However, over time, the latter's powers were expanded to rival that of the governor's ("Confusion, Conflict, and Currency" 161). Conflicted management of the colony ensued given that decisions often implicated both military and fiscal management. Class issues added further complications to this arrangement with governors being selected from the military, while *ordonnateurs* were from the nobility.

These administrative tensions created a situation that allowed for individual colonists to assume a certain autonomy over their lives that would not have been possible if there had been a more orderly and univocal administration from the metropole. Since the French colonists had to directly confront forces that often took their lives, such as natural disasters, disease, attacks, and starvation, they had to become self-sufficient and readily adapt to their changing conditions. Local agency was not only possible, it was necessary. Being less representative of France's interests and more representative of local Creole interests, the Superior Council enjoyed an autonomy that in many ways added to the divisiveness of the management of the colony, "The king's will did not prevail . . . The Superior Council had never functioned in the manner prescribed by royal law, and in its mature stage it differed radically from the institution designed by the French crown . . . The marked independence of the inhabitants has always been their greatest vice, and the group which should be the instrument for the maintenance of the king's authority [the Superior Council] acts in truth just like the others. From this spirit of independence in all the classes, there come cabals, intrigues, and muttering."[9]

Throughout the French period, this system of government had negative consequences for effective governance in the colony, in particular in New Orleans, because it promoted self-interest of administrators instead of thoughtful colony building. "The petty jealousy fostered by Louisiana's bipolar system of government was enhanced by the keen competition between the colony's executive officers who viewed their employment as a stepping-stone to a more important position in another part of the French empire. In New Orleans' closed society, the officials became acutely aware of, and tenaciously guarded, their social position. The competition between officials, coupled with their abrasive personalities, engendered clashes . . ." ("Confusion, Conflict, and Currency" 161–62). Thus, although Louis XIV had designed colonial governance with himself as the ultimate sovereign, a process that continued under the regency, the Crown's French administrators in the colony enjoyed unusual local agency and were more often than not motivated by self-interest or local political posturing when making their decisions and running the colony.

This spirit of independence evidenced in early New Orleans society is not surprising given that many of the earliest French settlers to New Orleans were lured into becoming colonists under false pretexts and promises that were not to be kept once they arrived in Louisiana. From its very founding with La Salle and later Iberville, "overcoming royal indifference would require great feats of rhetorical overkill, which is why early Louisiana is still remembered today as a place where fevered imagination often overtook reality" (*The Accidental City: Improvising New Orleans* 20). With John Law, the Mississippi bubble was created because of his treating the colony as a speculative financial venture for his Company of the Indies with Louisiana operating more like a commodity to be packaged, marketed, and sold, than a colony needing to be settled.

The Mississippi bubble was a stunning economic boondoggle where fevered imagination completely overtook reality. Just as in Law's other financial practices, he relied on hype and grandiose projects to garner stakeholders' confidence. To sell Louisiana to the people of France, Law needed to present an idealized picture of the colony that corresponded to French sensibilities, reinforcing its *mission civilisatrice* and its accompanying notions "civilization" and "order," so as to attract future colonists seeking a better life to immigrate to the colony. So, in collusion with French and French Canadian colonial administrators whose colonial charge made them essentially his employees, Law crafted ways to lure future colonists and entrepreneurs to the region, including through fictitious travel logs and other "official" documents. May Waggoner, in *Le Plus Beau Païs du Monde*, describes this vehicle for propaganda and its rationale as follows: "[I]t was clear to Law that potential settlers in Louisiana were frightened by the idea of going there. Law decided to use a form of indirect publicity to encourage colonization, and commissioned texts to be written in such a way as to present a rosy, attractive picture of what was, in fact, a very harsh reality. The best way to reach large segments of the French population, Law felt, was through newspapers and periodicals that were always eager to publish travel accounts. Since the French public loved these accounts, Law felt he could reach large segments of the population and capture their attention by publishing narrations written in the 'travel account' style" (19).

In one such travel account, *Relation de la Louisiane ou Mississippi: Écrite à une Dame, par un officier de Marine,* appearing in the *Nouveau Mercure* in February 1718, the author opens the travel narrative by stating that his purpose for writing his lady is for "making known to you a land worthy of your curiosity and which may one day become France's Peru" (Waggoner 49). That claim is substantiated further on: "The French who live among the Illinois, who trade with these natives of the Missouri country, state that the region is very beautiful and fertile, and that it will be possible to find numerous gold and silver mines there since these natives have shown them some pieces of these metals" (57). He goes into more detail near the end of the letter, "If you are interested in mines, as I know you are we . . . will visit the mountains along the Arkansas that has its headwaters in new Mexico and in which we will certainly find silver nuggets. Others have done so before with no difficulty, and the metals have been assayed to judge their value. I will point out to you that these mountains are in the same chain as those of new Mexico where the Spanish extract immense riches. These mountains will surely be just as bountiful for us" (77). Following the legacy of Spanish colonialism in the Americas, Crozat and later Law hoped that precious minerals, in particular gold and silver, would be found in these lands along the Gulf Coast. Law also hoped that the French would be susceptible to the promise of finding riches in the New World, making it easier to sell concessions in Louisiana to potential colonists. The *concessionaires* were investors "under Law's scheme who were given large land grants and a share in his exclusive trade privileges. In return, they were obligated to clear the land and recruit and equip settlers to plant crops. Some *concessionaires* came to Louisiana to oversee operations, others delegated this responsibility to a manager. Concessions varied in size from a few dozen acres to thousands of acres, but in general *concessionaire* denoted a settler of high social status in the early colony" (Dawdy 249). Propaganda in the newspaper the *Nouveau Mercure* helped to fuel the notion of precious mineral, as well as an idyllic space that settlers would find in the colony. These tales were believable because of their melding fact and fiction under the guise of discoveries put into an encyclopedic format, a format loved by the French at the dawn of the Age of Enlightenment.

Founding the Capital of *la Louisiane*

Early colonists understood so little about the geography of the vast Louisiana territory that many were fooled by false travel accounts, even Iberville himself. He relied on what turned out to be a fabricated travel narrative when he used Louis Hennepin's fictitious travel account supposedly written when Hennepin was among La Salle's party exploring the lower Mississippi River. Iberville offers the following lament in his *Journal*, "I found it difficult to believe that he could have been such a rogue as to publish a hoax to all France, even though I well know that in many passages in his relations he had told lies in what he said about Canada and Hudson Bay, in which he had lied with impunity" (60). In spite of Hennepins's questionable reputation, Iberville nonetheless used his account as a basis for charting his exploration of the Mississippi Delta. When Iberville realizes the complete worthlessness of Hennepin's account, he writes, "Today we kept going for thirteen hours; my men are very tired and, having only *sagamité*[10] to eat, are swearing and storming at the writers of forged narratives, who may be given the blame for my going so far" (66–67). Fictitious travel accounts of the geography of Louisiana had little to no basis in reality, so they contributed to creating, or reinforcing, false assumptions that the French held about the geography of North America. For example, French intelligentsia believed just beyond the Mississippi Valley could be found possibilities of vast mines of precious metals, and that beyond Louisiana was none other than the Sea of Japan.[11] These illusions were based on the colonial desire to find riches in the New World as the Spanish did, and establish new and easier trading routes, as had been the case throughout the Age of Exploration. For the French, just as for other colonial powers, the illusions they held about these unknown lands and waters were as significant as the reality they encountered in Louisiana.[12]

This ignorance of local geography in Louisiana caused the French to make completely false assumptions about geographical features that might be particular to North America or simply unknown in France, a case in point already described is Iberville's not recognizing the bird-foot delta of the Mississippi River and its accompanying mud lumps. Thus the early settlements in *la Louisiane* were chosen based on the settlers' false assumptions about the land. Furthermore, the settlers' own desire for personal economic gain and privilege greatly influenced where they settled, and with whom they cooperated. There appeared to be little interest to work collectively in making educated decisions about what might benefit the whole colony. This led to misguided decisions that cost countless lives and seriously compromised efforts at colony building. We have only to look at the places that they chose in their early attempts to create French settlements: Biloxi Bay, Bay St. Louis, Dauphin Island, and Mobile Bay. The first French attempts at establishing a permanent settlement in Louisiana were literally built on sand. Nonetheless, Native peoples did flourish in the region just beyond the coastal sand.

Who were the people on the ground, the locals whom the early French settlers encountered? In the area around New Orleans the Native peoples included Quinipissas (Colapissas, Alcolapissas), also known as the Bayougoulas (*Time and Place in New Orleans: Past Geographies in the Present Day* 20). From early colonist Le Page du Pratz we gain insight into the early colonists' encounters with the Amerindians of this region, as he explains: "We went up this creek for the space of a league, and landed at a place where formerly stood the village of the natives, who are called Cola-Pissas, an appellation corrupted by the French, the true name of that nation being Aquelou-Pissas, that is, *the nation of men that hear and see*. From this place to New Orleans, and the river Mississippi, on which that capital is built, the distance is only a league" (20). New Orleans was built on the high ground identified by the Quinipissas. They also instructed the early colonists about a shortcut from this high ground to the Gulf of Mexico via the portage leading to Bayou St. John, as Campanella explains, "While seeking this important piece of evidence during the month of March 1699, Iberville and Bienville gained crucial knowledge (courtesy of their Indian guides) of the geography of the lower Mississippi and deltic plain, naming features along the way. The information included the existence of shortcut portages to the Gulf Coast via the present-day Bayou Manchac-Amite River-Lake Maurepas-Pass Manchac-Lake Pontchartrain-Rigolets-Lake Borgne route and via Bayou St. John between the Mississippi River and Lake Pontchartrain, marking the future site of New Orleans (*Time and Place in New Orleans: Past Geographies in the Present Day* 20).

The "important piece of evidence" referred to above related to Iberville's uncertainty about which waterway he was exploring. Even after finding the mouth of the Mississippi River, he harbored serious doubts about whether he was indeed following the tracks of La Salle's exploration. The Quinipissas provided him with absolute proof that La Salle had passed there before. They had kept a letter written by Henri de Tonti, a member of La Salle's expedition. He wrote it during his futile search for La Salle in 1686 and left it with the Quinipissas in the event La Salle found them again. They saved the document and passed it on to Iberville. This document served as evidence that Iberville was following the tracks of La Salle and that he had indeed found the mouth of the Mississippi River (*Time and Place in New Orleans: Past Geographies in the Present Day* 20).

Other Nations outside of the new city included the Chitimachas, Choctaws, Chickasaws, Houmas, and Natchez. Innumerable Native Americans from these local nations were taken into slavery. Encounters between Europeans and Native Americans led to the formation of alliances, conflicts, and families. These local Native Americans also provided a model for trade oriented south throughout the Caribbean Basin, rather than east to the Atlantic. This allowed the early settlers to survive by reorienting trade and commerce to the New World north-south routes already in existence, as Dawdy explains, "The founding generation of Louisiana lived on intimate terms with Native Americans who were oriented toward a quite different Mississippi-Caribbean world. Their knowledge informed the selection of the site of New Orleans which, though soggy, had the advantage of being a major crossroads of the New World" (134).

In the early years of the colony, the number of European settlers remained paltry: 140 in 1702, just over 200 in 1714, with military personnel, mostly young soldiers, making up to largest demographic (*The Accidental*

City: Improvising New Orleans 34). As mentioned earlier, French Canadians had already settled in the area that became *la Louisiane*, mostly consisting of Canadian *coureurs de bois* and *voyageurs*. Not surprisingly, Iberville's crew consisted of many young Canadians, as well, hired to staff the garrisons. Furthermore, Iberville's leadership included providing for many of his relatives, including three brothers, nephews, and cousins, as well as other French Canadians in Louisiana who would ultimately "form the nucleus of an emergent colonial elite" (*The Accidental City: Improvising New Orleans* 35).

For Bienville, the most famous of Iberville's brothers, Law's company offered him a "new beginning" (*The Accidental City: Improvising New Orleans* 33). As part of his agreement with the French Crown, John Law agreed that his company would send six thousand men and women to settle Louisiana through land grants, or concessions, and three thousand African slaves to work plantations, especially to work on tobacco plantations that the company planned to establish (*The Accidental City: Improvising New Orleans* 31). In addition, there the company decided "resolutely to found a city to be called *La Nouvelle Orléans*" to be located thirty leagues up river with landings from either the Mississippi River or Lake Pontchartrain (*Bienville's Dilemma,* 109). Like others in the colony, Bienville sought personal profit and gain from spearheading a new settlement where he had already claimed considerable lands. He also understood the strategic importance of its location on the Mississippi.[13] With Bienville's sizable landholdings in area in and around New Orleans, establishing the capital of Louisiana in New Orleans would significantly enrich him. Initially, his plans played very well in his favor. The Company of the Indies appears to have fulfilled its promise to the French crown because between four thousand and six thousand Europeans arrived in Louisiana from 1719 to 1721 (Spear 44–45). However, Bienville was French Canadian rather than a French administrator, and this presented difficulties for him. In spite of the fact that the new settlers depended upon the knowledge of the French Canadians, with their understanding of the lands, cultures, languages, and ways of survival in these lands, the French-born administrators demonstrated enmity toward these French Canadians, including Bienville and his extended family.

By necessity, the expertise of the *coureurs de bois* and the *voyageurs* informed the process of colony building. Nonetheless, for the French-born administrators, their presence created tension and made the management of the colony difficult, or indeed impossible, as evidenced by this disparaging report: "The new *habitans* are not governable; they have no sovereign and are republican, as well as libertine with company they spend with the Indians and courting Indian women. They are without religion, without faith and without law. They are without discipline, without subordination, without weapons, most often without clothes, and must live off of what they find with the Indians. There is no fort, no place of retreat in case of attack. Their *magasins* are exposed."[14] Just as in Canada, there existed the attitude on the part of colonial administrators that the *coureurs de bois* and *voyageurs* were a disorderly bunch, and their habits did not represent rational, thoughtful exploration and colonization practices (Durand 20).

However, these early settlers represented a hybrid, new world order in Louisiana with this demographic having passed from French to Francophone, from colonizer to native, all of which contributed to the hemispheric shift in power from Europe to the Americas. As already mentioned, there existed in this early society tensions among virtually all who had an official or unofficial charge of contributing to the running of the colony and establishing settlements. Tensions existed between the French administrators and French Canadian administrators, as well as between the governors and the *commissaire-ordonnateurs*, and even between the French Canadians and the *voyageurs/coureurs de bois*. An attitude contributing to the divisiveness in early New Orleans society stemmed from the metropole's notion of exceptionalism in the colonies it established. Just as in other colonies established by the French, British, and Dutch, establishing European social structures in the New World was played out through "the inclusions and exclusions built into the notions of citizenship, sovereignty, and participation" (Cooper and Stoler 3). Thus the metropole established a semantic distancing, or "a grammar of difference that was continuously and vigilantly crafted as people in colonies refashioned and contested European claims to superiority" (Cooper and Stoler 3–4). The grammar of difference had been a tool of colonization for hundreds of years during which time "Europeans found themselves increasingly involved in trans-Atlantic ventures that depended on the exploitation of Africans and Indians. European ideas about differences between themselves and those who would become colonized others developed. As Europeans hungered for Indian lands and African labor, they transformed their ethnocentric notions of cultural difference into ideas of immutable, inheritable, racial difference" (Spear 2). Semantic shifts in language, naming and assigning group affiliation to groups of people, served as a means of ordering the emergent "disorganized" settlement in New Orleans. These shifts in naming and group affiliation attempt to reproduce European hierarchy on the part of French-born colonial administrators where being French functioned as a means to secure hegemonic privilege over other European nations—at least on a symbolic level. Thus, French-born colonial administrators took great pains to differentiate themselves and other French nationals not just from the peoples and African slaves, but from people of European descent in the colony.

This grammar of difference evident in the French records shows patterns of a sustained distinction between those administrators born in France and others who, although of French heritage, were born in French Canada. Throughout official records, and in the travel narratives treated further in this text, we see ample evidence of how those two groups were viewed as distinct, and therefore disassociated from each other.[15] Contributing to this distinction would appear to be an underlying concern about the political implications for the *ancien régime* of the "disorder" found in Louisiana as a threat to their European hegemony. So instead of engaging in a negotiation with actions that were considered troublesome to the Crown, such actions were dismissed as not being French just as they had in the Caribbean.[16] Not acknowledging or responding to such acts was a means to delegitimize them. This practice troubled the affective connections to France and contributed to the sense that New Orleans occupied an in-between space — one that was not quite "French," although it was a French colony, with a French colonial administration, a French army, and settlers from France. These gaps between what was considered authentically French and inauthentically French created semantic gaps in the culture, only adding to the hybridization of this newly found society.

The staggering gender imbalance in the colony contributed to the colony's hybridity and to its grammar of difference. The ways in which women's identities were crafted to suit the needs of the colony represent an extreme form of reappropriating identities to suit the needs of the metropole. For example, Louis XIV at one point, and only for a short while, went so far as to sanction marriages between Frenchmen and Native American women, provided the women converted to Catholicism. The Crown with the stroke of a pen went from considering these native women as soulless savages to considering them as worthy Catholic wives and legitimate mothers of the colony. The gender imbalance, however, could not be so easily reconciled. Later Philippe duc d'Orléans turned Louisiana into a penal colony, emptying the prisons and poorhouses, and sending men and women accused of questionable character to *la Louisiane*. Jennifer Spear in her landmark study *Race, Sex, and Social Order in Early New Orleans* examining women's and gender issues in colonial New Orleans contends that officials begged France to send more French women, "stressing that only marriage to French women would encourage the colony's young Frenchmen, many of them coureurs de bois, or discharged soldiers, to establish farms. As such, they saw the presence of French women as central to the goal of establishing a more stable and permanent economy based on family farming rather than a transient economy of Indian trade. French and particularly Canadian men had been at least partially blamed with their 'vigorous' appetites for 'debauchery,' but through marriage to French women, they could, it was thought, ultimately be redeemed" (43). Between 1712 and 1721 about twelve hundred women arrived in the colony, with the final shipment of *épouses, les filles de la cassette,* arriving in 1728 (Spear 45–49).

Bienville lamented the quality of the settlers, both male and female, sent by the company and tried to explain the consequences of sending the king's exiles to the colony and the problems they caused in the settlement of Louisiana. In particular, he argued that sons of privilege were incapable of contributing to building or public works projects, and Bienville expected their families to send them support of one kind of another. Since this type of support was almost never forthcoming, these individuals needed to be supported by the company. Because Bienville was not often pleased by the women who arrived on company ships, including some of the nuns, he sent women back to France on many occasions (De Villiers du Terrage, *Histoire de la Fondation de la Nouvelle-Orléans* 72–74). A ship captain, Vallette de Laudun, who transported some of the *forçats*, convicts, and other forced settlers, describes the condition of the women he transported in this passage: "I believe that the women sent here are so unhealthy and consumed by the gallantries they have had, that they were sterile even before their departure. This along with the scurvy that they all had by their arrival, and which they do not get over ashore, and you will not need to look for other reasons for their being sterile" (256). According to Dawdy, it was during the period 1717–1729 when convicts, social outcasts, and others were forced to emigrate from France that Louisiana's ill repute crystallized, and fear gripped Paris once again in 1750 when a rumor began that children were being abducted and sent there (150). It is no wonder that for the French in the Hexagon the colony was a terrifying place, *la terreur des hommes libres,*[17] with few men, much less women, choosing to immigrate there, in spite of official propaganda. In the early *concessionaire* Gérard Pellerin's letter to France, detailed further in this chapter, his first suggestion in his long litany of suggestions to future colonists is not to book passage on a ship carrying any convicts, even if it is well armed.

Of course the most significant of all the forced labor to arrive in Louisiana were the enslaved African men, women, and children who began arriving the year after New Orleans was founded from the Caribbean. New Orleans and its fledgling frontier economy represented a colonial backwater and the work of colony building was by necessity an egalitarian endeavor.

"Although a large influx of slaves entered the colony between 1719 and 1731, for the first several years those in the New Orleans area were put to work building levees, herding cattle, hunting, and tending gardens. Their labor tasks differed little from those of the idle soldiers in the city or the majority of free colonists, who were mainly concerned with feeding themselves" (Dawdy 83). The slippages in social and racial boundaries occurring in New Orleans existed despite official administrative decrees bent on separation of blacks from whites in order to preserve European notions of social hierarchy. Originally the French had planned for slaves to be housed outside of the city, a plan that was not viable in frontier New Orleans. "In early plans and maps of New Orleans, it appears that African slaves were originally intended to be housed entirely outside the proposed walls of the city. In the first several years, the majority of slaves who worked in New Orleans lived at one of two communities: at the Governor's plantation to the west, or at the Company plantation managed by Le Page du Pratz across the river. Thus New Orleans began as a segregated space reserved for free whites" (Dawdy 146–47). The governor's plantation belonged to Bienville who enjoyed further financial gain from New Orleans by importing African slaves to develop the city he championed.[18]

French colonial practices elsewhere in the Caribbean, where plantation societies already functioned, influenced the treatment of African slaves in Louisiana. The slaving society required rules to regulate its treatment of human chattel and to determine acceptable interactions between the races. Therefore, the French implemented *Code Noir* in the Caribbean (1685), which was in place in Louisiana until 1724 when a revised *Code Noir* was instituted. Spear compares the *Code Noir* of 1724 written for Louisiana to the earlier *Code Noir* written for Saint-Domingue in the following passage:

> The Code Noir was the metropole's response to the emergence of slavery
> in lower Louisiana. By the early 1720s, it became clear that the region's
> economy was moving away from that of New France, with its dependence
> on Indian trade and family farms, toward the Caribbean model of planta-
> tion agriculture and enslaved labor. As such, the Crown looked to the islands
> to determine how to govern Louisiana, and in 1724, it rewrote the Code
> Noir that had been implemented there in 1685, to regulate the relationships
> between slaves and their masters, the enslaved and the free, and those of Afri-
> can and of European descent. These 1724 regulations would shape how racial
> identities—with their particular rights and obligations—emerged in lower
> Louisiana, but they were, to a great extent, defined by a distant metropole

that was responding to situations within Louisiana, elsewhere in its colonial empire, and in France itself, as it sought to regulate racially exogamous relationships, manumission, and the status of free people of African ancestry. Codifying status and ancestry as important determinants of rights, privileges, and obligations, the 1724 Code Noir reflected the transition from a status-based hierarchy to one rooted in race, thus creating a niche for free people of African ancestry, albeit one that few were able to take advantage of during the French era. (Spear 53)

Thus at the dawn of the eighteenth century in France, regulating race relations and *métissage* in its colonies became of greater concern as the population became more hybrid and racially mixed. Dawdy offers further clarification regarding the implications of this new code to both France and Louisiana:

Comparing Louisiana's *Code Noir* of 1724 with its predecessor written for Saint Domingue forty years earlier (by the influential French finance minister Jean Baptiste Colbert) provides one of the clearest examples of the ways in which French ministers built up knowledge of their colonies and adjusted their tactics with each new venture. For the Louisiana version, several articles were dropped, recombined, or modified, and two new articles were added. The most significant changes entailed regulating intimate relations between blacks (*noirs*) and whites (*blancs*); controlling and limiting the free colored population; and intervening in the disciplinary regime of slavery. In the Saint Domingue code, only *concubinage* between whites and blacks was specifically prohibited. So long as the two parties were both baptized Catholics, interracial marriage *was* tacitly permitted. Further, a free man of *any* color could marry a slave woman and thereby free her. In contrast, the corresponding Louisiana article explicitly forbade marriage between whites and blacks of any station, and specified that manumission could result from marriage only in the case of a free *black* man marrying an enslaved woman. French ministers modified another article to restrict routes to freedom. In the original code, masters had the express right to free their slaves without needing to give a reason. The Louisiana version, however, dictated not only that owners had to justify a manumission, but that they had to obtain the permission of the Superior Council for it to be legal . . . With the Louisiana *Code Noir* of 1724, ministers attempted to design an "improved" slave society that did three things: made slavery more permanent by narrowing the chances of manumission; drew a starker color line between white and black by delegitimizing any kind of *métissage;* and intervened in the master/slave relationship in the area of corporal discipline. (198–99)

The 1724 code attempted once more to preserve the *mission civilisatrice* of France in the New World by going as far as criminalizing sexual relations between Europeans and Africans when such a mission represented a utopian ideal impossible in this new hemisphere. New hybrid populations emerged in this new world, populations not limited to the white-black binary notion of race, although that binary was the foundation on which plantation societies were built. The *Code Noir* of 1724 could not stop the new hemispheric genealogy from being established, as the code ultimately could not prescribe sexual interactions among the races. The result was a mixing, a *métissage* of the population forming "a community marked by slippages in the boundaries between classes and races fostered by the exigencies of frontier life" (*Masterless Mistresses* 67). The earliest New Orleanians represented a fundamentally multiracial society.

Examining Travel Narratives of Early Colonists

Not surprising, the travel narratives written by French colonists in the early eighteenth century present a very different picture of life in early New Orleans compared to the propaganda of the Company of the Indies. The "clearly defined" lines drawn between the races, and upon which the French colonial efforts depended, often appeared blurred; French notions of "order" and "civilization" touted in the travel accounts of the *Nouveau Mercure* simply did not exist. Instead Louisiana resembled much more the French colonies in the Caribbean already established by this time, with their "disorderly," "uncivilized" racial, gender, and social composition. Thus, far from being stratified, hierarchical, and bounded by European tradition, these societies represented Creole hybrids born by swift, haphazard fusion of Natives, Europeans, and Africans who quickly formed societies, families, and a new world order.

Manuscripts written by colonists, mariners, and administrators provide extensive and detailed accounts of the realities of early New Orleans and the efforts it took to survive and even thrive in this environment, often from very personal perspectives. Early travel writings include that of the ship captain of the *Toulouse*, M. Vallette de Laudun, in his *Journal d'un voyage à la Louisiane, fait en 1720;* of Adrien de Pauger, whose correspondence is included in the history of Louisiana written by De Villiers du Terrage; of Le

Page du Pratz, who wrote *Histoire de la Louisiane* (1758) from his observations while in Louisiana 1718–1734; of Chevalier Jean-Charles de Pradel (1692–1764), whose letters have been reprinted; of the Ursuline nun Marie Madeleine Hachard, whose letters from 1727 to 1760 have also been reprinted and edited by Emily Clark; of Charlevoix, whose travel account is perhaps the best known of all *Relations*; and of Marc-Antoine Caillot, who wrote *Relation du Voyage de la Louisiane ou Nouvelle France* in 1730, which has just been translated into English, edited by Erin Greenwald. This chapter also includes an important letter housed at the *Bibliothèque de l'Arsenal* in Paris that has been largely forgotten over the last century, and which has not previously been translated into English. It is written by the early colonist and *concessionaire* Gérard Pellerin, who details his arrival in the colony with family and servants aboard the *Toulouse*, and describes the process of establishing a settlement that took him to Natchez, via Dauphin Island, New Orleans, Manchac, and Baton Rouge. This invaluable manuscript tells of the challenges in establishing a concession, the shortcomings of the Company of the Indies providing for the settlers, an encyclopedic description of the geography and agricultural potential of the area, as well as his personal losses and how he eventually established himself in Natchez.

These writers offer a very different picture of New Orleans from the propaganda of the *Nouveau Mercure* and go as far as calling out the lies the journal had printed. When Father Charlevoix arrived in Louisiana at the beginning of 1722, he states: "Here I am in the famous city they call New Orleans . . . The eight hundred beautiful houses and the five parishes that the *Mercure* reported two years ago are reduced still today to a company store of sheds placed haphazardly, to one large company store built of wood, to two to three houses that would not grace any village in France and to the half of a miserable store that they were willing to loan to the Lord, and which had only just been given over for that purpose when the eviction notice came with the request to lodge it in a tent" (Letter dated January 10). In a letter dated January 26, the priest continues his lament, "The best idea that I can give you is to imagine two hundred people that were sent to make a new life, and who are camped on the banks of a great river where they only thought to set up protection from the elements, while waiting for a plan before building any houses." This paints a picture of rudderless, stagnated colonial management that neither suited the aims of the colony or the needs of the colonists themselves.

Coupled with the disorganization and mismanagement of the colony on the part of the Company of the Indies, these writers reference the company's dishonesty and profiteering that operated as common practice. Ship's captain Vallette de Laudun references important silver mines have been found in Illinois, supposedly three times richer than those in Mexico, adding the comment that it is probably from there that company stock got its worth (257–58), suggesting it was yet another example of company propaganda and economic exploitation. In the rest of the letter he states his opinion that instead of chasing after these dreams, and depending on suspicious and unreliable characters, it would be better to cultivate the soil, and raise corn, rice, and vegetables, to protect the coast and against growing Indian aggression against the colonists (259–61). He offers, as other writers also did, advice on how to adapt to the exigencies of life in Louisiana by demonstrating a commitment to settle the colony, invest in agriculture, and build an infrastructure there rather than by chasing the dream of get-rich-schemes and easy profits.

In their writings, the colonists also criticized how the *Nouveau Mercure* depicted Dauphin Island. Just as with New Orleans, the paper wove an imaginary tale of civilization and order on the island, just as it had done relative to New Orleans. Instead of its having one hundred houses and a fort, with two companies of fifty men, as *Relation de la Louisane ou Mississippi: Écrite à une Dame, par un officier de Marine* claims (14), Gérard Pellerin calls it a worm-infested sinkhole where newly arrived colonists rot, and Le Page only found one shack with a roof of palm fronds that Bienville had built (Book 1 34). The criticism found in these narratives was not limited to the company's propaganda, but also levied against its directors for their choice of beaches along the Gulf of Mexico as a place of landfall. Adrien de Pauger decries the faulty leadership of the company directors, their stubbornness, *leur entêtement,* and their abuse of authority, *leur trop d'autorité,* that led to considerable loss of life and opportunity because of these directors' insistence on having colonists make landfall on the sands of the Gulf of Mexico instead of in New Orleans (De Villiers du Terrage, *Histoire de la Fondation de la Nouvelle-Orléans* 87). Describing his arrival to Louisiana in 1718, Le Page du Pratz laments the sands of Biloxi, which Iberville had established as the first attempt at creating a capital for the colony. He says,

> I could never guess the reason the settlement was made in this place, nor why the capital should be built at it; as nothing could be more repugnant to good sense; vessels not being able to come within four leagues of it . . . But what ought to have been a greater discouragement against making a settlement at Biloxi, was, that the sand is the most barren of any to be found thereabouts; being nothing but a fine sand as white as snow, on which no kind of greens can be raised; besides, the being extremely incommoded with rats, which

swarm there on the sand, and at the same time ate even the very stocks of guns, the famine being there so very great, that over five hundred people died of hunger. (Book 1 31–32)

Pellerin explains his own attempts to move beyond Dauphin Island and the sands of the Gulf in his letter, describing how he was fueled by his personal determination not to follow the same plight as other concessionaires, "On the contrary, I ardently requested for them [company representatives] to provide me with the means to push forward. Otherwise I would be consumed like the others are. Or I would have made a decision when there would not have been enough time left. Ultimately I remembered that I had not come to Louisiana to fight the sand, but to work on a settlement equal to my strength." Pellerin asserts that his preparation for building a settlement was a product of the "long and well-known voyages that I have made by sea [that] have made me think differently from other concessionaires who, since they are tied to the company and need to be within reach of the easy supplies that they receive from the ships, do not want or do not seem to want to leave this island." His leaving Dauphin Island to obtain a concession, not surprisingly, marked the beginning of many challenges and losses, for in spite of his acumen and entrepreneurial spirit, he lost his wife and son within a few months of their setting out. He nonetheless remained undaunted in his desire to establish his own habitation.

These early narratives were written by colonists arriving directly from the metropole. When they got to Louisiana they distinguished between settlers, like them, from France and those from French Canada. For example, in Hachard's letters, she talks about potential colonists as representing families from France and Canada (*Voices from an Early American Convent* 89). Even if the family would be first-generation Canadian, as was the case with the Le Moyne brothers, Iberville and Bienville, they would still be referred to as Canadian. When French colonists arrived in Louisiana their experiences in this new land were mediated by French Canadians and in many ways followed their foundational footsteps in colony building. These writers, especially Pellerin, offer descriptions of Canadians language and ways of life to their French readers. When Pellerin first reaches New Orleans, which was two years before Charlevoix, he does not describe a French colonial space, but instead a settlement consisting of three houses for Canadians and a company store. The impression reflects that in its earliest iteration the city was a French Canadian, rather than a properly French, space. With Bienville being the city's champion, this does not necessarily seem surprising, yet it appears nonetheless interesting that as a French settler arriving in New Orleans Pellerin makes no mention of the Crown being present in this town. Instead the agents in charge of this colonial enterprise, according to his comments, refer to French Canadians. This problematizes the idea that they held secondary status to the French in the earliest years of New Orleans.[19]

In his text, Pellerin makes a point of explaining Canadian words such as when he says that the word bayou means "small river in Canadian." He offers a primer to his cousin, where he explains the ways that he learned as he pushed forward toward finding a concession:

> An explanation is due here to educate you on what it means "to make camp" (*cabaner*) or "to make the stew" (*faire chaudière*), terms used by the voyageurs in Louisiana. These are terms that come to us by the Canadians who use them during their voyages, as well as others. We would use other terms in their place to explain these things. At night be it on the seacoast or on the banks of the river, about one hour before dusk, they get out of the pirogues or the boats and come by land with equipment necessary for making beds and cooking. You see, one goes about making a bed by first gathering a pile of leaves on which one lays the mattress, then one takes some cane from the willows or another wood, bending it so that it can be stuck into the ground on both ends. That makes a circle on which one puts a large canvas so that on all sides the ends fall on the ground. On top of this canvas, another with tar is better still. Where it is waxed you sleep sheltered from the rain that can happen and from the mosquitoes who reign in this country from the beginning of April until October 15. When you go north, these animals reign for shorter periods. While some sleep, others "make the stew" for the next day's dinner so as not to lose any time. And at around noon they stop at the base of a willow tree to eat or they go on land, usually in the winter when there are no mosquitoes. So there you have it, what we call in this country *cabaner* and *faire chaudière*. And the canvas that covers the bed is the *berce*, it's the weapon for the voyage.

This account underscores how the ways of the French Canadians provided lessons for survival in the Louisiana wilderness as well as helped to establish patterns of colony building by how their ways allowed new colonists to camp, travel, and transport themselves.

Waterways, rivers, and bayous abound in Pellerin's narrative and impact almost every aspect of his existence in the area around New Orleans, especially since no levee had yet been constructed. With the mouth of the Mississippi River considered non-navigable in the early years of the colony, these alternate waterways, rivers, and bayous provided a means of transportation and allowed New Orleans to be settled. In addition, they also provided alternative routes for transportation of goods when the Mississippi River in New Orleans overflowed, which according to Pellerin happened six months out of the year. Little wonder why in this manuscript he draws up plans for the river relating to flood control. Nonetheless, Pellerin did not draw up these plans by virtue of his being an administrator of the colony, but rather he drew them up because he was an ardent colonist bent on settling in the area and was motivated to propose a solution to the flooding problem, the biggest impediment to establishing a viable colony.

Upon presenting these ideas on how to protect New Orleans from flooding, Pellerin articulates the colonial discursive space allowed to him by virtue of his unofficial status in the colony as he says, "So there is my idea. We all are free to talk until the time that good decisions come from France." This statement suggests that original, cogent ideas based on experiences in the colony are allowed free expression until the time the Crown assumes its role, given by Divine Right, to create order and live out its *mission civilatrice*, providing "good decisions." In Louisiana at that time, there were painfully few of these good decisions made, as Pellerin and other colonists attest. In this simple sentence, the colonist claims the right of agency for himself and other settlers, "we are free to talk," because of the profound lack of engagement by those who administer the colony, "until the time good decisions come from France," thus articulating a fundamental dynamic of Creole societies and the original cultures that emerge from this dynamic of local agency versus the metropole's control in the colony.

These writings then underscore the tenuous relationship that existed between the metropole and colonists who ventured to criticize the Crown. When the authors of these narratives criticized the ineffective settlement strategies and conflicted management of the colony throughout the French period, they did so understanding that it would be considered a criminal transgression by the French Crown and that they would be libeled. We see this especially with the Chevalier de Pradel and Pellerin. The documents they wrote were correspondence to family and friends, where they in fact knowingly included information and observations that could have put them and their families at risk. For example, in the Pellerin document this newly arrived colonist shares his concern about the mismanagement of the Company of the Indies when he says, "But oh my, just between us, the company that makes such a commotion in France, does not make much progress here for lack of getting involved and for not paying attention to the wellbeing of the colonists. I do not want to say more. *Nolite tangere christos* costs me a lot of butter."[20] He says all he dares to say because of the power of the "anointed," making allusion to the colonial administrators and the Company of the Indies. The order and civilization reported in the *Nouveau Mercure* were sadly missing from the colonists' point of view, and these texts serve as a testimonial to that campaign of misinformation.

In his letter, Pellerin often references the confounding indecision of the Company of the Indies, the inordinate time it took to accomplish basic tasks, and the broken promises made to the colonists concerning their future concessions in Louisiana. Not only does he speak about inefficient practices and a lack of organization, but he also tells of official corruption, explaining how the company takes the best merchandise and supplies for itself, and that the monopoly of trade is not only unjust but also forces the colonists to operate in contraband in order to survive. Pellerin was prosecuted for breaking the absolutist trade policies of the Company of the Indies and was libeled for selling his agricultural products from his concession in Natchez downriver in New Orleans. This act broke the terms of his agreement with the Company of the Indies. Pellerin justifies himself by saying his very life depended on his doing so because of the corruption of the Company of the Indies and the lack of supplies in its stores: "The court case in which Mr. de Gac did not want to understand me alleged that I am no longer the responsibility of the company. The beautiful reason given is that the company furnishes all its stores through its branches economically and equally, and a habitant should not need to leave his habitation for four to five months to make these one hundred leagues in order to come look for necessities. I console myself and I am convinced that I and the others would never come for the pleasure of coming unless the wound was mortal." When pushed to the brink, Pellerin like many others before and after him, relied on the commercial opportunities afforded by the Mississippi River, as well as the Greater Caribbean Basin, to buy and sell necessary goods that would not otherwise be available. Even the two French Canadian governors of the colony Bienville and later Vaudreil "violated the royal monopoly by aiding and abetting small-time smugglers . . . to keep Louisiana politically stable in the absence of French subsidies after the political divestment of the 1730s . . . Louisiana evolved over time from a buccaneer outpost to the base of a sophisticated creole syndicate" (Dawdy 102). Local agency was a form of alterity in spite of the metropole's ineffectual and divisive policies that led to starvation and death for many early colonists. The latter faced a daily choice of following the directives from France and perishing in the sands of the Gulf Coast. Or further north they might die due to lack of supplies and a dysfunctional colonial enterprise. To avoid such an unwelcomed fate, these people needed to adapt to their new surroundings. Adaptations would include learning from the "disruptive" *voyageurs* and *coureurs de bois*, or the Canadian leaders.

The most important guidance, however, would be from the Native American guides, viewed by the French as "savages" akin to animals. Pellerin says as much in recounting an episode about his Indian guide, whom he expected to lead him safely to shore from a shoal in the Gulf. Pellerin writes, "However I was still sinking along with a savage that had been given to us as a guide and who let us down. This animal only thought about saving a flask of brandy that he carefully carried in the air." Nonetheless, Pellerin later in the manuscript suggests that settlement patterns for future French colonists should follow the footprint of Indian settlements: "The more French who come, the more they would find because the savages upon the death of their chief traditionally abandon the village and the surrounding lands and go to live elsewhere." But he adds, "Thus a settler would have little trouble if the company would award him sufficient negroes, as were promised in France, and which until now has not yet been carried out in any way for us."

The colonial narratives put the tensions among officials and the consequences of their infighting in a personal context. Leaders contributing to ongoing conflict cited in these narratives included Bienville, who was both a general and a governor, Hubert, who was company director, and de la Chaise, who became company director and later *commissaire-ordonnateur*. The early colonists complain about the negative consequences they personally suffered on account of these officials. For example Pradel offers a considerable litany of consequences that he and his family suffered because of their personal connections to de la Chaise, whom Bienville considered an enemy. Pradel claims that Bienville was ultimately interested in his own personal wealth and when de la Chaise was company director, he had Bienville sent back to France, having accused him of malfeasance. So when Pradel married de la Chaise's daughter in 1730, he too became a target for Bienville's wrath (De Villiers du Terrage, *Histoire de la Fondation de la Nouvelle-Orléans* 78–79). Pradel was not promoted in the military; indeed he was passed over several times for promotion, and was sent on an agricultural expedition to Illinois as a much older commander than was typical. Conversely, thanks to his wife, he developed a friendship a few years later with then governor Kerlerec, so he was able to buy slaves at a lower cost because the governor had certain rights in the form of an account to buy slaves for less money than it would cost others. This added substantially to his personal wealth (Pradel 265).

Tension and competition existed between Bienville and Hubert, with Bienville's personal and financial interest being tied to New Orleans against Hubert's being tied to the settlement further north in Natchez. De Villiers claims that the development of New Orleans was stalled in large part because of colonists not wanting to rile Hubert or Le Gac. This caused people like Du Pratz and Pellerin to leave New Orleans or some like Breuil, Du Hamel, and les Chauvin to settle at a respectable distance from the town (De Villiers du Terrage, *Histoire de la Fondation de la Nouvelle-Orléans* 44–45). Pellerin alludes to this tension in the following passage in which Hubert, referred to as *M. le Commissaire*, persuades Pellerin to settle in Natchez rather than on Bayou St. John:

> I took it upon myself, or decided, if you will, to take my concession and the land that the General granted me through the help of Mr. Paillon, Major General. But Mr. Hubert cautioned me about it, saying that the company had reserved this land in order to establish a sizeable tobacco plantation. Personally I was not totally opposed to the situation, but I would not have been able to take possession of the land before the end of September, so I would lose time and it would cost to have to buy food possibly from the company. My spouse and I thought about what the *M. le Commissaire* had said. Mindful of public opinion that the best and most agreeable place was Natchez, we decided to place our concession in Natchez. My nephews who sometimes discussed things with the Canadians had begun to speak highly of this place. And it was for this reason that I asked *M. le Commissaire* for land in Natchez. He seemed delighted at the news. He assured me that it was the best port on the Mississippi and that there would not be nearly as many difficulties for me. In fact, further proving his point, he was going to settle there himself. It was for this land that I gave my word.

This passage clearly shows how decisions to settle in the Louisiana territory were motivated more by personal relations with those in power than by any colonial plan for settlement. Hubert possessed a strong personality and launched a personal campaign to create a settlement in Natchez. For Pellerin who appears as his ally Hubert is described as, "a very gallant man who engages a good bit in the interest of honest people." This allegiance extended to Hubert's development of Natchez over Bienville's New Orleans. "By this maneuver, M. *le Commissaire* will build up Natchez in under two years while downriver will not develop as it should for six years. This in spite of the fact that on the ships and in the lower river valley they have easy supplies for their consumption, while all that we have are leftovers that the voyageurs bring us from so far away. They do not ask if we need plums, however if we don't need them, they will come looking for us, in spite of the little bit that the ships bring to us. So here it is, my dear cousin, the normal situation in Louisiana, the state which all things are in. You can count entirely on this description to judge." However, Le Page had thought about joining Hubert and settling in Natchez but decided against it because he ultimately did not get along with Hubert, whom Le Page claims "endeavored to pay his court to the governor, at the expense of others" (Book 1 30). Such strong-willed, self-concerned characters would not have been able to wield such power and influence were the colonial administration more functional. It is evident in these writings that New Orleans was the territory's most important settlement well before it was officially named the capital of *la Louisiane* due primarily to its proximity to the mouth of the Mississippi River. Ultimately all those championing other settlements had to agree that New Orleans was indeed the superior location for the capital city, even Hubert (De Villiers du Terrage, *Histoire de la Fondation de la Nouvelle-Orléans* 100–102).

Perhaps the one thing that all administrators agreed upon was that there needed to be slaves to build the colony. The Company of the Indies promised a specific number of slaves to early concessionaires, a promise that, as Pellerin laments, went unfulfilled, "Thus a settler would have little trouble if the company would award him sufficient negroes, as were promised in France, and which until now has not yet been carried out in any way for us." Pellerin also complains about how the company controls access to slaves, keeping many for itself, "The company reserved the best and the largest number of those who arrived on the ships from Guinea. Now that there is the Company of Senegal, the company must not be lacking any and it can wait meanwhile, independently of the ships from Guinea, for a certain amount to come from the Cap to Louisiana by the boats that land there on their way to coming here." The slaves from Guinea, Pellerin explains, have been put to work by the company on levee building, "but they are currently working to make it more habitable by means of a great number of slaves or negroes who arrived from Guinea."

Newly arrived settlers from France would have to learn how to become slave owners and Le Page du Pratz concluded his history of Louisiana, with an extensive treatise providing information and lessons to colonists about how to become effective slaveholders, "[f]ancying himself an architect, Le Page set about designing slave quarters for the King's Plantation in the late 1720s" (Dawdy 147–48). Like other early settlers to the area, he abided by the notion that slaves needed to be segregated from the colonists. Le Page du Pratz situates the treatment of slaves in a discourse of the Christian colonist, stating in the conclusion to his treatise, "To conclude, one may, by attention and humanity, easily manage negroes; and, as an inducement, one has the satisfaction to draw great advantage from their labours" (Book 4 387). Being a master, as well as a humanitarian (of sorts), leads to order, profit, and success according to the author. He does not address here the question of miscegenation between the slave owner and slaves, although Le Page du Pratz himself had acquired Native American slaves upon his arrival, including a young woman who bore him two children.

When giving advice to future slave owners, he details how the purchase should be made, along with how to ensure the quality of the individuals who are being purchased. However, after the sale, he takes up the mantel of a Christian, expressing with a certain pride that a female slave shared a traditional cure with him because she had observed "the great care I took of both negro men and negro women" (380). It is with this attitude of "care" that he offers advice on how to welcome these new arrivals to the colonist household: "When a negro man or woman comes home to you, it is proper to caress them, to give them something to eat, with a glass of brandy; it is best to dress them the same day, to give them something to sleep on, and a covering. I suppose the others have been treated in the same manner; for those marks of humanity flatter them, and attach them to their masters. If they are fatigued or weakened by a journey, or by any distempers, make them work little; but keep them always busy as long as they are able to do anything, never suffering them to be idle, but when they are at their meals" (Book 4 380–81). When Le Page du Pratz was given the task of designing housing for the company slaves just across the Mississippi River in what is now Algiers Point, he explains his concept as follows:

> Prudence requires that your negroes be lodged at a proper distance, to prevent them from being troublesome or offensive; but at the same time near enough for your conveniently observing what passes among them. When I say that they ought not to be placed so near your habitation as to be offensive, I mean by that the smell which is natural to some nations of negroes, such as the Congos, the Angolas, the Aradas, and others. On this account it is proper to have in their camp a bathing place formed by thick planks, buried in the earth about a foot or a foot and a half at most, and never more water in it than about that depth, for fear lest the children should drown themselves in it; it ought likewise to have an edge, that the little children may not have access to it, and there ought to be a pond without the camp to supply it with water and keep fish. The negro camp ought to be enclosed all round with palisades, and to have a door to shut with a lock and key. The huts ought to be detached

from each other, for fear of fire, and to be built in direct lines, both for the sake of neatness, and in order to know easily the hut of each negro. (Book 4 381–82)

The order and symmetry of this compound functions for Le Page du Pratz as a sort of humanitarian prison, controlling the movement of these captives, assuring their well-being, all the while keeping them at a distance suitable to assumed white sensibilities. Further in this treatise Le Page du Pratz describes in great detail how to manage slaves within this space, both through encouragement and punishment, in order to establish a regime that preserves that health and well-being of the slaves. Encouragement includes asking the slaves not to work so hard, or sing so loud as to sap their energy for their labors, and a bit of tafia or rum to keep their "strength and spirits" (Book 4 384).

Regarding domestic slaves for the household, he takes a guarded tone and warns that female slaves should never be wet nurses to the family's children, since milk is the "purest blood of a woman" (Book 4 382). From his experience, he suggests that the only slaves to be allowed responsibilities for the household be those from Senegal because "they have the purest blood; they have more fidelity and a better understanding than the rest, and are consequently fitter for learning a trade, or for menial services. It is true they are not so strong as the others for the labours of the field, and for bearing the great heats. The Senegals however are the blackest, and I never saw any who had a bad smell. They are very grateful; and when one knows how to attach them to him, they have been found to sacrifice their own life to save that of their master" (Book 4 382). In this description of Senegalese slaves, the social hierarchy associated with color becomes a secondary notion to these slaves being deferential to their master's wishes, even to the point of the slave's self-sacrifice to save the slave owner. So the "blackest" of slaves gains value by a supposed tendency "to sacrifice" themselves, to be "grateful" to their owners, and all the while not to have "a bad smell."

A City Emerges

In spite of the corruption, disorganization, and local strife, by 1727, it appears that contributions of French Canadians, French administrators, and colonists, along with slaves, coalesced into making New Orleans into a recognizable city for those arriving in the city for the first time. When Marie Madeleine Hachard arrives in New Orleans that year she offers the following description:

Our city is very beautiful, well constructed and regularly built, as much as I am able to know of it . . . Before our arrival we were given a very bad idea of the city. It is true that those who spoke to us of this had not been here for several years. They have worked, and they continue to work, to improve the city. The streets are very wide and laid out in lines. The main street measures a league in length. The houses are very well constructed in collombage and mortar, whitewashed, paneled, and sunlit. The roofs of the houses are covered with little flat plates made of wood cut in the form of slate. One must know this, in order to believe it, for this covering has all the appearance and beauty of slate. It is enough to tell you that here one publicly sings a song in which there is only this city which resembles the city of Paris. This tells you every-thing. (*Voices from an Early American Convent* 76–77)

As opposed to earlier descriptions of a city where it seemed stagnant and rudderless, the city that Hachard describes represents a functional, orderly urban space. By 1730 Caillot's description of New Orleans shows well laid out roads, echoing Huchard's description, but his description also reveals a bustling city:

First you see the parish church, built of wood and bricked inside, 144 feet long and 60 feet wide, of a terrible wood that is found in this aforementioned place. One can sing the praises of the engineers who drew up the plan for this town, for it is a very fine creation for the country. It will become better and better, as much for the beauty of its buildings, which are being constructed, as for the layout of its streets, and also for its long levee, a quarter of a league long and 22 feet wide, which protects the city from river flooding. Along this levee is the customary promenade, and on one side there are two storehouses, each 220 feet long and 40 feet wide. The company headquarters are also very well built, both grand and spacious, consisting of an apartment for the direc-tor, a very proper main hall for hearings, and three offices joining it. They are as follows: one for the council, where the secretary and two assistants work; the second for the chief bookkeeper and his eight employees; and the third for the private accounts of the former administration, which has seven employees. What makes this building even more beautiful are two pavilions that have fine wrought-iron balconies. The munitions storehouse is found to the left of this building, and to the right you can see an arsenal, all situated opposite the river. (78)

Caillot continues to detail the various buildings, their function, and their importance to the city and the colony. Regarding the Ursuline nuns, which would include Hachard, he writes, "On Chartres Street there is a convent of Ursuline nuns, who are seven in number. There should be twelve more coming from France, and the convent will be at the other end of town, on the quay. They teach the young people without profit or anything else except for what people willingly want to give them. They have some boarders who pay room and board" (79–80). He describes an active community that interacts economically, socially, and religiously, and offers one of the few descriptions focusing on women's contribution to colony building in early New Orleans.

So in spite of the complex interactions and challenges to colony building on the ground, there is ample evidence that these early colonists remained optimistic about the future of Louisiana. Pellerin explains how he made that adjustment soon after his arrival in New Orleans, "This territory there is generally good, black, big and uniform, but full of trees in certain places like with poplars, sweetgums, laurels and green oaks. There are little rivers or bayous full of crawfish. All along one finds wetlands that are clear of vegetation. These would be quite a great advantage for the French who could find similar spots. The more French who come, the more they would find because the savages upon the death of their chief traditionally abandon the village and the surrounding lands and go to live elsewhere." What Louisiana can offer to France, according to Le Page du Pratz, is the following: "She has found in her lands neither the gold nor silver of Mexico and Peru, nor the precious stones and rich stuffs of the East-Indies; but she will find therein, when she pleases, mines of iron, lead, and copper. She is there possessed of a fertile soil, which only requires to be occupied in order to produce not only all the fruits necessary and agreeable to life, but also all the subjects on which human industry may exercise itself in order to supply our wants" (Book 2 198). Le Page du Pratz continues further on in his history of Louisiana:

> The real goodness of a country, will soon alter their opinion, and agree with me, that a country fertile in men, in productions of the earth, and in necessary metals, is infinitely preferable to countries from which men draw gold, silver, and diamonds: the first effect of which is to pamper luxury and render the people indolent; and the second to stir up the avarice of neighboring nations. I therefore boldly aver, that Louisiana, well governed, would not long fail to fulfill all I have advanced about it; for though there are still some nations of Indians who might prove enemies to the French, the settlers, by their martial character, and their zeal for their king and country, aided by a few troops, commanded, above all, by good officers, who at the same time know how to

command the colonists: the settlers, I say, will be always match enough for them, and prevent any foreigners whatever from invading the country. (Book 2 208)

Caillot talks about the potential of Louisiana by stating that if the company would send two thousand *nègres* and an appropriate number of whites, this would be a second Saint-Domingue (108). Pellerin states that the "river is deep, proud and majestic, as no other is in the world." And even Charlevoix concludes that this "wild and deserted place, still almost completely covered by cane and trees, will one day, and maybe that day is not too far off, become an opulent city and the capital of a great, rich colony" (98). These colonists' optimism for the future of Louisiana, and of New Orleans in particular, stems from the tremendous natural resources relative to land and water, its expansiveness, and its untapped potential for development.

Some of these colonists remained in Louisiana by choice, such as Pellerin, others by necessity such as Pauger. Many like Caillot continued their travels through his work with the Company of the Indies. Pauger died in New Orleans in 1726 despite years of pleading to be sent back to France. Succumbing to a tropical fever in his home on what is now Decatur Street between Conti and St. Louis, he was the first to be buried in St. Louis Cathedral (De Villiers du Terrage, *Histoire de la Fondation de la Nouvelle-Orléans* 115–20; Dawdy 65). But Caillot and Le Page du Pratz left while still in their prime of life. Caillot left Louisiana in 1731 after the huge losses the company suffered following the Natchez uprising that destroyed the tobacco investments. He requested a transfer and continued to work for the company in India (Greenwald xxix). Le Page returned to France in 1738, and it is generally believed that he had children with his Native American slave, who would have remained in Louisiana (Sublette 38). Pellerin's end was not a happy one, having lost everything in the Natchez Revolt of 1729 that destroyed the French settlement in the area now known as Natchez, Mississippi, he settled permanently in New Orleans. There he died in 1737 with a tarnished reputation. In his work as the storekeeper for the company store, he was accused of siphoning merchandise and even taking slaves that did not belong to him. This caused him to be fired as well as obligated to repay his debts to France.[21] And records of Pellerin's household lists one mulatto in 1732, which suggests that, just like Le Page du Pratz, Pellerin left behind at least one biracial child (*Census Tables* 124). Pradel succumbed to yellow fever in 1764, and his widow Pradel clearly considers Louisiana her home since she got so angry at her daughters for not wanting to return to Louisiana that she disinherited them.[22] Hachard died in the Ursuline convent in 1760 having spent over thirty years educating young women of New Orleans, a beloved member of her house according to her obituary (*Voices from an Early American Convent* 117–18).

During the time chronicled by these writers New Orleans grew from having a handful of buildings in a haphazard arrangement to a city that is well laid out, bustling and holding the promise of becoming the opulent capital of a great, rich colony. Within a generation, the local elite established itself, comprised mostly of French Canadians (*The Accidental City: Improvising New Orleans* 35). Creole society was taking shape with some of its characteristics still being recognizable today. A unique blending of fact and fiction created the fabric of New Orleans and shaped the identity of its people—the "French" "Creole." The "in-between" space created a colonial capital unique in how it built upon connections to the French colonizer, real and imagined, while it promoted local agency that was a Creole product. In the next chapter we will examine how this transformation of New Orleans into an emergent Creole society played out spatially, with traces still visible in today's French Quarter.

CHAPTER TWO

The French Quarter: Imagined Spaces

Introduction

Here I present an original interpretation of the urbanization of New Orleans as an attempt at transposing a "French space" onto the colonial wilderness through studying the design and construction of early New Orleans, today's French Quarter, thus extending the imagined connections between New Orleans and France to the spatial realm. The making of the French Quarter was a negotiated process occurring between the colonial officials representing the metropole, in their attempt to imprint French order onto what they considered to be savage land, and the local Creoles in the city, led and championed by Bienville. These locals had their own sense of how this city should be built. In this chapter, we will see how this urban design can be understood as representing a desire on the part of the local population to hold onto the stability of the French monarchy long after New Orleans ceased being French. I argue that from the founding of the city, the Catholic Church has served as a central organizing force in society. I also argue that the local population has demonstrated an unfailing respect for Bienville, as the patriarch of this city built on highland along the Mississippi River.

La Nouvelle-Orléans, the French Quarter

The French Quarter is the heart of New Orleans today both physically and symbolically. Originally the French Quarter comprised virtually all of *la Nouvelle-Orléans*, housing all of the components needed for this settlement to be an active colonial center.[1] From the mid-1720s within a relatively few square blocks were found the official administrative buildings of the colony, as well as the church, prison, schools, homes, hospitals, and other spaces that serviced the needs of the colony. These few blocks at the bend of the Mississippi River have been called various names over the last three hundred years: *la Nouvelle-Orléans, la Nueva Orleans, the French Quarter, the French Quarters,* and more recently *the Vieux Carré* (Lemmon et al. 308). This renaming mirrors the city's changing colonial history and its enduring association with its French heritage.

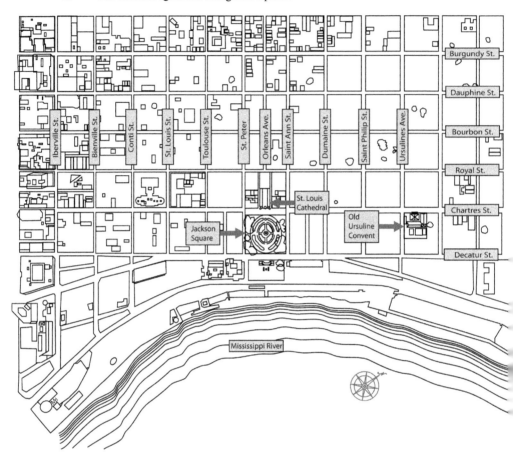

Once Americans started to settle in the city around the time of the Louisiana Purchase (1803), New Orleans grew well beyond the original few blocks at the bend of the Mississippi. The importance of the Mississippi River increased and along with it came an influx of settlers, investors, and transients connected in one way or another to the river and its growing port. Americans, especially wealthy ones, settled in what was called Faubourg Ste. Marie, now known as Uptown New Orleans, situated just upriver from the old city. The old city became known as the "French" Quarter and was separated from the American section by a median that was called a "neutral ground" in New Orleans, a term still used by New Orleanians today to mean "median." The lines of demarcation in the early years of the American colony were clearly drawn in the symbolic; the dynamics of "us," the French-speaking Creoles, versus "them," the Americans, appeared as a clearly drawn line on the cityscape, although the actual demographics of the city divide was more permeable than it first appears.[2]

As we have already established, New Orleans has not made the shift to becoming a "truly American" city, in spite of the importance of the long-standing American presence. It seems obvious that one of the main reasons can be found embedded in the cityscape of New Orleans that represents a minefield of French history. Unlike other American cities, such as Philadelphia, New York, or Chicago, whose histories as American cities are represented in their monuments, their architecture, and their cultural references, the historical references in New Orleans do not evoke American history but instead markedly French, as well as Spanish, histories, as Sublette muses: "To get around in New Orleans, you drive through history, navigating the dense web of references embedded in the street names. La Salle. Iberville. Bienville. Orleans. Chartres. Poydras. Ulloa. Galvez. Miro. Carondelet. Claiborne. St. Louis. St. Charles. St. Claude. St. Bernard. Frenchmen. Names New Orleanians negotiate every day. The street map is a time capsule" (5–6).

In spite of the visibility of historical markers, the interpretation of their significance remains much more subjective and hidden. Generally speaking, for Americans, including many American scholars, historical references to the French and Spanish colonial periods and their accompanying historical figures often remain vague, fragmented associations that suggest a somewhat monolithic notion of these colonizers' history. However, from the French perspective, as we have discussed earlier, there remains a notion that New Orleans as a part of *la Nouvelle France*, should have more in common with Québec than with the Caribbean or even the American South. The assumption implicit in this French perspective supposes that most aspects of the colonial process followed an order and a logic from France transplanted directly on the colonial landscapes first to Quebec and then to Louisiana.

French Imprint in New Orleans

Instead of viewing New Orleans primarily through a French or an American lens, this study attempts to gain a new understanding of the founding of New Orleans from a focus on how both the French colonizers and the local Creole colonists, comprised primarily of first-generation French Canadians, negotiated their stake in this colony through urban planning. We especially consider how the streets were ordered and named, and how the urban design and configuration of the streets represent both physically and symbolically the power of the French monarchy in the colony. We also consider this urban plan was a space in which Creoles negotiated aspects of their own identity, speaking back to the powers that exerted such influence on these colonists' survival. This chapter treats the changing cityscape during the colonial period and analyzes trends of urban development in both the local and the European arenas, and, as such, charts the social construction of the French Quarter in ways that have not before been considered.

At issue are how these urbanization efforts reveal the tensions between "empire" and the "colony," between how the metropole's policies, systems, and representatives negotiated with the local forces that were generally not controlled, defined, or limited by the French colonial agenda, and who in turn were able to exert influence not only on that colonial agenda but also on the monarchy itself. By focusing on the making of the French Quarter, we can see how a "grammar of difference" was constructed and constituted a staging ground for negotiation between the empire and the colony. French epistemological and theological forces attempted to make order and "civilize" what they perceived was savage wilderness. However the local Creole population had additional concerns, values, and desires relative to the design of this space. In considering the relationships of the hierarchies represented through the naming and renaming process of this streetscape, instead of arguing that the street names only reference individual historical figures, noble families, and these families' patron saints, as other scholars have done, the present analysis incorporates the notion of the "spatial imagination" of more symbolic French sociopolitical issues by considering how the connections between certain streets, especially those at the "center" of the French Quarter, represent cultural referents of France transplanted to the "new world" at specific historical periods.

The spatial imagination can be understood as "a conceptual process that combines relatively specific, if not always realized, social and functional urban intensions with deeper, more diffuse values and expectations. It operates in a realm beyond simple instrumentality, translating non-spatial goals and categories into spatial terms" (Upton 174). The spatial imagination at play in the making of New Orleans drew from French military history with its fortified cites and bastides, from the grandeur of Louis XIV's Versailles with its promenades and gardens, as well as the idealized logic and order of the Age of Enlightenment. Dawdy explains, "Planners and colonials seem to have hoped that New Orleans would have elements of all: it would be a well-fortified frontier town, an orderly port city serving mercantilism, a symbolic metropolis representing the king in a vast new territory, and a garden city of simple pleasures" (Dawdy 74).

Design of New Orleans

So while today it seems "natural" that New Orleans was conceived as a river city on the banks of the great Mississippi River, arguably the most important waterway in North America and therefore a "natural" location for the capital of *la Louisiane,* this was simply not the case. It took years of experimentation before these elements coalesced (Upton 174). At issue was the navigability of the Mississippi River because although the Mississippi's importance for colonization and commerce were evident to the French, in the early years of the colony, ships could not navigate up the mouth of the river. It took decades for engineers to come up with solutions to these challenges. So today it seems obvious that New Orleans would be a superior site over any of the competing sites, such as Biloxi, Manchac, and Natchez,[3] because of its location on the Mississippi River, its relatively short distance from the Gulf of Mexico, the portage that existed between the lake and the river, and the promise of a thriving port and its partial protection from floods and hurricanes (*Time and Place in New Orleans: Past Geographies in the Present Day* 36). Yet, as we have seen in the previous chapter, this was not the case. Besides the dissention and acrimony among these officials who were attempting to influence where the capital of *la Louisiane* would be located, part of the problem in initially understanding the enormous potential that New Orleans held strategically and commercially was due to the impossibility of navigating large vessels from the mouth of the Mississippi to New Orleans. Let us recall that the mouth of the Mississippi represents a bird-foot delta with shallow mud-filled channels. At the time New Orleans was founded, engineers were in the early stages of designing ways to dredge the river near its mouth.

In the travel narratives of the preceding chapter we have already seen how haphazard the development of the early years of the city appears and how much of a French Canadian space it initially represented. We also have seen how the mid-1720s saw the city transformed, as Hachard explains, "Our city is very beautiful, well constructed and regularly built" (76). This "order" was put in place by Adrien de Pauger, the city's urban designer and an early advocate of having New Orleans as the capital city of the colony (in spite of his being perennially at odds with Bienville).[4] He would have wanted to design the city much earlier than he did and understood how the hesitant, ill-informed, and self-interested patterns of settlement caused much suffering. In the following passage Pauger laments the cost in life and for the colony the delay in deciding to have New Orleans as the capital caused:

> I hurried to New Orleans to draw up a project of a symmetrical city that is to be the capital of this country, which would currently be much further along if the Company had provided enlightened settlers and directors who would have either seen for themselves or who could have listened to good advice when it was given to them. I have come to understand just how much their stubbornness and their power caused the vessels coming from France to stop in Biloxi rather than having them enter the Mississippi, which is the reason and the cornerstone for settling this country, where they would have disembarked both workers of the concessionaires and equipment on fertile ground that would have made life possible. There would have been beautiful houses but instead they disembarked in Biloxi on banks of sand that consumed them and where they saw their equipment and most of their best workers die. (De Villiers 87)

Pauger's plan borrows from the Spanish tradition of building colonial cities. The Spanish ideal consisted of a central square with a church and administrative buildings, with streets in a straight line, emanating from the central square, representing a grid. As the population might grow, development was meant to follow this grid design (Langlois 176). Although constructed later, we can understand Jackson Square, St. Louis Cathedral, the Presbyter, and the Cabildo as reflecting this Spanish influence, as opposed to Quebec City or Montreal with their "winding, organic streets cities, New Orleans and Louisbourg in Nova Scotia conform to the 'imperial' orthogonal grid" (Dawdy 72).

Pauger drew up these plans in 1721. The next year a major hurricane struck New Orleans destroying most of the buildings and an unexpected tabula rasa emerged for Pauger in the wake of the hurricane. Nonetheless, as we have already demonstrated, locals were quite accustomed to expressing their voice in the process of colony building, and many resisted building according to the limits this orderly grid imposed on them. Pauger, in turn, aggressively championed his design, not shying away from verbal, written, or physical conflict with residents or administrators who challenged him. Indeed within a few years the city was built according to Pauger's original plan, emerging as the most formally symmetrical of any city commissioned by the French (Dawdy 96). This plan did not include space to house African slaves, however.

As we saw in the previous chapter, Le Page du Pratz took it upon him-self to draw up plans for housing slaves in an enclosed settlement to be located on the other side of the Mississippi River. This segregation proved impractical in the long term. New Orleans emerged as a city where Afri-can slaves, free people of color, and whites lived in close proximity to one another in what would today be considered more like "racially integrated neighborhoods." Le Page du Pratz offers the following eyewitness account of the layout of this part of the city in 1728. In his account he describes New Orleans as being a more developed urban space:

> The place of arms is in the middle of that part of the town which faces the
> river; in the middle of the ground of the place of arms stands the parish
> church, called St. Louis, where the Capuchins officiate, whose house is to
> the left of the church. To the right stand the prison, or jail, and the guard-
> house: both sides of the place of arms are taken up by two bodies or rows of
> barracks. This place stands all open to the river. All the streets are laid out
> both in length and breadth by the line, and intersect and cross each other
> at right angles. The streets divide the town into sixty-six isles; eleven along
> the river lengthwise, or in front, and six in depth; each of those isles is fifty
> square toises, and each again divided into twelve emplacements, or compart-
> ments, for lodging as many families. The Intendant's house stands behind the
> barracks on the left; and the magazine, or warehouse-general behind the bar-
> racks on the right, on viewing the town from the river side. The Governor's
> house stands in the middle of that part of the town, from which we go from
> the place of arms to the habitation of the Jesuits, which is near the town. The
> house of the Ursuline Nuns is quite at the end of the town; to the right; as is
> also the hospital of the sick, of which the nuns have the inspection. What I
> have just described faces the river. (Book 1 54)

The basic design that Le Page du Pratz describes has endured for nearly three hundred years, including the layout of the streets, the "place d'armes," which today is Jackson Square with St. Louis Cathedral that overlooks it, and the location of the Ursuline convent downriver from the center of today's French Quarter.

A Fortified City

Le Page du Pratz, as well as other travel writers of the time, describes the city beginning with its relation to the Mississippi River. However the early plans of the city drawn up by Pauger suggested a different kind of a city center for the newfound capital of Louisiana. Instead of having the river and the access it provided to the city serving to frame this urban space, operating as its city center, Upton suggests that the original city planners de la Tour and Pauger relied on the pre-Vauban model of the walled Bastide for their design, rather than the model of a river settlement. This Bastide structure had a military function: "Bastides housed farmers in hostile settings. Typically a market square abutted by a church and the civil government's headquarters were placed somewhere near the town's center. Bastide planners assumed that their authority was threatened both from without and within, so they usually provided an interior strong point from which urban population could be controlled, along with the town's encircling walls" (175). When one considers New Orleans from the perspective of the Bastide model, the "interior strong points" in Pauger's design, as Upton posits, seem very compatible with those found in a typical Bastide and they include a place d'armes, a parish church, a corps de garde, and a clergy's residence (Upton 176). Just like in a Bastide, the most important administrative, religious, and security buildings were placed at the center of the city.

In the original plans there were walls or ramparts that surrounded the city. However, these were never built, although during the Spanish period five forts were built that had virtually the same function and they were built on the sites currently known as the intersection of Canal Street and Decatur Street, at the intersection of Canal Street and Rampart Street, at Congo Square, at the intersection of Rampart Street and Esplanade Avenue, and finally at the intersection of Decatur Street and Esplanade Avenue. In "Urbanization in the Old World and in the New," David Buisseret says that as far as fortified cities in North America are concerned, "none were as thoroughly carried out as that of New Orleans" (80). The city sought protection from Native Americans, especially in the wake of the Natchez Indian Revolt of 1729, which killed hundreds of settlers, thus destroying the French settlement there, as well as slaves from plantations upriver, downriver, and from Bayou St. John.

Since the Bastide concept is an abstract division of space essentially based on a clearly delineated center and on strong outer ramparts for defense, in New Orleans the Bastide model does not completely reconcile with the setting of the French Quarter and its position on the banks of a great river. Whereas bastides might have been built next to rivers, the integrity of the design depended on there being enough distance between the river and the settlement, as would be the case with hilly or mountainous riverbanks, so as to have a rampart or some other kind of defensive barrier built. However, *la Nouvelle-Orléans* did not occupy such high ground. Instead the earth consisted of low-lying alluvial rather than rocky ground. Indeed, no significant distance between the settlement and the river exists, and as we have already seen its proximity to the Mississippi was the settlement's greatest asset. So the Bastide model appears more like a vestige of colonialism where the empire, and more specifically French bureaucrats in the office of the Company of the Indies, attempted to imprint their own notions of order and organization on the colony without factoring in local realities, which were ultimately incompatible with the Bastide model.

On the local level, colonists found themselves in a position to incorporate other models of urban design, often by necessity, and use them to compliment those that do not completely account for the local conditions, creating moments of cultural fusion that suit the needs of this new environment. For the locals, for example, there was no ignoring the Mississippi River that impacted virtually every aspect of their everyday life. In his analysis of the design of New Orleans, we find an example of such cultural fusion when Upton suggests a second model of urban design with the river figuring more prominently than in the previous design. This model reflects the palace of Versailles. Whereas bastides were built to ward off attacks through their formidable defense, Versailles was designed in part to intimidate potential enemies of France. Instead of a military notion of defense relying on physical barriers so as to prevent attack, the model of Versailles uses the concept of majesty and order as a means of intimidation that begins on a symbolic level to ward off aggression from potential enemies. France's official architectural structures, both buildings and monuments, were traditionally a means by which to affirm French hegemony through these structures' grandeur as well as their sheer bulk as they functioned as the physical representation of the (supposed) colossal power of the monarchy, and would then be a formidable foe against potential aggression.

Versailles Transplanted

More than as a deterrent to its enemies, Versailles represented a culminating point of the *ancien régime* by virtue of, recalling Upton's words, the ways in which the palace successfully fused "physical and non-physical attributes into a kind of Platonic space that accommodates all connections, all relationships, all hierarchies at once" (174). Here is how Upton describes the way that Versailles served as a model for New Orleans and how this model was imprinted on the banks of the Lower Mississippi: "The approach from the river, as the planners imagined it, presented a unified urban image, a wall of authority centered on the three main institutions at the rear of the place d'armes, flanked by officials [*sic*] residences and warehouses and other public [buildings] stretching along the levee the length of the city. To step onto the levee and enter the place d'armes was akin to entering the *cour d'honneur* of a French Renaissance palace, and indeed the waterfront footprint of New Orleans resembled nothing so much as Louis XIV's Versailles. New Orleans's parish church and corps de garde occupied the *corps de logis*, the ruler's apartments at the Sun King's palace" (179).

The Grand Canal of Versailles's gardens can be understood as represented by "Rue d'Orléans ou grande Rue," as Pauger called it in New Orleans. Langlois posits that Rue d'Orléans functions as the *axe générateur*, the central organizing axis of the city, mirroring the same design as the park of Versailles with its central canal (225). Out of all the French colonial settlements, New Biloxi and New Orleans were the only ones to have a central axis (Langlois 179). The concept of a central point of power has preeminence throughout the *ancien régime*, especially during the reign of Louis XIV, where it functioned as a trope for social order and the French state. Versailles was in a very real sense the epicenter of French hegemony through its reason, its symmetry, its order. This palace and its grounds were the center of France. Louis XIV himself with his emblem of the Sun King was the embodiment of the French state, most obviously represented in his emblem of Apollo the Sun King, the center around which everything else revolved. This idea was reinforced spatially in the palace with the king's apartments being located in the actual center of the palace, while it was reinforced operationally through how the king's apartments functioned as the central administrative bureau of the French government.

Representing this notion of centralized power as an extension of the hegemony of the absolute monarch then can be seen as useful trope for this new colonial French city, with Rue d'Orléans as the *axe générateur*. Pauger's early map of the French Quarter then serves as an attempt to imprint through its very design French hegemony on the soil of *la Nouvelle France*. As such, the placement of a clear urban center represents the center of power of the monarchy both spatially and symbolically in this new urban landscape. The situation of having the monarchy referenced in the center of the urban grid afforded benefits to struggling colonists. One can imagine this transposition of European order in the Americas could have provided colonists psychological comfort during challenging moments. It also could have served as a convenient reference, as somewhat of a normalizing vehicle, to newly emerging hemispheric norms in this French colony.

New Orleans, just like Versailles, could be understood as being constructed "*A toutes les gloires de la France*." The centralized notion of power, of the state and of the monarchy, represented the known order of things, the pinnacle of French power and glory, and perhaps a necessary psychological reference point for making order out of the perceived chaos of this savage and dangerous wilderness. This idea is not at odds with that embedded in the Bastide model where the center of the grid is the most protected from threatening forces "both from without and within, so they usually provided an interior strong point from which urban population could be controlled, along with the town's encircling walls" (Upton 175). Both centers function as social organizers that project order, protection, control, and tradition on this colonial landscape, which would otherwise be wilderness. The fact that Louis XIV was dead, that there was a regency, and that the colony was being managed by a private company run by a Scotsman apparently did little to diminish the symbolic importance of the Sun King and the values manifest in his reign and his usefulness as a trope for colonists.

Mapping New Orleans

This section presents a detailed description of the changes in street names as they appear in chronological order on early maps. The next section "France's *Ancien Régime* on the Streetscape of New Orleans" analyzes these eponymous references and their significance. Generally speaking, the naming of colonial settlements was quite meaningful and operated on several different levels of significance relating to colony building. In particular in *la Louisiane*, naming of various parts of the colony also was a means by which to attract new colonists and to promote settlements in this new world, while appealing to French sensibilities. For example, Bienville thought that Indian names such as Biloxi or Natchitoches "would in Paris appear a bit savage" (De Villiers 21), so we do not see any Indian names in the street names of early New Orleans (Sublette 53). New Orleans was made feminine because it sounded more pleasing to the ears (De Villiers 22). Mobile seemed too unstable for Bienville, so he attempted unsuccessfully to have the name changed to Immobile in 1711 (De Villiers 21). And Isle Massacre, so named because the first colonists found bones in heaps there so that it appeared to have been the site of an Indian massacre, was swiftly changed once and for all to Isle Dauphine, which according to Le Page du Pratz, "as act of prudence, it should seem, to discontinue an appellation, so odious, of a place that was the cradle of the colony" (in De Villiers 20–21). This erasure eliminated reference to violence and to Native peoples at the same time.

In the context of New Orleans, although the earliest maps sometimes do not include the street names, a composite historical record allows for insights into when the changes in the street names of the French Quarter occurred. As the earliest maps show, very little has changed in the center of the French Quarter. Beginning with the earliest reference, Pauger's original plan included all of the streets that we now find in the French Quarter, that being the thirteen streets perpendicular to the Mississippi River and actually one more than the six streets running parallel to the river, as we see in *Plan de la Nouvelle Orléans* from 1722. However, due to a lack of population on the outlaying streets, maps drawn up later in the eighteenth century do not include all of the streets in Pauger's design. For example, streets running parallel to the river often do not reference to Dauphine and Burgundy because these streets did not have stable residences until the late 1700s or early 1800s. Pauger's original names for the streets of New Orleans are the following. Those streets perpendicular to the Mississippi River were named Saint-Adrien, Rue d'Anguin (or d'Enghien), Rue Bienville, Rue Saint-Louis, Rue de Toulouse, Rue Saint-Pierre, Rue d'Orléans ou Grande-Rue, Rue Sainte-Anne, Rue Dumaine, Rue Saint-Philippe de Clerment, and Rue de l'Arsenal. For streets running parallel to the Mississippi their names were Rue du Quai, Rue de Chartres, Rue Royalle, Rue de Bourbon, and Rue de Conty, Rue de Vendôme (De Villiers 114).

At the end of Caillot's 1731 book is a map that offers the following names. The streets perpendicular to the Mississippi River are called Rue de Bienville (rather than d' Anguin), Rue de Conty (rather than Bienville), Rue St. Louis, Rue de Toulouse, Rue St. Pierre, Rue d'Orléans, Rue Ste. Anne, Rue du Maine, Rue St. Philippe (rather than the longer St. Philippe de Clermont), Rue de l'Arsenal, and Rue des Religieuses (which appears for the first time). We see then that the only differences in names occur with the last two streets that are now called Ursulines and Governor Nicholls, respectively, and the streets that are the farthest away from the center are not yet on the map, those streets being Iberville and Barracks. The streets running parallel to the river are called Rue du Quay, Rue de Chartres, upriver from the Place d'Armes, and Rue de Condé, downriver of Place d'Armes (which appears for the first time), Rue Royalle, Rue de Bourbon (no longer having the second name of Condy for part of the street), and then two more streets on the grid that do not have names, so there is no longer a Rue de Vendôme. As we have already seen, it seems as though by the 1730s John Law's reputation has fallen so far out of favor that a direct reference to him has been eliminated from the cityscape of New Orleans. Another reason for the absence of references to these streets that were present in Pauger's model is that there was not enough population in the early 1720s for there to be development in these areas farthest away from the Mississippi River.

These streets were not developed until later in the colonial period, as the population of the colony grew, especially that of free people of color.

Besides offering a map of New Orleans, Caillot's travel memoir, as we have already seen, offers an invaluable glimpse of New Orleans of 1729 as he describes a more established urban center than Charlevoix witnessed seven years earlier. In his account, Caillot speaks about two company stores, each 220 feet long and 40 feet wide. The director's office is well built, large and spacious, and includes an apartment for the director, a very clean, large room used for meetings, and three adjoining offices all housing several employees and having various functions. There are two pavilions with two well-built balconies. The store for fortifications is to the left of this domicile and to the right is an arsenal, whose tower faces the river. He says that there are fourteen streets, not counting the Quay. The houses are built of wood, due to lack of stone, but one year ago they began using bricks. Instead of plaster, they use *chaux* made of seashells. He explains that there are two hospitals, 135 feet by 45 feet, and one of them is for black slaves. Nearby is a large building for the intendent. The Ursulines' convent is on Chartres Street and farther away live the two Jesuits remaining in the colony. He states that the prison is a beautiful building and is next to the guardhouse. There is also a Capuchin monastery with three priests; this space includes a nice but small residence, a pretty garden and a place to educate the young. He explains how it is presided over by the bishop of Québec, and he goes on to describe the executioner, who is black and who lives out of town, as well as the five or six wealthy planters living on the banks of Bayou St. John. He is one of the rare travelers to talk about the brewery, the inns, and the cabarets that also lie outside of town, where one is "well served." He also talks about stores selling contraband merchandise needed by the colonists but not sanctioned by the company (102–5).

On a map, the *Plan de la Nouvelle Orléans telle qu'elle était le 1 janvier 1732*, the names given are Rue de Bienville, Rue de Conty, Rue St. Louis, Rue de Toulouse, Rue St. Pierre, Rue d'Orléans, Rue Ste. Anne, Rue du Maine, Rue St. Philippe, and Rue de l'Arsenal for those streets perpendicular to the Mississippi River. Downriver are two more streets that do not have names. For those streets parallel to the river the names are Quay, Rue de Chartre (with no mention of the Rue de Condé), Rue Royale, and Rue de Bourbon. Furthest away from the river is one more street that does not have a name. As we will see, this map has the most in common with the naming of the streets that we have in the New Orleans French Quarter today.

On a map, *Plan of New Orleans the Capital of Louisiana; with a Disposition of*

its Quarters and Canals as they have been traced by Mr. de la Tour in the Year 1720,
dated 1759 and done by the English cartographer Thomas Jeffreys, the
street names are in a slightly different order. Streets perpendicular to the
Mississippi River are Rue de Bienville, Rue St. Louis (rather than Conti),
Rue de Conti (rather than St. Louis), Rue de Toulouse, Rue St. Pierre,
Rue d'Orléans, Rue Ste. Anne, Rue du Maine, Rue St. Philippe, Rue de
l'Arcenal, and two more streets that have no names. The streets running
parallel to the river are Quay, Rue de Chartres (spelled a second time on
the map as Chartre), Rue Royale, and Rue de Bourbon, followed by another street without a name.

One French map, *Plan de la Nouvelle Orléans,* drawn by Jacques Bellin
and dated 1764, was a reprint of his earlier 1742 map. This reprint was to
become the standard map of New Orleans in the late eighteenth century
(*Charting New Orleans* 315). The streets are in a slightly different order as
on the 1759 map, with streets perpendicular to the Mississippi River being
Rue de Bienville, Rue St. Louis, Rue de Conti, Rue de Toulouse, Rue St.
Pierre, Rue d'Orléans, Rue Ste. Anne, Rue du Maine, Rue St. Philippe,
Rue de l'Arcenal, and two more streets that have no names. And those
streets running parallel to the river are Quay, Rue de Chartres, Rue Roiale,
and Rue de Bourbon, followed by another street without a name. This layout is virtually the same as that of the 1759 map.

On the map, *La Luisiana Cedida al Rei N.S. Por S. M. Christianisima, con la
Nueva Orleans, é Isla en que se halla esta Ciudad,* drawn up in 1762 by Tomás
Lopez de Vargas Machuca for the king of Spain at the time that New Or-
leans became a Spanish city, we see the following names appear. Running
perpendicular to the Mississippi River are Calle de Bienville, Calle S. Luis,
Calle de Conti, Calle de Tolosa, Calle S. Pedro, Calle d'Orleans, Calle S.
Ana, Calle del Maine, Calle S. Phelipe, Calle del Arsenal, and then two
more streets without street names. Streets running parallel to the River are
Muelle, Calle de Chartres, Calle Real, and Calle de Borbón, followed by an
area that is a type of ditch. This map was inspired by Bellin's map of 1742.

On the 1803 map, *Plan de la Nouvelle Orléans et des environs dédié au citoyen
Laussat, préfet colonial et commissaire de la République française par Vinache, chef
de bataillon du génie sous-directeur,* drawn up for Laussat for the French at the
time of the Louisiana Purchase, there are thirteen streets running perpendicular to the Mississippi River: Rue de la Douane (the first time this street
has appeared since Pauger's original model), Rue de Conty (rather than
Bienville), Rue de Bienville (rather than St. Louis), Rue St. Louis (rather
than Conti), Rue de Toulouse, Rue St. Pierre, Rue d'Orléans, Rue Ste.
Anne, Rue Dumaine, Rue St. Philippe, Rue des Ursulines (rather than Rue

de l'Arsanal), Rue de l'hôpital (which appears for the first time since Cail-lot's map, where it was called Rue des Religieuses), and Rue du Quartier (which appears for the first time). There are five streets running parallel to the Mississippi River. Laussat does not give a name to the street normally called the Quay or Rue du Quay. The others are Rue de Chartres upriver from the church and Rue de Condé (this name appears for the first time since Caillot's map) downriver, Rue Royale, Rue Bourbon, Rue Dauphine (named for the first time since Pauger's plan of naming it Rue de Vendôme), and Rue Bourgogne (named for the first time).

France's *Ancien Régime* on the Streetscape of New Orleans

Given all of the uncertainty about the situation of New Orleans as the capi-tal and the tendency to alter the names of settlements in Louisiana, it is remarkable that the center of the city, the heart of the urban grid, has un-dergone very little change since Pauger drew up his plan for the city. The streets of Toulouse, St. Peter, Orleans, St. Ann, Dumaine,[5] Chartres (upriv-er from the Place d'Armes), Royal, and Bourbon remain unchanged since 1722. The unchanging nature of this cityscape from the French, through the Spanish and American periods, stands in remarkable contrast with the many changes in the street names that occurred into the nineteenth century for other streets farther from the center of New Orleans.

The heart of the city center is this intersection of the Church of St. Louis, whose name honors the canonized medieval king of France Louis IX, and which serves as the spiritual center of the capital. Originally the church faced away from the river, and toward the axial center of the city and the city's widest street, Orleans Street, also called Grande-Rue. This street represents the official political center of the city, named after the regent, Philippe duc d'Orléans, the leader of the French state when New Orleans was founded. While a French city of Orléans exists, at the time Pauger was drawing up his plans for the city, the reference would have been to the duc d'Orléans since he was ruling France. The intersection of the Catholic Church and the French monarchy at the center of this urban grid not only reproduced the spatial and symbolic power of each entity, but it also re-produced the hegemony behind the French monarchy's relationship to the Catholic Church of the early eighteenth century. In considering the latter part of Louis XIV's reign there had been no other country in Europe where state politics and Catholicism were more intertwined, not even in Spain or Italy, and no other country that assumed to have a king more power-ful than the pope himself. Under Louis XIV, Gallican policies were put in place to stem the tide of the growing numbers of Protestants in France. What helped to galvanize this relationship was the rising importance of the policies of the Counter-Reformation in France and France's intolerance of Protestantism and its "heretics." With his Revocation of the Edict of Nantes in 1685, being a Protestant in France, and by extension in its colonies, was a crime. Even as La Salle was continuing his exploration of Louisiana and the Gulf Coast expanding Louis's dominion over countless "*sauvages*," Louis XIV's domestic policies were becoming more intolerant and violent.

It was thought that under the regency of Philippe duc d'Orléans, beginning in 1715, there might be more religious tolerance in France and less abuses of power, but this did not prove to be the case.[6] Philippe continued in the tradition of his uncle, Louis XIV, and during his regency persecution of this type continued. In fact, the regent performed other acts of tyranny that went beyond religious intolerance through his decision to make Louisiana into a penal colony 1719–1720. This was an attempt to eliminate a broad range of "undesirables" from France—not just those serving prison terms, but the destitute, those accused by *lettres de cachet* of some dishonorable act, and prostitutes. Conversely, just as French monarchs before him had done, Philippe justified this colonial agenda through claiming that these were ultimately acts of evangelism to convert the heathens and save their souls. This discourse of evangelism is aptly represented by the presence of the Jesuits, the Ursulines, and the Capuchins at the founding of New Orleans, and with the Ursuline convent being the only building remaining from the French colonial period.

Moving from the intersection of Orleans Street and the St. Louis Church, there is St. Peter Street flanking Orleans Street upriver, and St. Ann Street flanking Orleans downriver. While it has been argued that these two references are based on their being patron saints of the House of Orléans (Hall-Quest 22; O'Neill, "The French Regency and the Colonial Engineers" 209), what if we consider that the naming of these two streets might be significant on a more symbolic level, one that would have been quite obvious to Catholics at the time? In Catholic tradition it is understood that Saint Peter is the patriarch of the Catholic Church, named by Jesus Christ just before his death to continue the legacy of Jesus on earth. Peter is the "rock" or the *pierre* upon which he built the church. Conversely, in the Catholic Church, Saint Ann is venerated because she occupies the role of matriarch, being the mother of Mary and thus the grandmother of Jesus. No matriarchal figure who is a forbearer to Ann exists in the Catholic tradition. Furthermore, Ann had long been the patron saint of French sailors and was an important presence throughout *la Nouvelle France*.[7] Therefore, having these two streets named after the symbolic patriarch and matriarch of the Catholic Church functions as a tangible means to embed the capital of Louisiana at the symbolic bedrock of Catholicism. Further reinforcing this idea, these streets flank and support Orleans Street, the symbolic center of this urban environment, at its intersection with the Church of St. Louis. Having the church at the center of this space fortifies its being a Catholic rather than a protestant or "savage" city.

Flanking St. Peter Street upriver is Toulouse Street and flanking St. Ann Street downriver is Dumaine Street. As historians of New Orleans have often noted, these Toulouse and Dumaine refer to two legitimized sons of Louis XIV who were born of his relationship with Athénaïs de Rochechouart de Mortemart, better known as Madame de Montespan. The eldest child born of this union was Louis-August, duc du Maine (1670–1736), and the second born was another son, Louis-Alexandre, comte de Toulouse (1678–1737). There were a total of six children that Madame de Montespan bore Louis XIV, and they all enjoyed, generally speaking, a most privileged status at court, evidenced by the fact that Philippe duc d'Orléans himself was married to the fourth born, Françoise-Marie, Mademoiselle de Blois (1677–1743). The symmetry of the placement of these two streets Toulouse and Dumaine relative to the axial center of the French Quarter suggests that these individuals not only occupied a privileged place in the colony, but that they also shared the same level of privilege in the eyes of the colony given the complementary pairing of these streets.

These historical figures loomed large in the reign of Philippe as they were pawns, in a sense, that helped to define his reign and the limits of his power. During his regency, uncertainty about Philippe's desires as regent abounded. Historians assume that just as regents before him, he was more interested in ascending the throne himself than he was in his role as steward for Louis XV, or other Bourbons who could have made a case for assuming the throne if Louis XV were to die at a young age. There were clear reasons to suspect Philippe's motives. Namely, in spite of the fact that the status of his own wife would be implicated, Philippe attempted to solidify his hold on power by "rebastardizing" du Maine and Toulouse, who would have been next in line for the throne were young Louis XV to die. This plot to remove the legitimized status of du Maine and Toulouse was inspired by John Law, who saw it also as a strategic move to further disenfranchise the court nobles and to enhance the status of Law's chief benefactor, the regent himself. This represented a radical departure from what was considered acceptable practice at court that had surprising consequences. In *France 1715–1804: Power and the People*, Gwynne Lewis offers the following descrip-

tion of this most unusual episode in French history, which coincides with
the year that New Orleans was founded:

> By the summer of 1718, Dubois and Law, increasingly anxious about resis-
> tance from court aristocrats, the Paris parlement, and financiers like the Cro-
> zat and the Pâris brothers, decided to convince a rather skeptical Regent that
> liberal policies were no longer appropriate. The "old guard" would have to
> be sacrificed on the altar of "modernisation." Dubois, who regarded himself
> as the reincarnation of Richelieu, was desperate to don a cardinal's hat, and
> thus had little time for the pro-Jansenist antics of the parlements. Like his
> role model, he was more than prepared to sup with Protestant devils abroad
> in order to make France safe for Catholic absolutism at home. His friend
> Law was also facing increased hostility over his moves to further depreciate
> the value of gold and silver coins in favour of his paper money. The Regent,
> however, conscious of how many political cards were being stacked against
> him, took some convincing; but his eventual conversion to the authoritarian
> cause was facilitated by the conspiracies of the duchesse du Maine and the
> Breton nobility.

This represented a turn of events from which Law and his cohorts would
not recover. Gwynne Lewis goes on to suggest the following interpretation
of events:

> It is easy, with the benefit of hindsight, to dismiss these events as "comic-
> opera," but it would be wrong to underestimate contemporary fears of
> noble resistance, foreign interference and popular rebellion, in other words,
> a reversion to the days of the mid-seventeenth century Frondes. A feisty
> granddaughter of one of the grandest of *les Grands,* the prince de Condé, the
> good duchesse had been incensed by the Regent's move to "rebastardise" her
> husband, the illegitimate son of Louis XIV and the latter's choice as guardian
> of the young Louis XV. Living in her turreted fantasy land, she succeeded—
> to most people's astonishment—in getting the Spanish foreign minister,
> Alberoni, and the Spanish ambassador to France, Cellamare, to join her in
> a plot to secure both the return of the Stuart pretender to London and the
> replacement of the Regent in Paris by Philip V of Spain; in other words, to
> destroy the Treaty of Utrecht. The duchesse de Maine also became embroiled
> in a less harebrained revolt by the Breton parlement—the most independent
> and aristocratic in the country—over the government's attempt to force new
> taxes on the province in the spring of 1718. By September, several of the

members of the parlement had been arrested or exiled for opposing "these assaults on the rights and privileges of our estates." (28–29)

With these court intrigues in mind, when the Law financial bubble burst in 1720, it represented a victory for the French nobility. In particular the duc and the duchesse du Maine and for the comte de Toulouse enjoyed a most significant political victory over the usurpers Law and Dubois. Du Maine and Toulouse were able to keep their most privileged position at court, as well as their potential claim to the French throne. This act also signified a restoration of the traditions put forth by Louis XIV, and the accepted economic and political practices of his time, that were displaced when Law had power over the French economy and commerce.

Pauger's plans for New Orleans were drawn up in 1721, thus after the status of du Maine and Toulouse had been reestablished. Du Maine remained an important figure since he was given the tutelage of the young Louis XV, and Toulouse remained very implicated in affairs at court and abroad. In fact he was supposed to review Pauger's city layout (De Villiers 84–87). There was a fort named for him, and Charlevoix named an island for him. Taking all of this into account there is a clear argument to be made that the naming of Toulouse and Dumaine Streets was not only in honor of these two royals but also signified an affront to the legacy of John Law and his Company of the Indies in Louisiana. As we shall see, these are not the only streets to celebrate individuals who helped burst Law's financial bubble and bring down his financial empire.

One more point that should be made about the place that du Maine and Toulouse occupied in French society: There was always the chance that one of them would ascend the throne since at the moment New Orleans was founded, the future of the Bourbon line sat squarely on the shoulders of the crowned prince Louis, the great-grandson of Louis XIV. The crowned prince was the last-born child of the duc de Bourgogne. His two siblings had died several years earlier, and his father and grandfather the Dauphin both died in 1711. In biography of the last years of the reign of Louis XIV, Max Gallo poignantly captures the sadness at the court of Louis XIV, when he describes the aging king losing so many of his offspring in a few short years and then dying with the knowledge that there would only be one child left to carry on the Bourbon dynasty, one great-grandson still a boy. Therefore when we consider the placement of Dumaine and Toulouse Streets on the urban grid of New Orleans, we can see that they are the nearest to the center of the city, in fact closer to the center than streets that reference

Louis XIV, Philippe duc d'Orléans, and the crowned prince. This suggests that the colonists, too, understood the potential role these two historical characters might play in the future well-being of the colony. We can imagine that the city planners might have been hedging their bets on which of these potential sovereigns might end up controlling the colony.

Moving to the next pair of streets, we find the last complimentary pairing of streets in the French Quarter: St. Louis Street flanks Toulouse Street upriver and St. Philip Street flanks Dumaine Street downriver. Given the complimentary position of these streets in the urban grid, St. Louis Street can be understood to refer to the immediate past king and the crowned prince, that is, Louis XIV and Louis XV, respectively, while St. Philip Street can be understood to represent Philippe duc d'Orléans.[8] A complimentary relationship to the placement of these streets exists, linking the past, present, and future rulers of France to this urban space and the political stability. These streets tell the story of the sociopolitical hegemony of the time that included uncertainty and doubt, especially the prevalent doubt as to whether young Louis XV would survive to his majority and actually ascend the throne. This collective doubt might explain why the paired streets of Toulouse and Dumaine are closer to the axial center of the French Quarter than are St. Louis and St. Philip, and as such are closer to the symbolic hegemonic center of both the colony and the empire. Finally, the pairing of St. Louis and St. Philip Streets would seem to serve as a kind of topological end point where the elements within this topology symbolize the relationship between the Catholic Church, the saints, and the Bourbon line, Louis and Philip, which was then imprinted in this New World structure. The other streets in the current French Quarter do not follow the same pattern of mirroring one another, and they also have had their names changed over the years. Thus, these streets will be examined after a treatment of the streets that run parallel to the Mississippi River.

In examining the discernible patterns and significance of the street names that run parallel to the Mississippi River, we begin at the river's edge only to see that for Pauger the name of this first street was simply a function of its position lying next to the water, with its being referred to as the Rue du Quai. For many years, well into the American period, it was also called Wharf or Levee Street, until given its current name of Decatur in 1870 when the street was no longer along the levee due to the action of the dynamic Mississippi River (Chase 52). The fact that this street's name was completely functional for the entire French period, and well beyond, reinforces the notion that in the original design for la Nouvelle-Orléans the center of this urban space was not meant to be the opening onto the Mississippi River, but rather the center was intended to be the Rue d'Orléans-Grande Rue.

The next street away from the Mississippi and running parallel to it is Chartres Street. It is on this street that the Church of St. Louis was built. As we have already noted, in earlier maps the part of the street downriver from the church was named Condé, although this reference does not seem to be a constant because it is listed on the Caillot map of 1731 and is not found again until Laussat's 1803 map. The name Chartres once again serves as a reference to the regent, with his official title being Philippe II d'Orléans, duc de Chartres, duc d'Orléans. This interpretation then further plays upon the notion that this street was one that framed the center of the Vieux Carré, delineating an outer imaginary boundary toward the river, in the same way that St. Louis Street did upriver and St. Philip Street did downriver. When considered from this perspective, these "outer" limits of the center of New Orleans suggest that this heart of the colony were framed by references to the eighteenth-century rulers of the house of Bourbon, Louis XIV, Philippe duc d'Orléans, and the future Louis XV, the heads of state responsible for the colonial past, present, and future.

The Condé family was one of the *grandes familles* of France and like the Conti family was a branch of the house of Bourbon (Ripley and Dana 585). A member of this family, Louis IV Henri de Bourbon-Condé, who was also known as the duc d'Enghien (Ripley and Dana 585), looms large in the early history of New Orleans, and will be treated later in this analysis. However, by 1803 there was no single figure in the Condé family who would be implicated in Louisiana or New Orleans. We are left to consider, then, why this name reappears after seventy years. Could it be a return to the original name of the street? If the answer were that simple, then all streets should have had their original names, which of course is not the case. Might it be that the street was referred to as Condé over the years, and that this was simply overlooked by eighteenth-century cartographers? This too does not appear the case because on the maps of 1759 and 1764 the name Chartres (or Chartre) is given to the street both upriver and downriver from the Church of St. Louis. What we do know about the situation of the Condé family in 1803 was that they were fierce royalists and the head of the family, Louis Joseph de Bourbon, Prince de Condé (1736–1818), had emigrated to England after the revolution, and fought against France. His son was executed by Napoleon in 1804 (Gilman et al. 122). So the Condé family was clearly an enemy of Napoleon. We are left to wonder about the unexpected reappearance of their name etched upon the landscape of New Orleans, at the same time as Napoleon sold the city to the United States, and whether this was another example of how the colonists in New Orleans expressed their unhappiness with a political situation that implicated them and their city by bringing back the name of a family that was fiercely royalist and not happy with Napoleon as emperor.

Let us now consider the remaining streets running parallel to the Mississippi River as a single complimentary unit. The streets are Royal, Bourbon, Dauphine, and Burgundy, and they can be understood as representing a toponymy of the French monarchy, with the first street in this series, Royal Street, representing the overarching principle of the *ancien régime*. It was by virtue of royalty that allowed La Salle to found *la Louisiane* in the name of the king:

> By his very high, very powerful, very invincible and victorious Prince Louis the Great, by the grace of God, king of France and of Navarre, fourteenth of this name, today, this 9th of April 1682, I, by virtue of my commission by His Majesty, which I hold in my hand, ready to show to whomever its rightful owner, have taken and do take possession in the name of His Majesty and of his successors to the crown, this land of Louisiana, and its adjacent seas, harbors, ports, bays, straits, and all nations, peoples, provinces, cities, towns, villages, mines, mining, fish, rivers existing in the area known as Louisiana. (Margry 190)

It is by virtue of Louis XIV's royalty that the colonial enterprise is legitimized. Just as the king's power is legitimized through his coronation, a ritual as political as it is religious, so is the taking of this land in the New World by this sovereign legitimized because of how his royal powers were seen to give him this license to further the interests of his empire.

In this proclamation we see the importance of another dimension that is crucial to legitimizing the claim to this territory for France: the notion of origins of the royal line. This act of claiming Louisiana as French details the current monarch's ancestry as a product of a bloodline that ascended the French throne in 1589, with the crowning of Louis XIV's grandfather, Henri IV de Navarre, the first of the Bourbon kings. In the toponymy of this group of street names in the French Quarter, we see that Royal begot Bourbon in the year 1589, as the Valois family's reign ended while through the marriage of Maguerite de Valois to Henri de Navarre the Bourbon line was born. The next two remaining streets, Dauphine and Burgundy, also represent the future generations of this royal lineage because *le Dauphin* was the first in line for the throne and the *duc de Bourgogne* was the eldest son of the Dauphin, and as such the second in line for the throne. It would appear that the feminine form of the word comes from its modifying *rue* which is also feminine. Just as La Salle's proclamation claimed Louisiana for the current king, ruled by Louis XIV and his successors, the names of these four streets, Royal, Bourbon, Dauphine, and Burgundy, reinforce this sense of permanence, with the order of the empire and its monarchy being imprinted on the banks of the river for the present and into perpetuity.

Interestingly this toponymy was not given by Pauger. According to De Villiers, Pauger's map of 1724 assigns the street known today as Dauphine as Rue de Vendôme (114). This name is not found in Caillot's 1731 description of the street grid of the Vieux Carré. If we take Vendôme to be a reference to the Place Vendôme in Paris, then it is the place where John Law lived, representing the center of monetary wealth in France. It was a series of imposing buildings that served as a residence for Law and his financial empire, as well as serving as the residence of none other than Antoine Crozat, who was still one of the richest men in France. These buildings were so opulent that they still are associated with wealth today, with part of this development serving as the Ritz Hotel in Paris.[9] We can understand that the name of this street served perhaps as a short-lived reference to Law, a vestige of his importance to Louisiana. But this vestige did not live much beyond the Mississippi bubble that burst in 1720 and announced the demise of the Company of the Indies. John Law was vilified; pamphlets were written satirizing him. The financial progress and the promise for riches that he represented at the outset failed miserably. His entrepreneurial banking system that stimulated the economy made the poor rich and changed some fundamental aspects of the social hierarchy in France at that time. This quickly turned into scorn, ridicule, and a return to more traditional French values in France. In this colony whose existence and well-being on a very real level depended on Law and his Company of the Indies, this serves as evidence of not only his fall from grace but also of a new order being established in New Orleans with promise for the future of the colony and its empire: The Rue de Vendôme is not just eliminated, but it is replaced by a reaffirmation of the importance and value of the monarchy. Calling the street Rue Dauphine suggests a renewed confidence in the order that the monarchy represented socially, culturally, and financially for that time and for the future.

However, yet another level of this analysis should be considered. The names of Dauphine as well as Bourgogne do not appear on maps before New Orleans became a colony of Spain. In Pauger's original plan the last named street was Rue Vendôme, with two more streets on the grid that had no name. We also know that the population of the French Quarter during the French period was concentrated on the streets closest to the river.[10] So it is not surprising that these streets were late to be named. However, in light of the argument we have made regarding how the naming of streets in the French Quarter was a negotiated process pitting the empire in some ways against the colony, it would follow in this example that the names of these two streets, Dauphine and Burgundy, appear as an act of defiance against the Spanish colonial regime. This act can also be interpreted as a longing for the established order that being a colony of France represented. Burgundy Street marked the edge of the French Quarter, with Rampart Street, which is today considered a boundary of the French Quarter, appearing later in the period. Thus, Burgundy also can be understood as a fourth boundary framing what we have called the "center" of New Orleans, along with St. Louis, Chartres, and St. Philip Streets. It is as if these four streets represent a symbolic bulwark preserving its identity as a French colony, even after it was no longer a French territory, functioning as a reference point for a collective desire to remain part of France.

Let us consider the significance of the names of streets that run perpendicular to the Mississippi that we have not yet discussed. Upriver from what we have called the "center" of the French Quarter, are Iberville Street, Bienville Street, and Conti Street. These three streets did not originally have these names. In Pauger's original plan Iberville Street, according to De Villiers, was St. Adrien Street, obviously referencing Pauger himself. Surprisingly it took almost 150 years for this street to be named Iberville, after the founder of the colony. For much of the American period it was known as Custom House Street because of where the Custom House was located. The next streets' names shifted over time, as we have seen on the description of the maps. D'Enghien was the first name given to the street that is now Bienville. Given that the name only appears in reference to the original names that Pauger gave to the streets of New Orleans, it is likely as has already been mentioned that it was a reference to Louis IV Henri de Bourbon-Condé (1692–1740). At the time plans for the urban grid of New Orleans were being drawn up, the duc d'Enghien was not only a member of the board of the regency of Philippe, but he, along with his cousin the Prince de Conti, had just caused John Law's system to burst by wanting the *Banque Générale* to convert his paper money to gold. Also, upon the death of Philippe, d'Enghien was appointed prime minister. The fact that this individual's name is not on any later map would also appear to correspond to the duc d'Enghien's own disgrace at court, from which he was banished in 1726, a mere three years after being appointed prime minister. It can be argued that was the most important factor for the name of the street changing to Bienville, whose stature was certainly growing at this point in New Orleans' history.

In considering the reason that Conti Street was so named, we can argue that it was a reference to the Prince de Conti (1695–1727), who along with his cousin made a run on John Law's bank (Wiston-Glynn 155–56). In addition, his daughter-in-law was Philippe duc d'Orléans youngest daughter, Louise Diane d'Orléans (1716–1736), who became the Princesse de Conti at her marriage. We can see evidence of John Law's disgrace by the fact that two men who caused the run on his bank were given names of streets, just as we see that Vendôme Street was a short-lived name for the street that was to become permanently known as Dauphine Street. Both Dauphine and Conti Streets endure as evidence of the acrimony felt by those in New Orleans whose very lives were at the mercy of John Law and his failed Company of the Indies, while at the same time they serve as a reminder that the colonists of New Orleans chose at this juncture to reaffirm their dependence on and their devotion to the French monarchy.

Downriver from the Quarter's "center" we have the streets now known as Ursuline Street, Governor Nicholls Street, Barracks Street, and Esplanade Avenue. Ursuline Street was originally called Rue de l'Arsenal and then St. Adrien Street and St. Ursule before receiving its current name. This is the street that houses the Ursuline convent, which is the only building remaining from the French colonial period (Sublette 168–69). Governor Nicholls seemed to have been referred to as Rue de l'Arsenal as well as Rue de l'Hôpital under the care of the Ursuline nuns. As we can see, the arsenal was relocated several times, and this continued during the Spanish period. The streets in this last section of the French Quarter when they had names at all were given names that for the most part had little symbolic meaning but instead followed their function.

La Nouvelle-Orléans as Contested Space

In conclusion, the story of the urban design of the French Quarter reads as a palimpsest of contested spaces. In blending the physical and the non-physical dimensions of the French Quarter, insights emerge relative to the confluence and divergence of colonial and local desires. As we have seen, with Bienville being present on every map of New Orleans since its founding, there is an abiding affection for him and his importance as the founding father of New Orleans seems to have always been important to the settlers of New Orleans. Conversely, it certainly seems as though the early Creoles were quick to embrace the demise of John Law. It also appears as though they refused to accept that their ties with France were severed as evidenced by how references to the French monarchy and structures of the *ancien régime* endured through the ages and even remain today. Although there is ample evidence that Napoleon would have been welcomed in New Orleans upon his exile with the existence of the Napoleon House and by virtue of the fact that his death mask resides in the Cabildo Museum, the reappearance of the name Condé on the map drawn up for the Louisiana Purchase suggests anger on the part of local French Creoles toward him.

We have seen that names Dauphine, Burgundy, and Iberville Streets suggest the social collective remained connected to France, even when New Orleans no longer belonged to French physically. Nonetheless, in the hearts of many living in the French Quarter, especially French-speaking Creoles, there was a stubborn resistance to let go of French connections that became more of a cultural and social construct living more in the collective imaginary world than in the physical one. This imaginary space is rich in significance because after the French colonial enterprise ended in Louisiana, many of the French-speaking Creoles of the city continued to live there, as opposed to living in the American section of the city that was known as the Faubourg Ste. Marie, now called Uptown New Orleans. The identity for the French-speaking Creoles that differentiated their concept of self from the American "Other" was reinforced by this notion that theirs was a space where they could live surrounded by cultural references that they named and that reminded them of a lost time and place.

New Orleans remains one of the most important river cities in the world. Its center, its heart, can be found on its riverfront, which opens onto the Mississippi River, revealing its most recognizable icons, Jackson Square and St. Louis Cathedral. However, these icons did indeed take years "of experimentation to coalesce" before becoming the iconic structures they have become today. These icons had not yet been built in the French colonial period; instead these structures were constructed upon those earlier ones, and the coalescing that occurred can be understood as a product of the creolization process that will be treated in the next chapter.

CHAPTER THREE

Creolization
or Necessary Interdependence

Introduction

The creolization process occurred in New Orleans through the French, Spanish, and American colonial periods. The collective imaginary informed the construction of individual identities, as well as the emergent culture in the city. The term *creolization* in the French colonial context refers to the rapid transformation of native land and people in the Americas due to the arrival of Europeans and Africans, who were implicated in colony building of slaving societies in the Caribbean Basin in the sixteenth and seventeenth centuries.[1] By virtue of its location on the north coast of the Caribbean Sea, New Orleans shares many elements with the islands geographically, economically, and culturally, as this study has treated in previous chapters. Regarding the relationship of New Orleans to the French islands of Saint-Domingue, Martinique, and Guadeloupe, arguably the most important element these colonial spaces shared was that they were all intended to be slaving societies. The context of slaving society provides a framework within which to analyze the cultural production found in New Orleans revolving around issues of race and the collective imaginary that represent original, unscripted New World constructs.

This analysis incorporates the concept of *la créolité* as established by prominent Antillean theorists Edouard Glissant, Raphaël Confiant, Patrick Chamoiseau, and Jean Bernabé. The basic premise of this theoretical framework posits that relational identities produced in these New World societies, rather than root identities especially from Europe and Africa, emerge as operative in the creation of the Caribbean's original societies with their unscripted narrative. The explosion of cultures that rapidly intermingled produced new peoples, languages, and societies. The result constituted a new hemispheric genealogy. During much of their colonial history, New Orleanians self-identified as Creole due to their speaking French and being Catholic. This meant that whites, blacks, and biracial/multiracial people were all considered Creole if they identified as local Francophone Catholics. This chapter considers how the term Creole was redefined by

New Orleanians who identified as white around the time of the Louisiana Purchase, creating the notion of the "white Creole."

The chapter proposes that the changing definition of "Creole" implicating race coincides with the city assimilating into the southern United States in which race was defined along a "black and white" binary. Thus from a southern US perspective, the racial mixing that had occurred in New Orleans society throughout the French and Spanish colonial periods made the society racially suspect because the "whiteness" of the population claiming European descent was questionable. Thus being Creole in this context was a maker of (potential) blackness. Consequently assimilation of Creoles of European descent into the southern United States beginning in the mid-nineteenth century required them to prove their whiteness, which resulted in redefining the term Creole to mean being only of French and Spanish descent.

In the chapter's conclusion I consider how the trope of "French" functions relative to "Creole," with French being a term bringing together the very diverse elements and players that made history in New Orleans, a history that is often portrayed or considers itself as exceptional. The tendency to self-fashion a French identity made it a useful umbrella term serving to recast the unruliness of the multicultural, multiracial people of New Orleans into being an expression of a respectable and legitimate hegemonic culture. The chapter presents the argument that identifying as French contributes to creating a space that is neither black nor white. The term then allows for the city to remain distinct in North America through the exoticization of its culture when represented as French, while it also gains cultural value by this association with French hegemony. The chapter considers how these self-fashioned associations have allowed for renewed cultural ties to emerge between France and Louisiana that coincide with the transnational emergence of *la Francophonie* in the twentieth century with former colonies of France claiming a shared transnational identity by virtue of their shared colonial history and language.

Multicultural Settlement

As we have already established, early New Orleans society was profoundly diverse, formed by the cooperation of those who would be considered elsewhere as belonging to disparate groups. Furthermore, for early colonists such as Pellerin New Orleans at its founding appeared more as a French-Canadian space, rather than a properly French one, with Bienville and his extended family preeminent. That diversity of early inhabitants coalesced into a hierarchal society in which by "the second generation of creole rule, the offspring of bootstrap *voyageurs,* noble adventurers, indentured female domestics, and an unknown number of native American, *métis,* and African-descendant women comprised a local aristocracy of sorts" (Dawdy 183). Although the French were initially intent on preserving the separation of the races, through the *Code Noir* of 1724 and evidenced by Le Page du Pratz's designing slave quarters across the Mississippi River from the city, this practice proved unsustainable, particularly after the first Creole generation became established in 1730 (Dawdy 146). Hall explains the multiracial, multiethnic collaborative efforts necessary to colony building in the following way: "The folk culture of the Gulf South was born in the face-to-face, global villages of French Louisiana. The folk were from three continents: Africa, Europe, and North America. Theirs was a[n] insecure, frontier world where peoples met and mingled biologically and culturally, adopting and adapting each other's technology, skills, economy, culinary arts, traditions, and cultural strengths. Almost all of the population of colonial Louisiana was poor. Out of necessity, most of these varied folk got along well with each other most of the time. None of them were easy to control and subordinate to the interests of the slaveholding colonial elites, the colonial bureaucracy, or to the larger designs of the metropolis" ("Epilogue" 293). Life in the early colonial years focused on survival, and that survival could only happen with mutual cooperation of all settlers, free and enslaved. In this way, society functioned as a very rudimentary social collective of a profoundly diverse group of people in the earliest years.

In spite of the French Crown's calling for distinctions in terms of ethnicity, religion and, perhaps most important, race in its colony, by the 1730s New Orleans society was racially mixed and the terms "white" and "black" were little used. Groups were defined more on the grounds of their culture and religion rather than along racial lines, as Dawdy explains, "New Orleanians of all colors grew up in more intimate and integrated quarters than had the founder generation. At the same time, they began to form more definite ideas about 'race.' Through these concepts, they chose a segregation of the mind rather than the body" (Dawdy 175). The choices made by these New Orleanians resulted in a society characterized by fluid boundaries and the necessity of collective cooperation to develop settlements drawing upon the affective ties to France. These ties inspired the sociocultural constructions in this budding society, with French society serving as its implicit model.

The self-fashioning of identities built on French notions of class distinctions, and in particular on the importance of noble titles as reflecting elite status and privilege, as Clark explains: "The officials of French Louisiana in the 1720s worked hard to replicate the performance of these class distinctions in the colony. Although not all petty officials could claim to be members of the nobility, most appended to their names whatever honorific designation they could. Perhaps more than other inhabitants of colonial Louisiana, officials of the proprietary Company of the Indies and their families engage in the game of social posturing and elegant living that prevailed in their homeland" (Clark 66). Dawdy furthers this argument, stating, "As the self-invention of noble titles in Louisiana suggests, upwardly mobile immigrants may have modeled themselves more after the rural cavalier than the capitalist grain trader . . . While the founder generation may have initially resisted these adaptations, their creole children showed no such hesitation" (84). By the second generation, then, New Orleans Creoles constructed self-fashioned identities from collective memory and affective associations with France, which served to elevate their stature in New Orleans society. These residents were able to forge associations with France that suited them, by virtue of the freedom that their Creole society allowed and the French language they spoke.

Defining Terms: Creole and *La Créolité*

The etymology of the term Creole can be traced from the Portuguese *crioulo,* the Spanish *criollo,* and the Wolof *kréyol,* to describe a person of Old World parentage born in the New World (Thompson 8). So in its most basic sense, the term Creole can be understood as being a transplant to the New World from elsewhere. In early eighteenth-century Louisiana, Bienville is the first local resident known to have used the term *créole* (Dawdy 163). As we have posited above, "creolization" can be understood as the rapid transformation of native land and people due to the arrival of Europeans and Africans implicated—willingly or unwillingly—in colony building. This occurred primarily in the sixteenth and seventeenth centuries in the lands of the New World. The vastest Creole space is found in and around the Caribbean Sea and includes New Orleans situated on the North Coast of this transnational Creole region. Throughout the Caribbean Basin, the process of creolization stemmed from the necessary interdependence of Europeans, Africans, and indigenous populations thrown together to build new settlements in indigenous lands. The demographic transformations occurring through this period of colony building were swift and profound, with new communities, indeed new peoples, being formed with their accompanying cultures, languages, and identities—all of which can be understood as Creole, whose identity was forged by the creolization processes.

Although New Orleans is most tied culturally and historically to Haiti (Saint-Domingue), for a number of reasons, especially political dictatorships of the twentieth century, writers in Haiti have avoided theoretical—and therefore overtly politicized—writing. Thus, they have refused theoretical codification (Glover ix). Instead the island's literati have sought "to narrow the divide between the written and the lived" (Glover xii).[2] This stands in contrast to writers from elsewhere in the Caribbean who have developed theoretical schools of criticism such as *négritude, bovarysme collectif, antillanité, guyanité,* and *métissage.*[3] The present study relies on theoreticians from Martinique because of that island having produced the most prominent theorists in contemporary Francophone Creole studies, especially Edouard Glissant, Raphaël Confiant, Patrick Chamoiseau, and Jean Bernabé. Their theoretical works treat questions of identity, language, and place and are often referred to under the umbrella term of *créolité.* Relative to New Orleans there have been few texts exploring New Orleans in the theoretical context of *créolité.*[4] The current volume seeks to consider New Orleans history and culture informed by *créolité* in order to shed light on the city's relationship to the Caribbean and the larger Creole world.

According to Glissant, the process of creolization happened on multiple levels. In his seminal *Poetics of Relation,* Glissant describes this creolization process as follows:

> What took place in the Caribbean, which could be summed up in the word *creolization,* approximates the idea of Relation for us as nearly as possible. It is not merely an encounter, a shock (in Segalen's sense), a *métissage,* but a new and original dimension allowing each person to be there and elsewhere, rooted and open, lost in the mountains and free beneath the sea, in harmony and in errantry. If we posit *métissage* as, generally speaking, the meeting and synthesis of two differences, creolization seems to be a limitless *métissage,* its elements diffracted and its consequences unforeseeable. Creolization diffracts, whereas certain forms of *métissage* can concentrate one more time. Here it is devoted to what has burst forth from lands that are no longer islands. Its most obvious symbol is in the Creole language, whose genius consists in always being open, that is, perhaps, never becoming fixed except according to systems of variables that we have to imagine as much as define. Creolization carries along then into the adventure of multilingualism and into the incredible explosion of cultures. But the explosion of cultures does

not mean they are scattered or mutually diluted. It is the violent sign of their consensual, not imposed, sharing. (33)

So for Glissant, the creolization process "defracts," "opens," and "explodes" these new societies as they are being (re)formed making them new and original hybrids. Glissant situates his theory as a poetics of Relation where the identities resulting from this explosion of cultures operate as "relational" rather than "rooted" identities, and contrast ideas of Creole in Spanish and British colonial histories with their notions of separation and distinctions relative to race. For Glissant, relational identities are the conscious and contradictory experience of contacts among cultures, produced through chaos, circulating through errantry and totality (*Poetics of Relation* 143–44). A plurality of coexisting dynamics in both the "internal" and "external" dimensions of Relation are at play, and as such Relation rearticulates oral and written forms of expression within a new world order, a new utopia. This Relation is therefore original, by definition unpredictable, and always a collective product.

Bernabé, Chamoiseau, and Confiant build on Glissant's notions of creolization in their *Éloge à la créolité* and declare: "Neither Europeans, nor Africans, nor Asians, we proclaim ourselves Creoles" (75). They offer the following exploration of the meaning of Creoleness, especially as it evokes the originality of the Creole condition:

We declare that Creoleness is the cement of our culture and that it ought to rule the foundations of our Caribbeanness. Creoleness is the *interactional or transactional aggregate* of the Caribbean, European, African, Asian, and Levantine cultural elements, united on the same soil by the yoke of history. For three centuries the islands and parts of continents affected by this phenomenon proved to be the real forges of a new humanity, where languages, races, religions, customs, ways of being from all over the world were brutally uprooted and transplanted in an environment where they had to reinvent life. Our Creoleness was, therefore, born from this extraordinary "migan," wrongly and hastily reduced to its mere linguistic aspects, or to one single element of its composition. Our cultural character bears both the marks of this world and elements of its negation. We conceived our cultural character as a function of acceptance and denial, therefore permanently questioning, always familiar with the most complex ambiguities, outside all forms of reduction, all forms of purity, all forms of impoverishment. Our history is a braid of histories. (87–88) (Italics in the original)

One braid of history most important to the notion of *créolité* is the connection to Africa, with *créolité* building on the earlier Afrocentric *Négritude* school whose theoreticians included Aimé Césaire, Léopold Senghor, and Léon-Gantran Damas. These thinkers explored the notion of Africanness rooted in the displaced blacks of the diaspora, and their shared common identity born from their African heritage. Césaire, Senghor, and Damas provided the theoretical foundation upon which *créolité* sprang through their writings on critical theory and in their literature. One of the foremost Francophone Caribbean authors and critics, Maryse Condé, observes, "Francophone and Anglophone literatures were born in different ways. West Indian Francophone literature emerged from protest engendered by the Négritude movement, while Anglophone literature was born out of an immediate awareness of Otherness" (Pfaff 108). As proclaimed in *Éloge à la créolité*, "Césairian Negritude is a baptism, the primal act of our restored dignity. We are forever Césaire's sons" (80). These theorists of Creoleness, while indebted to these thinkers who laid the foundation for their own theories, nonetheless could not reconcile their notions of the creolization process to simply one historical place, rooted in just one single "braid of history" connected uniquely and essentially to Africa. With Glissant positing Creole cultures as relational rather than rooted, he implicitly rejects Aimé Césaire, Léopold Senghor, and Léon-Gantran Damas's notion of *Négritude*, and the "root identity" of being African due to its essentializing and over-determining identities relative to the Caribbean. Instead the cultures of the Caribbean bear "both the marks of this world and elements of its negation" with the various braids of history engendering a fluid, interconnected, hybrid identity, where life had to be "reinvented."

The Creole language of these communities represented a marker of their reinvention. Building on the foundations of African, colonial, and indigenous languages, a new kind of language emerged. In this Creole culture "people who met speaking mutually unintelligible tongues developed a linguistic medium to communicate among themselves. They restructured the existing languages of the colonizers and colonized, creating new Creole languages" (Baron and Cara 3). Originally the function of language was to allow slaves to communicate with one another without their masters understanding what they were saying: "The Creole language serves as a fundamental metaphor for the complex exploration of this phenomenon of creolization; the product of the experience of colonization and slavery that was developed on the plantation, it was engendered by the attempts at communication by slaves deliberately separated by ethnic group to forestall the hatching of revolutionary plots. The Creole language and the cross-fertilization it symbolizes bring a new importance to the richness of regional, cultural and ethnic admixture: ultimately, the language reinforces those key aspects of pluralism and transformation that undergird the heterogeneity of the Caribbean experience" (Murdoch 267). Just as the language functioned to counter white hegemony, the birth of Francophone West Indian literature, as Condé posits, occurred as an act of protest.

The protest was against the supposed legitimacy and the primacy of colonial hierarchy established by French policies in the Caribbean. By disassociating the colonial enterprise from local Creole societies, the machine of colonialism becomes visible, a delineated other. This "othering" of the French is all the more radical because the French colonial enterprise itself operated under a utopian notion of universalism, where it assumed an unassailable hegemonic role. Thus, from this position the French systematically resisted a negotiated relationship with its colonies. Glissant explains, "Our aim here is to advance the notion that, within the limited framework of one language — French — competing to discover the world and dominate it, literary production is partly determined by this discovery, which also transforms numerous aspects of its poetics; but that there persists, at least as far as French is concerned, a stubborn resistance to any attempt at clarifying the matter. Everything just goes along as if, at the moment it entered into the poetics of worldwide Relation, ready to replace the former hegemony, collective thought working within the language chose to cover up its expressive relationship with the other, rather than admit any participation that would not be one of preeminence" (*Poetics of Relation* 23). Glissant attempts here to make explicit France's ultimate resistance to "expressive relationship with other" that has historically been concealed under the cloak of French universalism.

This resistance to engage in a discursive relationship with its colonies was treated earlier in the current study where we saw that the French systematically applied a grammar of difference toward its colonies that served to delegitimize these New World spaces and peoples. By this exclusion and exclusivity the French established a semantic distancing that was continuously and vigilantly crafted (Cooper and Stoler 3–4). This grammar of difference is evident, for example, in the French records showing patterns of a sustained distinction between French administrators, policies, and aesthetics as opposed to those of Francophone Canadians, Creoles, and later the Acadians. Lifting the veil of French universalism, Glissant argues, would reveal the underlying exploitative, xenophobic, and racist motives at work in French colonialism. Glissant continues, "It is not merely a pleasant option to consider this 'movement' within the context of French literature. Quite simply, two conditions have come together here: a culture that projected onto the world (with the aim of dominating it) and a language that was presented as universal (with the aim of providing legitimacy to the attempt at domination)" (28). The desire to control the colonial landscape, however, was a utopian ideal that could not be actualized. As history has shown, colonialism set in place a new social order that could not be controlled or predetermined by the metropole in spite of these utopian ideals. When confronted with this new social order that did not replicate European realities, the collective response on the part of the French in particular was to view this new society as chaotic, unruly, and ultimately all the more in need of the civilizing order French colonialism promised. Thus Caribbean societies created in these colonies could only have marginal rather than equal status vis-à-vis France with its desire for colonial domination.

Insidiously, the process of exposing the colonial desire for domination at the same time exposes the innate vulnerability in being Creole, a product of the creolization process. And the fact that historically these Creole societies were largely plantation societies built on the African slave trade only exacerbates this vulnerability to external exploitation and racist practices. Creole societies have historically been marginal rather than dominant on the world's stage, thus tempting Creoles to develop an exoticized view of their Creole selves. This circularity allows for Creole societies to be further devalued, dismissed, and ultimately exploited for the colonizer's own purposes.

An avenue that breaks this cycle of marginalization and suppression is the solidarity found in the collective experience of Creole societies throughout the Caribbean that serves as one vehicle to counter this menacing hegemony of the colonizer's desire for preeminence. If we consider the implications of the hegemony of French universalism, and in particular what could be produced through binary opposition to it, then *Négritude* could ironically be seen as the other side of the coin of French colonialism. This braid of history functions as an essentialized, distinct, and coherent response to the French, and could explain the reasons why "West Indian Francophone literature emerged from protest engendered by the Négritude movement," as Condé says. The literary traditions inspired by the Négritude movement and by *créolité* theory were born not simply through alterity to the colonial process, as in the Anglophone islands, but through a discernible, coherent opposition to a colonial entity that itself pretends to be universal.

Of all the writers on Creoleness, it is only Glissant who speaks about the connections between the Caribbean and Louisiana. This is not surprising since he lived in Louisiana and taught at Louisiana State University from 1988 to 1995. Specifically he speaks about the Creole artifacts of zydeco music from southwest Louisiana, and the tradition of the Indian marching clubs that parade on Mardi Gras Day in New Orleans:

> In Louisiana, for example, the creation of zydeco music is an application of traditional Cajun music and the powers of jazz and rock. In Louisiana are found Black Indians who are tribes born from the mix of runaway black slaves and Indians. I went to see the parade of ethnic Black Indians and there is something there that is completely unforeseeable and that goes beyond the simple fact of miscegenation. These cultural and linguistic microclimates that creolization creates in the Americas are crucial because they are the very signs of what really happens in the world. And what really happens in the world is that linguistic and cultural micro and macroclimates of interpenetration are created. And when this cultural and linguistic interpenetration is very strong, then the old demons of purity and anti-miscegenation resist and set fire to these infernal points that we see burning throughout the surface of the earth. (*Introduction à une poétique du divers* 19)

In hearing zydeco music and witnessing the Mardi Gras Indians march, Glissant sees evidence of a Creole hybridity that was original, transcending its historical elements and emerging as a unique form of self-expression. Glissant also makes it a point to situate these examples as part of what is occurring in the "Americas" and not just in the Caribbean, underscoring a distinction between the lands of the Caribbean and the continents of North and South America. For him New Orleans is both a distinctly Creole space and a part of North America.

Contrasting New Orleans with the Francophone Antilles

When we consider how New Orleans exists as both Creole and North American, we are indeed confronted with divergent sociocultural issues. While Guadeloupe and Martinique still remain part of France and continue to struggle with the ramifications of their relationship to the colonizer, one that continues its attempt to overdetermine economic, political, cultural, and environmental systems and policies even in this postcolonial age, Louisiana by contrast was released by France on two different occasions. During the French and later the Spanish periods "New Orleans was the marginal capital of a peripheral colony that mattered to both France and Spain mostly for its strategic value in stemming British and later Anglo-

American expansion across the continent" (Spear 11). The effect of France severing ties with Louisiana abruptly and unceremoniously in 1762 and again in 1803 through the Louisiana Purchase seems to have produced a mythical longing for connections to a lost homeland, adding another layer to the many ways France has been mythologized throughout the history of New Orleans. For example, in what is perhaps the most popular book on New Orleans history and culture ever written, *Fabulous New Orleans* (1939), the author Lyle Saxon states: "As a matter of fact the day of the transfer of Louisiana to the United States was a day of mourning in New Orleans. And it is easy enough to understand this . . . [t]he general feeling was that New Orleans had been handed over to the vandals" (160). Locals experienced a collective trauma of being adrift on the North American continent, exposing the vulnerability of being a Francophone Creole in Anglo-America.

However, this change was also understood as an opportunity for newfound freedom. Once the locals were convinced that they could not negotiate with the Crown to have it reconsider its decision and take back Louisiana, France became a convenient trope of self-fashioning, allowing New Orleans Creoles to distinguish themselves not only from other Caribbean areas and their North American neighbors, but from Spain, their new colonizer. This passage for *Fabulous New Orleans* represents a typical twentieth-century version of the self-fashioned identity constructed by New Orleanians a century earlier to preserve their ties to French privilege and exceptionalism even as the city was cast off by France: "New Orleans was cut off completely from the French world to which it belonged. The city felt itself thrown away, and lost indeed. But it must be remembered that, in a sense, except for the scattered archipelago of its plantations and hamlets — an archipelago as French as the city itself. So remote was New Orleans from other communities of the United States, that it might have been on another continent" (135). We see represented in this attitude a sense of political, geographical, and cultural displacement, with New Orleans and other "French" areas being islands lost in the sea of North America. We also are presented with an accompanying nostalgia, a longing for a past now lost. These notions of displacement and nostalgia represent the seeds of a mythology of "Frenchness" that has helped to root New Orleans as a French space in North America, distinct from its Spanish and English-speaking neighbors.

Another distinction between Louisiana and the Caribbean stems from Louisiana's relationship to the United States, as compared to the relationship that Martinique and Guadeloupe have with France. Whereas the islands have had marginalized status relative to France since the colonial period, exerting limited influence on the metropole, the Louisiana Purchase served to significantly redefine the United States, by doubling the size of its territory and furthering its notion of manifest destiny. New Orleans at the time of the Louisiana Purchase was already a vibrant port city of enormous economic importance to the United States. So as Louisiana's future was changed by becoming American, America itself was changed by acquiring Louisiana, making the semantic dissonance between colonizer and colonized less distinct, less obvious in the context of New Orleans as compared to the islands. In Lawrence Powell's recent article "Why Louisiana Mattered," he reflects on the importance of Louisiana to the history of the United States, and offers the following reflection:

> What happened here refused to stay put. Key developments in Louisiana history rippled across American laws, culture, and politics. Indeed, their influence did more than reflect national trends. They started them. . . . Under the Bourbons (both French and Spanish), the Crescent City had already taken charge of Louisiana's economic destiny, serving up bounties of forbidden pleasure even as the sinful city stirred the kettle of envy and resentment. And it was this combination—an alternative politico-cultural tradition that not even in-pouring Americans could easily sweep aside, and a major town in a milieu of master-slave agrarianism—that endowed Louisiana with its unique influence within the union. What flowed through here would swell the main currents of American history along any number of tributaries—musical, racial and political. Envisaging the contours of American history *sans* Louisiana is a pointless exercise. Even making the effort can tax the resources of language. (390–91)

Furthering the notion of the importance of Louisiana to United States history, Shirley Thompson in her *Exiles at Home: The Struggle to Become American in Creole New Orleans*, suggests that New Orleans and the United States experienced a shared process of Creolization:

> When we scratch the surface of the history of nineteenth-century New Orleans, though, any strict distinction between processes of Americanization and Creolization begins to erode. For one thing, the U.S. national identity itself has incorporated and facilitated powerful narratives of vibrant becoming. Likewise, Creole identities have often masked enduring commitments to racial essentialism and other forms of determinism. The process of Americanization, therefore, is not as limited or limiting as it seems, and creolization is not as unrestrained or as freeing a concept as it is often taken to be. More importantly, though, the "Creole" city of New Orleans, from the early de-

cades of the nineteenth century on, has functioned as a chief site of American-ization in two respects. From New Orleans, U.S. officials incorporated the vast territory and diverse peoples of Louisiana into the nation and engineered a brand of imperialism that would influence decades of domestic and foreign policy. Also, as a bustling port city, New Orleans acculturated countless im-migrants—particularly during the 1840s and 1850s—to the opportunities and strictures of becoming American. (7–8)

New Orleans has functioned as an unadulterated cultural contact zone for new arrivals to America and the experiences, relations, and opportuni-ties granted to immigrants set in motion elements that these immigrants took with them elsewhere. The fact that the city was so diverse and its pop-ulation so fluid made it inclusive in ways other cities could not be. Instead of having to assimilate to America immediately, New Orleans allowed these newcomers the freedom to make choices about their lives that were not possible elsewhere, thus affording them unique types of agency not found in other cities serving as points of entry to the United States.

A further point of comparative difference between Louisiana and the Francophone Creole islands that appears meaningful concerns the ques-tion of French versus Creole language. The role of French language in Louisiana during the Spanish and American periods has functioned as a unifying force of the disparate communities that immigrated to and mi-grated through New Orleans. The French language in this context appears to have a diametrically opposed function when compared to Martinique and Guadeloupe where the French language represents—historically and still today—the voice of the colonizing other. By contrast after the end of the French colonial period, the French language in Louisiana served as a marker of distinction from, and a point of resistance against, Spanish and American rule. Thus, when it was no longer a French colony, the French language functioned in New Orleans as an important sign of displacement and nostalgia in the same way politics, geography, and culture served as markers to differentiate New Orleans from the rest of North America. The French language operated, through the Spanish and American colonial pe-riods, as a recognizable link to France and other Francophone areas, and served to advance the immigration of the Acadians in the late eighteenth century and the refugees from the Hatian Revolution in the early nine-teenth century. The French language also allowed for familial and cultural ties to be cultivated abroad. Many New Orleans elite both white and of color were educated in France, and had careers and families there as well, while others nurtured economic and family ties to postrevolutionary Haiti.

In contrast, the voice of unification in the Caribbean islands is the Creole language, which operates as a marker and touchstone for (re)claiming a specifically Creole identity. The sociolinguistic specificity of this language serves, as we have seen above, as the primary vehicle for theorizing Creoleness. In New Orleans and throughout south Louisiana and the area of Cane River near Natchitoches, Creole language developed much as it did throughout the Caribbean. Historically the Creole language in New Orleans played a very similar role to that of the Francophone Caribbean as a means of communication, with its being a uniquely hybrid product of French, African, and American influences. However, while in southwest Louisiana (Acadiana) and the Natchitoches area, there remain a significant number of speakers of Creole, in New Orleans today, the Creole language remains an oral form of expression limited to fairly small linguistic communities of color in the city. Furthermore in the eighteenth and nineteenth centuries, as represented in the literature of that time, in New Orleans proper, and on plantations throughout southern Louisiana, Creole language functioned primarily as the language of slaves and those free people of color who were not a cultural elite. Young Creole elites, whether white or free people of color, were often nurtured and raised by enslaved women. For these elite New Orleanians, Creole was the language of their privileged childhood. Once educated and grown, these Creoles "lost" their Creole language and communicated in what would be considered a more standard form of French.

The result of these differences is that theoreticians such as Confiant and Glissant can present a much more cohesive portrait throughout history of the role the Creole language has played and how it has informed the processes of creolization than can those studying New Orleans. Whereas in the Caribbean, the term Creole enjoys primacy as a term uniting the Creoles as evidenced in the declaration: "Neither Europeans, nor Africans, nor Asians, we proclaim ourselves Creoles."

The existence in New Orleans of a *créolité* has been acknowledged, by scholars such as Sybil Kein, who in the book *Creole: The History and Legacy of Louisiana's Free People of Color,* states, "While not as uniformly defined as that of the West Indies, a *Créolité* is indeed identifiable in the United States" (xvi). It is a qualified statement, alluding to the conflicted definitions of the term in New Orleans. Perhaps the cultural artifact in New Orleans that might most closely resemble in function the Creole language of the islands is the early music of New Orleans that is still played by musicians today, such as in the form of zydeco music or jazz, as alluded to by Glissant. These are recognizable forms that have made their way into popular American culture, and especially with jazz, come to be claimed as an American genre.

The *créolité* that allowed for these types of music to be formed, by contrast, does not translate into the American sociopolitical landscape. When considering why the Creole language virtually disappeared from New Orleans in the early twentieth century we are left wondering what role race, and the ensuing issues of access to education, economic privilege, and white hegemony have played in its demise.[5] Generally considered as a language of blacks, although there is ample evidence that it was also spoken by whites, it did not enjoy the privileged status nor did it serve as a motor for transnational culture and economic gain as the French language did.

The Making of the White New Orleans Creole

Here we touch upon what is perhaps the biggest difference between the Francophone Caribbean islands and Louisiana. The majority population of Haiti, Martinique, and Guadeloupe is of African descent. Furthermore the theoreticians of *créolité* are all black with their movement having been engendered by the *Négritude* school. While New Orleans has seen moments where its population of color was larger than its white population, at the time of the Louisiana Purchase, it became officially a part of the American South, and thanks to Thomas Jefferson, it continued to be a slaving society after joining the United States. This action served to disenfranchise its black population.

From a southern US perspective, the racial mixing that had occurred in New Orleans society throughout the French and Spanish colonial periods made New Orleanians nonetheless racially suspect because the "whiteness" of the population of European descent was questionable. Being Creole in this context was a maker of (potential) blackness. Therefore in order to assimilate into the southern United States, Creoles of European descent had to prove their whiteness. Not surprisingly, over the course of the nineteenth century New Orleans assimilated into the United States' binary system of race and the racist practices from elsewhere in the South. In *Confronting Modernity,* Megraw summarizes the Americanization of New Orleans as follows:

> For all of the presumed racial openness of antebellum New Orleans despite
> the size of its free black population or its legacy of race mixing, segregation
> began during Reconstruction and radicalized thereafter. Disfranchisement
> followed, and sporadic violence enforced systems of political exclusion,
> economic peonage, and social separateness. Three race riots rocked the city
> between 1866 and 1900. There, too, in a less violent if equally telling develop-

ment, a raging debate redefined the term "Creole," purging it of racial taint and equating it with white purity. Less is known about the postwar black community outside New Orleans, but, as numerous scholars have shown, the central issues and concerns of free blacks in New Orleans fit a pattern common throughout the urban South. Beyond the city and across the parishes, like the region at large and the nation which acquiesced, the nadir of Louisiana's race relations coincided with the dawn of the new century. (25)

After the Louisiana Purchase the term was redefined by the Creole elite to mean "white" and only of French and Spanish decent, reminiscent of the Spanish codification of the *limpieza de sange.* In this Creole "mixture," Spanish heritage was explicitly linked to the French. It recalls (perhaps not coincidentally) the original Spanish definition of Creole as meaning belonging to the planter class of white Catholics born in the New World.

Consequently in New Orleans the elites systematically disassociated themselves with Africa and any connection that might exist between themselves, as white, and others of African descent, creating "racist attitudes [that] are constructs deliberately created over time and imposed upon the population from above" ("Epilogue" 292). Thompson explains: "For those seeking to recreate themselves in antebellum New Orleans, as elsewhere in the United States, 'whiteness' was a particularly powerful tool. Minimizing distinctions of class, trivializing any particular cultural heritage, and overcoming glitches in individual genealogies, whiteness produced a condition of equality before the law and created opportunities for economic gain and social prestige" (10). Whites, and those passing for white, then strategically appropriated the term Creole for themselves as a term for whiteness mirroring in this effort to gain status and social prestige in America. Thompson describes this strategy as follows:

In the late nineteenth century, allegations of impurity prompted those New Orleanians with stakes in the whiteness of their bloodlines to "purify" the definition of *Creole.* Turning the original sense of the term on its head, they argued that a Creole was a native solely "of European extraction, whose origin is known and whose superior Caucasian blood was never assimilated to the baser liquid that ran in the veins of the Indian and the African native." In a formulation reiterated over and over again in the late nineteenth and twentieth centuries, New Orleanians contended further that while the noun *Creole* was to be reserved for whites, the adjective *creole* could be made to modify lesser beings and inanimate objects "creole horses, creole cattle, creole eggs, creole corn, creole cottonade," and creole "negroes." (12–13)

Thus, in New Orleans the term Creole itself diffracts meaning, as Thompson explains:

> The symbiotic relationship of Americanization and Creolization is mirrored in the way the term *Creole* itself morphed its way through nineteenth-century New Orleans. A chameleon of a word, *Creole* has, in the most general sense, both masked and exposed anxieties over place, culture, and race. Wherever it is used, the term confronts the challenges posed by a radical pluralism. It attempts to name an ethic of in-between-ness—to connect multiple allegiances and to channel them into a singular identity with deep roots in a particular context . . . On the ground of nineteenth-century Louisiana, the term *Creole* displayed an impressive elasticity, taking on a variety of forms to fit a range of individual and communal needs. When used with a lowercase *c*, as it often was in the antebellum period, the term benignly attributed native birth or origin. When used with an uppercase *C*, the word took on an overtly political cast from the early nineteenth century on. (8–9)

How was history rewritten to make Creole a term for whites? Daniel Usner's study, "Between Creoles and Yankees: The Discursive Representation of Colonial Louisiana in American History," treats the question of how New Orleans was understood in the historiography of nineteenth-century America, by both Anglophone and Francophone historians, and he concluded that toward the end of the century Francophone Louisiana historians such as Alcée Fortier exaggerated the colonists' attachment to France and along with Anglophone historian Grace King, tried to document a racially "pure" origin for the Creole population (13).

In order to see how such a claim could find its way into popular culture, let us look to this most popular history of the city, *Fabulous New Orleans* (1939), to see what came to be the accepted narrative of the definition of a New Orleans Creole and Creole society in the early twentieth century. The author was Lyle Saxon, the "recognized literary voice of Louisiana" (Megraw 155). In his most famous work he writes: "Almost from the beginning there was a sort of society—a group of men and women who held themselves aloof from the rabble and who, as best they could, preserved the manners of the court of France" (89). Continuing to cast the founders of the city as aristocratic elites, he continues: "Bienville lived in a more aristocratic neighborhood. His neighbors were M. de Chavannes, secretary of the Council; M. Fleuriau, attorney-general; Dr. Alexandre, surgeon-major of the Hospital, and other dignitaries. . . . The population in 1726 was 880 free white men and women, 65 indentured servants and 129 slaves, all living within the town's boundaries" (93). Had he chosen to quote from the census the next year, he would have been forced to include the first mention of free people of color.[6] For Saxon, Creoles were born from the "Latins," the French and Spanish in particular, who settled New Orleans: "These were Latins and they brought with them their Latin frankness as to eating and drinking and as to matters pertaining to sex. And from these first settlers a definite type emerged, a type known a few years later as the Creole" (91). According to Saxon, New Orleans Creole society was created by Europeans: "It was not long before the Spanish officers had married into the Creole families—which, oddly enough, the French officers had not done to any great degree—and French and Spanish blended into a pleasing Creolism" (141).

This definition is found in later texts from the mid-twentieth century and seems to borrow from the Spanish use of the term Creole meaning Spaniards born in the New World. For example, Harnett T. Kane's *Queen New Orleans: City by the River* (1949) offers the following explanation: "Spaniards courted Frenchwomen, and from their alliances emerged a new designation—Creole. The New Orleans Creole is a descendant of both elements, or of either, and the word denotes white, without admixture" (9). This is perhaps the reason that scholars sometimes mistakenly believe that the term Creole was first used in the Spanish period.[7] In the American period Saxon posits the following melding of Creole and American: "It was not long before the Creole mothers were anxious that their daughters marry the rich Americans, and more than one impoverished Creole lad exchanged his aristocratic name for good American dollars" (163). This Creole lineage passes from French and Spanish to American, on a path of whiteness "without admixture," that is, therefore, pure and thus valued within the context of American ideals and hegemony.

When having to explain the existence of the population of free people of color in New Orleans history and their place in this Creole society, Saxon obfuscates: "Here were laws in the colony prohibiting white men marrying negro women, and also laws prohibiting white men from living with negro women. Well, we all know something of prohibitions. I shall not go into the matter except to say that a great many mulatto children were born" (180). This obfuscation serves to disassociate the free population from their historicity, as it also delegitimizes biracial unions, not to mention multiracial ones, by reducing all interracial relationships as illicit affairs begun through Quadroon balls. He continues: "In addition, there came many 'free people of color' from the West Indian islands. Very early we find these free mulattoes with a society of their own—a society neither white nor black, but between the two" (180). In this narrative, typical of the twentieth-century white Creole perspective, freed blacks are not only seen as apart and separated from whites, but as an anomaly, neither black nor white and in a society of "their own." This group is presented as having no genealogical ties to either race, but more importantly in this equation, having no ties to whiteness biologically or culturally; this group is completely separate, and follows the Jim Crow mentality of the time. Furthermore the name free people of color that this population claims for itself, one that has been part of recorded history since the New Orleans census of 1727, appears to be an expression that for him is not common usage. By putting the term free people of color in quotation marks it makes it appear as though he has borrowed the term and that it lacks a generally accepted meaning in the historical narrative, whereas the term mulatto sans quotes situates this term in common usage.

The term mulatto refers to the racial lineage of an individual, their degree of blackness and how much of "the tar brush" they possess, and follows the cast system where "mulatto" refers to being half black, "quadroon" as being one-quarter black, "octoroon" being one-eighth black, and so forth.[8] More important, perhaps, is that a mulatto could represent a free or enslaved individual, whereas the term "free person of color" functions more as a sociopolitical or socioeconomic reference defining, rather than dissecting, a member of a free community. This passage, then, ultimately serves to render suspect the citizenry of free people of color in New Orleans history, and along with it, the tripartite racial system in New Orleans history. By aligning all people of African descent with slavery, this passage does not allow a legitimate status to free people of color. Thus we see evidence of the narrative that white Creoles imported from the American South, with its the binary system of race, resulting in the erasure of the history of free people of color from New Orleans history. While the presence of Creoles of color in New Orleans history could not be denied the complex history of these Creoles, unique in North America, could be easily reappropriated and attributed to white men's indiscretion, according to the tale this narrative weaves.

The year 1812 looms large in Louisiana history, corresponding with the Battle of New Orleans, and Saxon describes it in detail in his book. This battle represents the first time that New Orleanians and Americans worked as military partners aligned against a common enemy, the British. In this description of the fighters on the battlefield, we see that Saxon replicates the social structure of the American South with its hierarchy and binary system of race as he describes the troops taking up the fight against the British:

> And it was not only the Creoles and the English-speaking citizens of New Orleans who gathered there. With them were companies of lean Kentuckians, men who had come down the river aboard flatboats, each with his rifle in the crook of his arm — men who had come to help protect Creole New Orleans because Louisiana was now a part of their United States. From the streams and bayous of inland Louisiana came the bronzed Acadians, to take their places in the line. Down the levee from the German Coast trudged the descendants of those flaxen-haired pioneers who had come to America a hundred years before. Companies of negroes — "free men of color" — came bearing arms and took their places quietly, ready to do their part. Surely a strange group of men these were, gathering there under the oaks at Chalmette. But it was a group no longer merely French or Spanish, or a mixture of the two. Here was America! (164)

So for Saxon in New Orleans, now part of America, free men of color are the last to be named, and appear as if out of the shadows taking "their places quietly, ready to do their part" to serve the cause of freedom, illustrating Thompson's claim that white Creoles had "superior Caucasian blood . . . never assimilated to the baser liquid that ran in the veins of the Indian and the African native" (12).

Vying Definitions of Creole in Louisiana

The social foundation of Creole New Orleans was, according to this narrative, composed of French and Spanish elements, with the African and Native peoples being excluded by this definition of Creole. This same narrative continues today for some New Orleanians. For example, in *Gawd, I Love New Orleans* (1996), the author Frank Schneider opens his "potpourri of remembrances, folklore and history," as the book cover states, by delving into the meaning and use of the word Creole. He states: "Early French families accepted one definition — theirs. . . . Some historians and writers suggest that their colleagues treated facts loosely, and thereby contributed to confusion of the word's meaning in Louisiana. Recorded statements of Creoles (with a capital C) insist that a 'Creole is a native Louisianian of French or Spanish ancestry, or both.' As late as 1886 Creole gentlemen attempted to identify themselves by organizing the Creole Association of Louisiana . . . to disseminate knowledge concerning their true origin and real character, and to promote the advancement of the Creole race in Louisiana" (6).

The passage demonstrates a desire, still operating in certain circles of New Orleans, to belie the historical record by carefully choosing evidence. However, if we jump ahead to the late twentieth century this has become more tenuous when compared to the tone of Saxon and Harnett Kane. Furthermore, in this passage, there appears to be a tacit acknowledgment that the historical record, as disjointed and confusing as it might be, does indeed say something different and that Creole elites were striving to reinvent themselves as another race, nonetheless still white. This association's records go on to state, according to Schneider, "the Louisiana Creole is one who is a descendent of the original settlers in Louisiana under the French and Spanish governments, or, more generally, one born in Louisiana of European parents, and whose mother tongue is French" (6–7). This perspective is not as generally shared as in decades past, but it still does persist in the minds of many in the city.

The view seems to reflect a more generally accepted definition of the term Creole today in popular culture and gives more primacy to people of color, but there still is a color line dividing Creoles of color and white Creoles. Even now, the term Creole is not applied to whites and blacks together. For example, while New Orleans presents itself to tourists as a multicultural place, there is still a resistance to have the term Creole refer simultaneously to blacks, whites, and multiracial groups, as we can see from the Website of the New Orleans Tourist Marketing Corporation: "Any discussion of Creole culture in New Orleans needs to start with how ambiguous the word 'Creole' is. Early on, the term might refer to slaves born in the New World, to *gens de couleur libres* (free people of color), or to people of mixed racial heritage. Especially after Louisiana transferred to American control in 1803, the white descendants of the French and Spanish who lived in New Orleans increasingly adopted the term 'Creole' for themselves to distinguish themselves from the influx of Americans whom they disdained."[9] This contemporary definition suggests that whites started to call themselves Creole after the Louisiana Purchase, echoing to a degree the idea that we have just considered, that the definition of Creole as relative to whites was still coming to be after New Orleans became an American territory, demonstrating a continued anxiety about the city's history as a racially mixed colonial space. The term Creole still is associated with African heritage, as in the French Caribbean and in Brazil.

Whereas the narrative that Saxon recounted in *Fabulous New Orleans* defined early French and Spanish settlers exclusively as Creole, making the term exclusively a white reference, in this twenty-first-century narrative scripted in post-civil rights New Orleans, early Creoles were defined as nonwhite, being of African descent exclusively. In this twenty-first-century version, whites during the French and Spanish colonial period are simply called "descendants of the French and Spanish" who lived in New Orleans. And they are made to sound as if they appropriated the term in the nineteenth century for the very first time, thus suggesting that until the nineteenth century there existed whites who did not identify as Creole, but as only as French and Spanish. Ultimately, French is allied to Spanish just as in the narrative presented by Saxon to define whiteness and to establish a clear color line in New Orleans history between "Europeans" and "Africans." Of course in New Orleans things are never that simple, that reducible to the simple binary opposition of "white" and "black."

As opposed to the view of many white Creoles and the picture that is painted of New Orleans for tourists, the concept of a color line existing within the definition of Creole is far from universally accepted. For many Creoles of color the term has not been associated with whiteness or blackness but rather in an inclusive manner. For example, in *Creole: The History and Legacy of Louisiana's Free People of Color,* Kein relies on Gwendolyn Midlo Hall's definition of Creole, as "a person of non-American ancestry, whether African or European, who was born in the Americas" (*Africans in Colonial Louisiana* xv). The usage of Creole as an inclusive, umbrella term without reference to race or intimating a racial divide not only respects the etymology of the term—the Portuguese *crioulo,* the Spanish *criollo,* and the Wolof *kréyol*—to describe a person of Old World parentage born in the New World (Thompson 8), but this inclusive definition also remains truer to the historical record and what history has chronicled about New Orleans. It also remains truer to New Orleans' shared history with the larger Caribbean Creole region, where new societies were formed "with the most complex ambiguities, outside all forms of reduction, all forms of purity, all forms of impoverishment. Our history is a braid of histories" (*Éloge à la Créolité* 87–88). It should not be surprising that the community of color has sustained this historically accurate definition. There would be a number of reasons to do so. Besides being a simple truth, this community would have more to gain than lose by keeping this truth alive, especially when confronted with American racism. We've seen ample evidence of how for whites and those passing as white, there was a concerted attempt to lose the multiracial connotations that had been associated with the term Creole; for Creoles of color, it would appear that the opposite is true, thus allowing

Creoles of color forms of self-expression in politics, newspapers, literature, music, and commerce that did not exist elsewhere in America.

Nonetheless, because the term Creole remains a contested term in the context of New Orleans history and because one finds contradictory definitions and tendencies to apply the term to what one desires to be the case, especially within the white Creole mindset, rather than what is indeed true, the term is not a stable signifier of meaning. In spite of the inclusiveness of the definition of Creole held by Creoles of color, on a practical level it cannot function as an umbrella term in New Orleans because its meaning is far too contested. Kein opens her introduction saying as much: "When examining the history of Louisiana French, one may wonder why the Louisiana Creoles have been marginalized by scholars, and why no extensive study of the group has been done before now. One reason may well be the seemingly infinite number of possible definitions of *Creole*" (xii). Functionally speaking, the term Creole in New Orleans has become so creolized that it does not have a sustaining referent, and therefore it has no "root" meaning. In this way, the term reflects Glissant's conceptualization of how creolization operates: "creolization seems to be a limitless *métissage*, its elements diffracted and its consequences unforeseeable" (*Poetics of Relation* 33). The meaning of the term has become so diffracted and hyperlocalized that it is only operational in these "historically linked connotations," to quote Dominguez, by those who claim it for themselves, no matter how inclusive or exclusive that group might be.

Becoming French Once More

What this study suggests is that the term French, by contrast, can be understood to function as a more desirable umbrella term to represent "Creole" New Orleans. By holding fast to this evidence of New Orleans being a French colonial product, it follows a tack put in place by the French colonial enterprise, with its domination always remaining rooted in its desire for universalism and as such displaced from its colonial spaces, as Glissant explains: "Moreover, as French spread, it simultaneously strengthened the illusion that its place of origin remained (even today) the privileged womb and promoted the belief that this language had some kind of universal value that had nothing whatsoever to do with the areas into which it had actually spread. Consequently, the situational competence of the language became overvalued and at the same time 'upheld' in its place of origin" (Glissant, *Poetics of Relation* 117). The French colonial enterprise then set in motion a maternal kind of relationship with its colonies in the Caribbean and Louisiana, where it represented the "privileged womb" that bore these colonies. New Orleans, it appears, continues to hold on to this notion of being the child of France, the product of the metropole.

New Orleans through its self-fashioning and mythmaking gained through this mindset. Since the customs, the food, the music, the social structure, the economic foundations, the political systems not to mention the geography do not come close to replicating French systems, models, and practices, this apparent upholding of French origins and acquiescence to French universalism, it appears, veils a subversiveness to those very same notions. Because New Orleans has not actually functioned as a French colony since 1762 it has enjoyed the freedom to appropriate this label in ways that Martinique and Guadeloupe, for example, cannot. In New Orleans, being "French" has served as a trope that unified the diverse and changing dynamics in the city throughout its colonial histories, affording this space a recognizable, distinct identity. The association with France in this context is not a rooted but a relational term, borrowing from Glissant. This process of self-fashioning an identity through myth and language is posited by Glissant as follows: "Identity will be achieved when communities attempt to legitimate their right to possession of a territory through myth or the revealed word. Such an assertion can predate its actual accomplishment by quite some time. Thus, an often and long contested legitimacy will have multiple forms that later will delineate the afflicted or soothing dimensions of exile or errantry" (*Poetics of Relation* 13). In the case of Louisiana, the appropriation of a French identity as an identifier not only predates, but postdates the accomplishment, signaling an ongoing desire to reclaim a lost past, forged through association, desire, and perceptions of self and other. There continues to be value, status, and differentiation associated with French hegemony that made it a desired social identifier, with these self-fashioned associations allowing for renewed cultural ties to emerge between France and Louisiana that coincide with the transnational emergence of *la Francophonie* in the twentieth century. The following chapter on the Spanish colonial period treats what is perhaps the most Creole of all periods in New Orleans history. Affective ties to France helped chart systematic resistance to this unwelcome colonizer, making the Spanish colonial enterprise a deeply negotiated process with the local Creole elite that resulted in the colonizer being creolized.

CHAPTER FOUR

The Spanish Period:
Creolizing the Colonizer

Introduction

The Spanish colonial period is arguably the period of the most intense creolization in New Orleans history. My argument is based on how Spain had
no interest in the Louisiana territory, a "gift" the Spanish Bourbon king
Carlos III received from his cousin, Louis XV, for his military allegiance to
France during the Seven Years' War. Consequently the Spanish metropole
acted in a most deferential way to the local Louisiana population in administering the colony, affording local Creoles freedom not allowed in other
Spanish territories. Also due to Spanish manumission practices slaves were
allowed to buy their freedom, resulting in the emergence of a remarkably
large population of free people of color in New Orleans, further adding to
the creolization of the city by implicating new social order, mobility, and
self-determination for this significant population of African descent.

Throughout the Spanish period, the local Creole population overwhelm-
ingly resisted Spanish rule. The chapter posits that the locals' mytholgized
associations with France and the process by which the act of remaining
staunchly French in their collective imaginary suited local resistance to colonial rule and contributed to uniting the disparate, sometimes competing,
Creole elements against a common foe. In other words, by self-ascribing a
posteriori associations as "French" during the Spanish and later American
period this population created a semantic space of opposition to the colonial yoke. Associations with France in the colony after it was no longer
French sustained the "in-between-ness" of New Orleans as a hybrid space,
which could not be controlled or for all intents and purposes governed by
the Spanish and later the Americans. Much of this hybridity consisted of
mythmaking and illusion, with associations with France masking a fierce
independence and antipathy toward any colonizer, and by displacing that
resistance the colonized were able through their own agency to shift their
hemispheric allegiance without appearing to do so.

The French Quarter reinforced the French presence spatially, as a physical reminder that social collective remained connected to France, even when New Orleans was no longer officially a colony. King Carlos III was himself a Bourbon, thereby already implicated in this socially constructed French landscape. By not severing these (imagined) spatial and cultural ties to France, New Orleanians enjoyed more freedom from their colonizers since this mythology disguised radicalism and a degree of self-determination that ultimately would be a threat to European colonialism in the New World. In fact, New Orleans Creoles attempted the first rebellion against colonial rule in the New World, as we will see, when they sought self-determination in establishing the Republic of Louisiana and drove out the first Spanish governor in what is known as the Rebellion of 1768.[1]

Another goal of this chapter focuses on the importance of the influx of former slaves into the class of free people of color in the creolization processes in the city. This demographic shift happened within the perpetually compromised Spanish political system and significantly altered the developing constructions of race in New Orleans. This occurred in part because the Spanish reopened the slave trade, and the influx of newly arrived Africans further reinforced the shared sense of community among Creole New Orleans with their common language, culture, and religion, all of which differentiated these established New Orleanians from the recently arrived Africans. During the later American period this community coalesced in historic ways, producing the first literary works, the first newspapers, and the first political manifestos of African Americans in the United States, which will be studied in the next chapter.

End of the French Period

The French colonial period ended in the 1760s as a result of the Seven Years' War, often referred to in the United States as the French and Indian War. After several years of battling between Great Britain and France, the French Crown wanted to be free from the burden of part of its colonial responsibilities and secretly offered lands west of the Mississippi River and New Orleans to Spain, ostensibly in recognition of their support of the Bourbon cause against Britain. So it was that by the secret Treaty of Fontainebleau of 1762, New Orleans became a Spanish city, along with the all territory west of the Mississippi River.

New Orleans at this time had a population of over 2,500 people (Dawdy 158). The social fabric was beginning to reify, and a group of economic elites emerged, as Dawdy explains: "Through our modern eyes, the creole generations of the 1730s to 1760s could be characterized by 'mixture' of various kinds, but also by segregation of a new type. Slaves, Indians, soldiers, and poor freemen continued to drink, gamble, socialize, and conduct business in the city's cabarets, although efforts to regulate these establishments were becoming more strident. While *métissage* probably contributed to slow but steady population growth among free people of color in New Orleans, the ranks of wealthy merchants and slaveholders began closing through endogamy. The *petits gens* continued to mingle, while elites began to hold themselves apart. Giving up on the difficulties of spatially segregating others in a wide-open port town, creole merchant planters instead decided to genetically segregate *themselves*" (181–82). So while New Orleans was at its root a multiracial, multiethnic city, "by the 1750s slavery and trading wealth had begun to harden into caste-like distinctions" (Dawdy 142). The newly formed elite represented through their "genetic segregation" an emerging white demographic, at least among their offspring classified as "legitimate."

More generally speaking, at the end of the French period, New Orleans society appears multicultural, with free people of color estimated as 20 percent of the population (Dawdy 179). Social bonds uniting this society included French language and Catholicism, as Spear explains:

> By the second half of the eighteenth century, people of African and of European ancestry probably knew each other far better than their parents or grandparents had. Because both African and European immigration into the colony had virtually ceased after the early 1730s, by midcentury, Louisiana-born Africans and Europeans were coming into their own. Whereas language, culture, and religion had separated the previous generation, those becoming adults in the 1750s and 1760s grew up with each other, speaking French and sharing Catholic religious practices. Cultural endogamy had probably deterred family formation, although not more casual and exploitative sexual relationships, between Africans and Europeans earlier in the century, but by midcentury the city's second and third generation creoles of African and European ancestry shared enough language, religion, culture, and customs that their relationships had become culturally endogamous even as they remained racially exogamous. (142)

Hanger echoes the multicultural fabric of this Creole city that existed into the Spanish Period:

> With few exceptions, persons of all colors and classes worked and played together. In the still primarily frontier environment of Spanish New Orleans

libres, whites, and slaves commonly mingled in the streets, markets, taverns, dance halls, churches, and private homes of the city . . . [L]ibres and whites formed common-law unions, usually without the church's blessing but at least with its toleration. Free blacks also married or had relations with slaves, but they often had to live apart . . . Census and notarial records attest to the lack of residential segregation in colonial New Orleans. Free blacks bought, sold, and rented accommodations adjacent to whites . . . A perusal of census re- turns indicates that libres resided not only next door to whites and slaves but also in the same households with them. Economic considerations drew free blacks into white households, where they worked as apprentices, domestics, and laborers. In addition, libres rented rooms or floors to and from white persons. Libres, whites, and slaves also came together within the St. Louis Parish church, after 1794 a cathedral. (138)

Cultural bonds in colonial New Orleans, as we see, were more import than racial divides. So while this was a slaving society, the black-white bi- nary notion of racial difference that existed in plantation society outside of New Orleans, did not exist in this urban, creolized space. Thus economic opportunity was not limited to those individuals of exclusively European descent. Cultural practices and social identities were emerging at this time as distinct to the urban environment, informed by shared language and re- ligion that were transplanted from France onto American soil. As I state in chapter 2, the design of the city was in effect an attempt at binding this place to France for future generations, in physical as well as in imaginary realms. However, New Orleanians of the mid-eighteenth century lost that bet, when the secret treaty of Fontainebleau was signed November 3, 1762, and adding to the affront was the fact that it was made public a full year and a half later to New Orleans locals by the royal decree sent by Louis XV on April 21, 1764.

As we have already seen, the accepted narrative and shared cultural ref- erences since the founding of New Orleans were rooted in the city being a French city. The stubborn resistance in the hearts of French-speaking Creoles to let go of French connections, real or imagined, only exacerbated their shock and disbelief of hearing the news in 1764 that political ties had been cut, indeed over a year earlier, as a simple repayment for Spanish costs incurred in the Seven Years' War. Creoles of New Orleans experienced collective trauma at being severed by their "mother country." The reac- tion from the now former colony was for political and economic leaders to meet and discuss how best to respond to the news. The group of this newly emerging elite met to discuss their options and this group included

Lafrénière, the attorney-general; Jean Milhet, the wealthiest merchant of the colony; Joseph Milhet, his brother; St. Maxent; De la Chaise; Marquis; Garic; Masan; Massange; Poupet; Noyan; Boisblanc; Grand-Maison; Lalande; Lesassier; Braud, the king's printer; Kernion; Carrière; and Dessales (Gayarré, Vol. 2 127). They decided to send a representative to France to argue their case. Chosen as emissary was the wealthy Jean Milhet, who traveled to France with the goal of persuading King Louis XV to change his mind. These locals hoped by sending Milhet that "the king of France, when made aware of their love and devotion, would retract his donation, and that they would thus prevent what they all dreaded so much" (Gayarré, Vol. 2 126–27). Milhet, accompanied by the aged Bienville, who lived in Paris, met with Prime Minister Choiseul, who refused to give them an audience with the king. Such a refusal constituted another staggering blow for the Creoles in Louisiana. A French man of letters, Abbé Raynal, represents the colonists' trauma in his history of colonialism that was published just a few years after the transfer of Louisiana to Spain: "Unbeknownst to me, you struck up a deal whose very secret was treasonous. Unfeeling, ungrateful Mother, how could you have broken what Nature intended, broken the ties that bound me to you through my very birth? When I honored you through my labors, with the blood and milk that I had received from your veins, I could only hope for the consolation to live and die under your laws. You did not want this. You ripped me from my family to give me to a husband that I did not want" (Vol. 6 133). The trauma of French Creoles, abandoned by France when Louisiana was ceded to Spain, was exacerbated when the Creoles suffered further silencing and marginalization, lost amid the colonial hegemony that sought to control them, "It was not enough that the colony was divided and that one part was given over to England, it was also yet necessary that the portion that remained with France was made to swear allegiance to a foreign sovereign! There were no more French in the former Louisiana; there were only English and Spain."[2]

Becoming a Spanish Colony

King Carlos III of Spain approached the governing of Louisiana cautiously. As the first governor he chose a renowned scientist, man of letters, and military officer, Antonio de Ulloa, who received the following instructions from the Spanish king: "I have resolved that, in that new acquisition, there be no change in the administration of its government, and therefore, that it be not subjected to the laws and usages which are observed in my American dominions, from which it is a distinct colony, and with which it is to have no commerce. It is my will that it be independent of the ministry of the Indies (*ministerio de Indias*), of its council, and of the other tribunals annexed to it; and that all which may be relative to that colony shall pass through the Ministry of State (*ministerio de Estado*), and that you communicate to me, through that channel alone, whatever may be appertaining to your government" (Gayarré, Vol. 2 158).

Governing Louisiana was to be through a different channel, by different laws and procedures than in Spain's other colonies. The Spanish built on the foundation that they had inherited from the French rather than a system they themselves established. This was the first time that Spain took over such a territory that was already functioning as a colony with economic, political, and social systems in place. Added to the complexity of the situation was the fact that Spain did not seek to colonize Louisiana, having little interest in this territory. Rather than by his own design, King Carlos III was obligated to take the territory offered to him by France as part of the Bourbon allegiance; neither he and nor his government wanted to take on what they considered as a burden. Consequently Spain put forth no vision or sense of purpose, relative to Louisiana: "One of the cardinal ideas that must be taken into account when judging the Spanish administration of Louisiana is that Spain never proposed, in reality, to hispanicize its new colony. On this point we must remind ourselves, once again, that the Court of Madrid showed no enthusiasm upon accepting the French gift and that neither did it feel much displeasure when it was compelled, forty years later, to return the territory to its original owners" (Montero de Pedro 20). Given this lack of enthusiasm, vision, and sense of responsibility for its new colony, the move to take over the colony proceeded cautiously, and very slowly, taking a full three years for Governor Ulloa to arrive to Louisiana.

In those long, uncertain, and most challenging years, New Orleans remained governed by the French. Denis-Nicolas Foucault, the *commissaire-ordonnateur*, was responsible for administering "justice and regulated the colony's commerce, finances, internal improvements, royal warehouses, and police" ("Confusion, Conflict, and Currency" 161). The replacement for the last official French governor, Louis Billouart de Kerlerec, recalled to France to face criminal charges, was Jean-Jacques Blaise d'Abbadie. D'Abbadie arrived in June 1763 having been appointed director general of the colony rather than governor. His appointment signaled a desire on the part of the French, especially Choiseul, for a smooth transition of these vast lands to their new sovereigns. "With trans-Appalachian Louisiana ceded to the British as a result of the Treaty of Paris, and occidental Louisiana transferred to Spain in the secret Treaty of Fontainebleau, Choiseul apparently feared that intragovernmental strife might disrupt or impede the transfer of the colony. Under d'Abbadie's administration, the colony weathered the transfer of trans-Appalachian Louisiana without internal squabbles" ("Confusion, Conflict, and Currency" 163). However, upon d'Abbadie's death in early 1765, Charles Aubry replaced him, and this era of collaboration between the *commissaire-ordonnateur* and the director-general ended. The tensions within the French administration during this time of uncertainty and transition to future Spanish rule were exacerbated by the dire economic situation in Louisiana. On the heels of the Seven Years' War, Louisiana suffered economic collapse and a devaluation of its currency, putting many families on the brink of starvation ("Confusion, Conflict, and Currency" 166).

To further complicate the political, cultural, and economic concerns, this was also the time that the first waves of Acadians began to arrive in Louisiana, having been chased by the English from Acadie in 1755 in what has come to be known as *le Grand Dérangement,* or the Great Upheaval.[3] These Francophones began arriving in April 1765 and in correspondence to France sent by Aubry and Foucault beg for assistance, making it clear that their situation is dire and they are in urgent need of support from France. The king's store is empty, and there is no money to purchase needed provisions and supplies to help in the settlement of these Acadian families. To make matters worse a smallpox epidemic has broken out.[4] In an attempt to convince the Crown to comply with their request for help, Aubry and Foucault compliment the Acadians for their industriousness, religious, brave, attached to their king and capable of making this colony a flourishing colony in the hopes of convincing the king to send support to the colony.[5] This ploy worked and in the end, the French had to "spend over 40,000 *livres* in royal funds to subsidize the settlement of the Acadians during 1765–1766" ("Confusion, Conflict, and Currency" 164).

When Ulloa finally arrived in Louisiana, Aubrey and Foucault assumed that he was going to immediately take possession of Louisiana.[6] Instead he remained in Balize at the mouth of the Mississippi River from September 1766 until his arrival in New Orleans in March 1767. Once arriving in New Orleans "[t]he paucity of Spanish troops, the impossibility of recruiting French troops into the Spanish service, and the lack of operational funds prevented Ulloa from taking possession of the colony, and, in time, he became totally dependent upon the French administration" ("Confusion, Conflict, and Currency" 164). This dependency lasted for his entire term as governor, with him never taking formal possession of Louisiana because Spain never did send the number of troops that he requested for the transition. So confusion even among the highest echelons continued: "Aubry himself referred in his reports to the strange situation in which he found himself, actually having to govern a colony belonging to the King of Spain, using troops to do so who were in reality loyal to the Kings of France. He even reached the point of complaining about the unpleasant task which had been placed upon him of having to govern the affairs of a colony without knowing with certainty whether it was Spanish or French. It is impossible to think of a more absurd situation" (Montero de Pedro 28).

When Ulloa arrived in New Orleans, he had only ninety soldiers and three civil servants in his entourage (Montero de Pedro 26). "Ulloa faced difficult issues during his thirty months as governor. The unpleasant reception he received on arriving had disillusioned him. His efforts to redeem the inflated paper money then in circulation had been unappreciated. Moreover, many of the later French accusations against his conduct were spurious and had little to do with real issues. Ulloa's problems in the colony centered on his jurisdictional conflict with the French Superior Council, which represented a privileged group of residents, mainly planters and merchants, who enjoyed economic control of the province" (Din and Harkins 41). In 1767, the Spanish government reconsidered its initial decision to leave French institutions unchanged, and Ulloa began to assume the duties of the Superior Council, which he finally dissolved (Din and Harkins 43). Ulloa decided to dissolve the Superior Council, which constituted local government for New Orleans Creoles. He published his decree of his intention to enforce Spain's restrictive trade policies, which could seriously undermine the economy in Louisiana and pose a threat to the status of Creole elite. With this move, the scene was set for conflict between Ulloa and the Creoles harboring resentment against this new governor and their new sovereign.

Locals well understood Ulloa's ongoing vulnerability due to Spain's lack of support for his administration, one characterized by uncertainty, confusion, and inaction. Although technically a Spanish colony, Spain refused to claim Louisiana. No longer a French colony, the French Crown nonetheless paid the colony's bills. King Carlos III treated New Orleans and his Louisiana territory as exceptional, and this exceptionalism operated as ferment for the local Creole population, especially the elite, to be emboldened and chart their own, self-determined course.

The Republic of Louisiana

Creoles of New Orleans were willing to obey France, to be loyal subjects of the French Crown, and not to question — excessively — the role that the metropole played in their determination. It was however France who broke that bond, that social order. Consequently, the pain felt by locals, combined with a sense of abandonment at being so easily discarded by France, led to a sense of freedom and liberty that the colony had not known before. And once that order was broken, New Orleans Creoles acted very much like their Canadian forebearers the *coureurs de bois* and the *voyageurs*, seeking to create their own New World social order and identity. Just as the Creole identity had melded to "France" and negotiated that existence by affective, imaginary ties to France, so was it that once France no longer held the function as colonizer, or as the official role of "mother country" to the colony, many locals especially among the elite class adapted a more authentic name, that of being a Lousianian. The Lousianians did not shift in their position through this change in name; it appears that they simply changed their label and claimed what was already true, that their collective identity was rooted in Louisiana rather than in Europe, in the New World rather than the old. They were therefore already independent from their former "mother country" and released from a sense of duty not only to the French Crown, but to any crown.

As we have seen already Creole collectives operate in original, unscripted ways, with relational identities having import. Thus lacking directives from France gave license to Francophone Creoles to pursue all the more what they had done when New Orleans was the capital of French Louisiana. They engaged in the process of collectively scripting an identity based on their sense of exceptionalism and their living in the New World. The agency allowed them to generate their own narrative. Let us recall the words of early colonist Pellerin, who said, "We all are free to talk until the time that good decisions come from France." In the space of absence, Creoles fill the gaps with their voices, sense of self, and self-interest through their own actions in order to weave a narrative they constructed. No good decisions were forthcoming from France, nor for that matter from Spain, so the Creoles put forth a completely audacious goal.

Their goal was to establish the Republic of Louisiana through staging what we call today the Rebellion of 1768. Their first step was to rid themselves of Governor Ulloa, and on October 29, 1768, the Superior Council voted to expel the governor and virtually all Spanish officials from the colony, except for the handful that they held as hostages (Din and Harkins 45–46). The resolution of the Superior Council read: "[The council] enjoins Mr. Ulloa to quit the colony allowing him only the space of three days, either in the frigate of his Catholic Majesty in which he came, or in whatever vessel he shall think proper, and go and give an account of his conduct to his Catholic Majesty" (Sublette 92). Ulloa retreated and the Rebellion of 1768 marked the first time that colonists in North America staged a rebellion against a colonial power on the grounds that they wanted self-determination.

Lest we begin to fancy the notion that this was a collective, populous effort, let us recall the legacy of the French colonial structure, and how those in power were able to gain wealth and influence within a fragmented and divisive system. Furthermore, the organizers of this rebellion were convinced that the Spanish were not committed to settling Louisiana, that they had little interest in governing the colony, and that they were completely unwilling to invest meaningfully in the territory. Judging from Ulloa's governorship, it could accurately be said that France rather than Spain continued to govern Louisiana. Nonetheless, there was not unanimity around this uprising, especially since those who were most prone to rebellion would have been those with the most to lose under Spanish rule. As such the rebellion did not have the full support of all New Orleans Creoles; this was the first of many situations where the tensions between those who valued liberty, self-determination, and republicanism were at odds with royalists in the colony who believed in the importance of the sociopolitical and economic order found in the monarchy. As is often the case, the roots of the Rebellion of 1768 were largely economic in nature. These tensions between revolutionaries and royalists played out in Creole New Orleans throughout the Age of Revolution that was to follow.

The Rebellion of 1768 occurred in the context of shifting times where world order was shifting away from Europe toward the New World, and the Enlightenment was ushering in new questions about the role of government and new ideas about the rights of peoples. At its core were both deep economic concerns and a desire for liberty. For rebel leaders in New Orleans, the basis of their power and wealth had more do with their connections to circum-Caribbean trade, rather than a reliance on France or Europe as trading partners. If we recall the correspondence between Aubry and Foucault to France, they pleaded to the Crown for assistance because of the king's stores in the colony being empty, and they lamented that support from France was slow to arrive in Louisiana. However, while the situation was difficult, neither the Creoles nor the newly arrived Acadians suffered outright famine and the project of settling the Acadians occurred in spite of this crisis.

This can be explained by how in the mid-eighteenth century Creoles were well versed in illegal trade of contrabands. Since the earliest French colonists, smuggling, contraband, and privateering flourished in Louisiana, and indeed were essential for the development of the colony. The ties that bound New Orleans to Saint-Domingue, Havana, Veracruz, and elsewhere in the Caribbean far outweighed in importance any connection to Europe that was wracked by war and ensuing crises. Local agency on the part of New Orleanians provided them a means of avoiding famine and total ruin during this ongoing economic crisis of the 1760s. So when the transition to Spanish rule finally happened, locals were justifiably concerned that some of their livelihood would be adversely affected by implementation and the enforcement of Spanish trading policies. As we have already established, while France had imposed strict limitations on trade in the colonies, they spuriously enforced them. So in spite of how policies limiting mercantilism were in place in both the Spanish and the French colonies, Spain more vigorously enforced policies beginning in 1760 (Dawdy 131–32). Locals rightly were concerned that their contraband commercial routes spanning the Caribbean Basin would be disturbed and that the complex web of trade would be eliminated. The Creole societies of the Caribbean enjoyed a web of north-south interdependence that had a basis in economics, but also in significant sociocultural dimensions that were reinforced constantly in the context of maritime trade, and the patterns of migration and immigration. In spite of concerns for disrupting this north-south web, during the Spanish period contraband and privateering among Spanish territories, especially Havana, grew significantly.

Ending the Rebellion of 1768 and the Arrival of "Bloody O'Reilly"

Unlike successful revolutions happening later in the eighteenth century, this attempt at self-determination, while audacious, ultimately failed. In August 1769 Alejandro O'Reilly, the second Spanish governor of Louisiana, arrived ready to take possession of the colony for Spain. His arrival was a study in contrasts with that of Ulloa. O'Reilly came to the Place d'Armes, known during Spanish rule as the Plaza de Armas, with his soldiers, taking swift political and military control of the colony. Whereas Ulloa had just ninety troops, O'Reilly commanded over two thousand troops. Immediately O'Reilly sought to render justice to those Creoles responsible for the rebellion, and within days had the leaders arrested, and five of them, including La Frénière, executed by a firing squad (Sublette 95). The others were given prison terms in Havana, and their property confiscated (Montero de Pedro 31; Sublette 93–94). Thus he put an end to the uprising and earned the sobriquet "Bloody O'Reilly" for this action against the local Creole population. The site of the execution has come to be known as Frenchmen Street, although those who were executed were Creoles. The name of this street serves as an example of how the Spanish viewed the local population through the lens of European identity, as French rather than as Creole.

O'Reilly then formally replaced the Superior Council form of municipal government with a cabildo, a council of local landowners acting as representatives and a form of government found in other Spanish territories (Din and Harkins 49–53). His term provided a foundation upon which the rest of the Spanish colonial period was built, and historians have more recently claimed O'Reilly showed astuteness that often goes unrecognized. For example, he included local Creoles as members of the Cabildo, thereby presciently acknowledging "the City's powerful ethnic roots. Spaniards never outnumbered the French and French creoles in Louisiana, and, although Spanish became the official language of church and state, the lingua franca and the cultural milieu of New Orleans and its environs remained French" (*Masterless Mistresses* 123). The order that O'Reilly brought to New Orleans reflected his understanding of Creole dynamics comprising New Orleans society. Spanish rule as instituted under him existed in an in-between space where Spanish "ruled" in a conciliatory way within a Francophone Creole sociopolitical and linguistic context. Nonetheless, with the rebellion squashed, Louisiana became a part, albeit exceptional, of the Spanish empire, seven long years after having been ceded to Spain.

Race in Spanish *Luisiana*

The conciliatory approach of Spanish rule added to the process of creolization in important ways, especially regarding free people of color. Under Spanish rule New Orleans became the most African of cities in North America, and the legacy of that demographic shift represents that most important legacy left by Spain. Caryn Cossé Bell in her seminal study of the revolutionary history of Louisiana's free people of color states that Spain benefited by promoting a tripartite, as opposed to a binary, system of race in Louisiana since it was a counterweight to the Francophone elite of the city because "the free black class had served as a crucial counterweight to planter ambitions. Lenient manumission practices, a lax social regimen, and the exigencies of colonial management promoted economic and social mobility for the free black population" (36). Furthermore, Bell argues: "In seeking to establish their own authority and bring tranquility to the multiracial and multicultural colony they had inherited from the French, Spanish officials endeavored to organize New Orleans' society into three corporate bodies: Euro-Louisianans, libres, and slaves. They imposed a new legal apparatus that encouraged manumission and strengthened the rights of both slaves and freed persons of African descent, thus profoundly reinforcing the development of New Orleans' tripartite racial system that the Code Noir had initiated by codifying the distinctive position of free Afro-Louisianans within it" (100–101). This tripartite system fit within the Spanish tradition of *limpieza de sangre* with its extremely codified social hierarchy based on an individual's "whiteness." Spear explains, "Conflating honor and status with lineage, limpieza de sangre constructed a socioracial order that was based on a concept of whiteness that held that only those of pure European ancestry possessed honor, legitimacy, respectability, and rank" (129).

This policy of Spanish rule regarding slaves' rights was the right of *coartación*, or self-manumission, and it is estimated that during the Spanish period two thousand individuals became free through self-purchase. Bell explains: "The Spanish slave code, Las Siete Partidas, which provided for slave self-purchase (*coartación*), became the most important means of manumission. The new measure permitted slaves to accumulate personal funds by selling their extra labor to the masters or other people in need of their services. This source of income enables slaves to purchase their freedom. An accompanying measure required the slaveholder to set a fair purchase price" (18). Furthermore under the Spanish regime, "lenient provisions of Las Siete de Partidas had also provided for the legitimation of mixed-blood children born in concubinage. The statues entitled the offspring of such relationships to become legal heirs" (Bell 76). Change happened quickly. Jennifer Spear in her exhaustive study of race relations in colonial Louisiana says that it "took only four years under the Spanish for the number of manumitted slaves to surpass all those freed during the five decades of French rule. Almost two thousand slaves received their freedom during the four decades of Spanish rule" (110). Thus in the early 1770s, one slave in 126 became free. There was both resistance and complacency among whites. Whites helped secure freedom for slaves for a number of reasons, intimacy, kinship, or religious, social, or economic ties (Spear 100).[7]

Dynamics of self-fashioning relative to newfound freedom under Spanish rule are described by Spear as follows: "But, perhaps most important for slaves seeking freedom was the introduction of Spanish rule and the precariousness of Spanish authority over the inhabitants of the formerly French colony. The Spanish regime provided slaves with greater options than had been the case under the French, and they quickly learned how to take advantage of them. Spanish laws did little to mediate the actual experience of enslavement, especially in conjunction with a rising plantation economy, but the codes and the response they engendered from local elites reveal how competing interests shaped the developing constructions of race and offered slaves a chance to remake themselves as free" (101–2). Predictably the growing number of free people of color was cause for concern among a considerable portion of the economic and political elite. These leaders' concerns were assuaged by acts by subsequent Spanish governors to accommodate them. This included marrying into elite families with the third governor of Louisiana, Luis de Unzaga y Amezaga, and his successor, Bernardo de Galvez, marrying daughters of Gilbert Antoine de St. Maxent, one of the ringleaders of the Rebellion of 1768, thus taking the notion of conciliation to a very personal level.[8]

Galvez has gone down in history as the most famous of Spanish governors. First he was a military leader helping the revolutionaries in the southern flank with his multiracial troops win battles in Baton Rouge and Manchac: "Spain's participation in the American revolutionary war against Great Britain was perhaps the most exciting time in the Spanish era in Louisiana. Upon learning of Spain's declaration of war, Governor Bernardo de Gálvez worked to amass supplies, foodstuffs, and men to attack the British forts in west Florida. Gathering his troops, militia, and volunteers, he first led his soldiers up the Mississippi on August 27, 1779. His victories at Manchac and Baton Rouge gave him possession of Natchez as well, and he took a large number of prisoners down to New Orleans by October" (Din and Harkins 14). The multiracial troops consisted of different companies of militia grouped together by their skin color, explains Bell: "The Spaniards divided free black soldiers into separate military units on the basis of color as part of a general policy of creating more rigidly defined racial categories. They separated dark-complexioned free black soldiers (*morenos*) from lighter-complexioned free black soldiers (*pardos*) in segregated companies. Spanish officials awarded free black soldiers silver medals, cash bonuses, and military pensions for exemplary service. The Spaniards also advanced black soldiers to positions as commissioned and noncommissioned officers. Membership in the Spanish corps was considered a mark of high status by the city's Creole of color" (16).

Furthermore, Galvez encouraged more people to settle in Louisiana, such as hundreds of settlers from the Spanish Canary Islands, known as *Los Isleños*. He also facilitated the migration of more Acadians who arrived to join their families already settled in Louisiana. And he reopened the slave trade, a move welcomed by Louisiana planters. In addition to the Acadians, Canary Islanders, and Africans, the newly arrived to Louisiana included Iberian officials and soldiers and Anglo-American and British merchants (*Masterless Mistresses* 124). The multicultural, multiracial, and multilingual diversity continued to grow. For Creole New Orleanians, it added to their sense of local identity, as belonging to a distinct culture. The arrival of Africans, Anglos, and other Europeans enhanced "the sense of shared community among New Orleans' French-speaking Catholics of both European and African ancestry. Thus, while many Euro-New Orleanians sought to form families with those who shared European ancestry, despite cultural, linguistic, and religious differences, others seem to prefer cultural familiarity to shared European ancestry" (Spear 143). Therefore, beginning in the 1780s there were more *sang-mêlé* children who were acknowledged by their blanco fathers in church records (Spear 143).

However, given the influx of newly arrived Africans into slavery, by the end of the Spanish period the conditions for Africans or those of African descent were both much worse and much better than under French rule. Spear describes this dichotomy as follows: "On the one hand, far more people of African ancestry found themselves enslaved in Louisiana as the reopened slave trade fueled the growth of a plantation economy, which, in turn, created rapidly deteriorating conditions for the enslaved. On the other hand, the Spanish government opened new avenues to freedom and often defended the rights of slaves against their owners" (128). She concludes by saying that a very important element of this system was the agency of the slaves themselves in working toward their manumission. "Not only did the population of free people of African ancestry increase dramatically during the last third of the eighteenth century, but so too did the number of those individuals who had African, European, and occasionally Indian ancestry, a consequence of the growing numbers of families formed by women of color and Euro-Louisianan men. It was this combination of freedom and mixed ancestry that became the essence of the gens de couleur libre by the end of the Spanish era" (128). Once again we see evidence of growing ties with the Spanish Caribbean at this time in the context of creolization and racial mixing at this time. The system of *coartición* developed in Cuba. This system "received royal recognition and legal sanction in the late 1760s — just as the Spanish arrived in Louisiana" (Spear 109). In his text *No More, No More: Slavery and Cultural Resistance in Havana and New Orleans,* Daniel Walker draws parallels between this multiracial Creole city and Havana:

> In these cities, the enslaved came in contact with a host of Europeans and Euro-Americans, a diverse mix of native Africans, free black and mulatto populace, and, in the case of Havana, Chinese laborers and others imported from the Yucatán Peninsula. When one adds the significant numbers of Native Americans still residing in close proximity of New Orleans throughout

this period, it becomes clear that slave life in these areas was much more complex than what is generally proposed. In contrast to the relative isolation of the outlying plantations, urban slaves participated in mutual-aid societies, conducted large public festivals, engaged in organized African and Afro-Christian religious practices, and like their rural counterpart, at times threatened the institution of slavery through their violent resistance. (ix)

Colonial New Orleans remained distinct from other areas of the Louisiana Territory because it was never a plantation economy and slaveholders were never in the majority in the city. The complexities of the social structure created by slaves only grew due to the manumission of so many people.

With the reinstitution of the slave trade that occurred simultaneously with the shift in manumission practices, there emerged the desire to reinstate the *Code Noir* of 1724 under O'Reilly, but instead other policies were instituted. Some were written by officials in Spain in the metropolitan trying to reorganize the Spanish empire. And local officials also promulgated their own desired changes that suited local circumstances. "Contemporaries on both sides believed that Spanish policies were more moderate. Spanish officials defended their laws as 'just and fair,' while local elites protested they were too lenient and inadequate for their circumstances" (Spear 103). In 1789 the Spanish presented their *Código Negro*, but the local Creole elite protested this and attempted to write their own slave law, the *Code Noir ou Loi Municipale* of 1778, which implicated that all free people of color had "literal or at least figurative connections to slavery" (Spear 108). It also sought to reverse the ease with which slaves could be manumitted. The *Código Negro* was revoked in 1794 after protests throughout the Spanish colonies, and the local *Code Noir* was never officially sanctioned. These two codes were not completely dissimilar, with both insisting on instructing slaves in Catholicism and for masters providing for the basic needs of slaves, but the *Código* focused more on their status as persons, and the *Code Noir* more on their status as property. The Spanish Code did more to punish those who mistreated slaves, even if done by the slaves' masters. Spear argues that the Spanish code's purpose was motivated by the desire for more tranquility in the colonies rather than having humanitarian aims.

Nonetheless, threats to the institution of slavery mounted as the eighteenth century drew to a close, especially due to the French Revolution based on its the Declaration of the Rights of Man and Citizen, leading to widespread discontent that fueled the establishment of independent republics in North America and the Caribbean (Bell 19). With the dissolution of slavery in France at the end of the French Revolution, and then the successful slave revolt in Saint-Domingue, a direct result of the Declaration of the Rights of Man and Citizen, slaving societies everywhere were reeling. This was especially true in New Orleans due to its close proximity to postrevolutionary Saint-Domingue, now known as Haiti. It was Spanish governor Baron de Carondelet who found himself having to quell thoughts of rebellion in Louisiana in light of those events further south. Disturbances did occur in Louisiana, with Carondelet and his governments unsuccessfully attempting to insulate free people of color and slaves from events elsewhere. Bell gives the following account: "The outbreak of revolution in Europe and the French Caribbean produced considerable repercussions in Spanish Louisiana. Spanish authorities could not insulate free people of color and slaves from events underway in France and the Antilles. The ideal of racial equality, given political expression in the French Convention of 1794, and the realization of national independence in Haiti in January, 1804, presented a radical challenge to slavery and racial oppressions" (24). The revolution in Saint-Domingue affected New Orleans in many ways, including Carondelet's mostly unsuccessful attempts at restricting social interactions of his subjects of color. "As paranoia about a second Saint-Domingue sweeping Louisiana spread in the 1790s, official proclamations prohibited free blacks and slaves from masking during carnival and established separate balls for whites and libres," explains Hanger (143). She continues explaining, "Although local authorities preferred separate dances for whites, libres, and slaves, residents of New Orleans usually cavorted in mixed company. Free blacks provided the music at many white gatherings. Masked slaves and libres occasionally disrupted carnival balls, their identities hidden behind ingenious disguises" (146). In spite of attempts to "manage" the population, it was impossible in this fluid Creole society, a society of slippages with culture historically more important than race in defining social bonds.

Governor Carondelet's concerns were in part based on the arrival of refugees from the Haitian Revolution in Louisiana that began during his time as governor, with one hundred refugees arriving in New Orleans between 1791 and 1797 (Bell 37). This was the beginning of a groundswell of migration that would double the size of New Orleans in the next decade. Carondelet did not mince words when he complained to Cabildo officials in May 1795, "the colony, by means of secret and undercover plots, is on the verge of being submerged in the horrors which have ruined the French colonies" (quoted in Bell 28). Indeed the governor arrested and deported "several French individuals who tried to propagate republican ideas in the province" (Montero de Pedro 68).

Given the composition of Francophone Creoles in New Orleans, Caron-delet's fears should have been somewhat assuaged since in general free people of color did not embrace revolutionary ideals, at least not during the end of the eighteenth century. Hanger describes this society as follows: "As loyal Spanish subjects and members of the free pardo and Moreno militias, many libres defended Louisiana against a likely invasion by French radicals attacking from both the Gulf and the upper Mississippi, as well as from internal disturbances fomented by pro-French agitators and discontented African and Creole slaves. Throughout Spanish America administrators continued to rely on free blacks to contribute to their colonies' defensive and labor needs . . . [M]ost libres were reluctant to go so far as to take up arms against white persons, not only because whites could call on well-trained police forces, but also because many libres were linked to whites by kinship and patronage networks and had a direct stake in Louisiana's slaveholding system" (151). The free people of color's resistance to revolu-tionary ideals should not be confused with acquiescence to white European hegemony. They were bent on reforming the system in which they lived, rather than overthrowing it. They resisted overdetermination of their so-cial and economic status based on race, as they sought more recognition for their achievements and more equity in their life chances. Nonetheless, their society "reaffirmed the city's patriarchal, Eurocentric social hierar-chy" (Hanger 136–37). Thus, the culture and sense of community in New Orleans appears to have changed very little from the end of French colonial rule. The city remained multiracial and multicultural united by its identify-ing as a community of French-speaking Catholics.

The Catholic Church in Spanish *Luisiana*

A surprising institution of contested space that provided a context for social resistance to white hegemony was the Catholic Church in New Orleans. When Spanish clerics arrived in New Orleans, even late in the Spanish period, they were "profoundly scandalized" by the "low level to which re-ligion and morals had sunk in the colony" (Montero de Pedro 69). Atten-dance at mass and other observances were not followed, and the habits of lifestyle of the local French Capuchins, the only order in the colony, were no less scandalous. Paradoxically, the absence of whites participating in Catholic observances allowed for a connection, an economy of sorts, where the presence of free people of color allowed them to gain more of a voice in the church. Among other things, it was an avenue of social advancement for them. Hanger explains, "Although slaves and newly freed Africans practiced their non-Catholic religious beliefs overtly—but cautiously and usually within a controlled setting—most libres followed the prescriptions of the dominant Catholic religion . . . They aspired to white acceptance and patronage" (139). Bell delves further in the economy existing between the Catholic Church and free people of color: "Opposed to interference in the master-slave relationship, white Creole planters withdrew from active participation in the church and generally refused to comply with statutes designed to protect their slaves' spirituality and religious obligations. Free blacks and slaves, perceiving the Spanish clergy as a useful ally, filled the resulting vacuum by taking the place of whites as godparents for unbaptized African and Creole slaves" (65).

Research on the history of the Ursuline convent, treated earlier in this study, by Emily Clark in her *Masterless Mistresses: The New Orleans Ursulines and the Development of New World Society, 1727–1834* details the dynamics of race relations as played out between the Francophone Creole and French Ursuline nuns as opposed to the newly arrived Spanish Ursulines. Ultimately the presence of Spanish nuns as well as ecclesiastics forced cultural, racial, and gender norms to be reconsidered. The newly arrived Spanish nuns in particular objected to the fluid sense of race permeating the convent that opposed their more rigidly codified notions causing divisiveness and friction among the women. By the 1780s and 1790s, the tensions between these groups "erupted in fractious convent politics. Yet the Spanish era also brought real prosperity to the convent and the extension of its educational program to an unprecedented number of colonial women and girls. At the end of the eighteenth century, the Ursulines were more financially secure and less susceptible to interference from male authorities of church and state than they had ever been (3). Enhanced financial security of the Ursuline convent mirrors the enhanced economic situation of New Orleans at the end of the Spanish period with its booming port and growing merchant class.

The End of the Spanish Period

When considering the overall contributions of the Spanish to the urbanization of New Orleans, development of New Orleans between 1779 and 1803 attests to Spanish practices of building strong cities and investing in infrastructure. This was in part by necessity since during the two generations of Spanish rule, the city experienced challenges, both natural and manmade, including three major hurricanes (1779, 1780, and 1793) and two fires (1788 and 1794). The fire of 1788 destroyed over eight hundred buildings, nearly 80 percent of the city, and the fire of 1794 destroyed over two hundred buildings.

An account of the 1788 fire in the *Relation de l'incendie qu'a éprouvé la ville de la Nouvelle-Orléans, le 21 mars 1788* describes the terror of this huge fire that destroyed all but three buildings in the city, the chaos of the residents, and how the pumps were of little use and were consumed by fire at times. It also describes the exploding powder that had been secretly kept in individual homes. The narrative explains in painful detail the complete lack of coordination and procedure about how to save what could be saved, as it also describes the residents of New Orleans on the day after the fire, who could only walk around stunned and dazed at the sight of such destruction. It then describes the welcome response by the governor and the intendent, who promise to aid the residents. The article ends with an appeal to His Majesty for sufficient aid to offset this suffering and need (n.p.). However, it was only after the Fire of 1794 that building codes were established under Governor Carondelet to make them more fire resistant, that they should be made of brick and have tile roofs (Din and Harkins 31–33).

Due to these new regulations, there remain over thirty buildings from the Spanish period in the French Quarter today. Adding to Spanish urban improvements such as sidewalks (*banquetas*), Carondolet had street lamps installed, and a canal built connecting the French Quarter to Bayou St. John, allowing the shipment of building materials to the city. The Spanish government accommodated the Creoles in many ways, including creating special militia units for Francophone Creoles (Din and Harkins 23). Other less-tangible improvements occurred such as safety codes, procedures for fighting fires, standard weights and measures, regulated access to the levee and assumed responsibility for its maintenance, and set licensing requirements (Sublette 95).

As the eighteenth century drew to a close, the little interest that Spain had in continuing to rule Louisiana began to wane, just as Creole involvement in the Cabildo also waned. The design of having this area act as an advantageous buffer against British and later American aggression, protecting mineral resources of Texas and Mexico, was a costly enterprise. So the Spanish readily gave Louisiana back over to France by the secret Treaty of San Ildefonso in 1800. "Spain did not much care about the colony anymore. The governors were lame ducks. Law enforcement was lax. No matter who was ostensibly in charge, the Anglo-Americans would keep coming into the region. They could not be stopped" (Sublette 176). The French promised to hold on to the colony for three years, but instead the French were slow to take possession of the territory and only officially held it for twenty days, as Napoleon arranged for what the French still call today, *La Vente de la Louisiane,* or the selling of Louisiana in 1803. When the French regained the colony it was a thriving commercial center, and this was because of the reestablishment of slavery in 1777 and the furthering of trade along the Mississippi that built on peace with Great Britain and the development of Anglo-America, underscoring the shifting hemispheric hegemony.

The Erasure of the Spanish Period in New Orleans History?

The result of the hesitancy to govern on the part of Spain, the continued implication of France years after Louisiana was no longer a French colony, as well as the resistance on the part of New Orleans Creoles to acquiesce to Spanish rule resulted in a kind of collective erasure from New Orleans culture, with the Spanish period remaining a vague historical moment. The myth then persists that New Orleans retains no significant place for the Spanish presence in its history. However, this way of thinking represents a rescripting of historical moments in order to reestablish an imagined French presence in the city. This discursive space falls back on the family ties of the Bourbon dynasties in Spain and France, with the territory remaining in the family, as it were, during the Spanish period, therefore still fundamentally a French space.

The irony here belies the historical record and how it was under Spanish rule that New Orleans developed into an important port city. As we have established, it was the Spanish who invested in the infrastructure and who rebuilt the city on several occasions after disaster struck. The buildings from the Spanish period that survive in the French Quarter include the most iconic Presbyter and Cabildo that flank St. Louis Cathedral. For many today the most obvious vestige of the Spanish period is found in the tile street Spanish names found on many corners in the French Quarter, a fairly recent addition to the cityscape. The Spanish hispanicized the names of the streets in the French Quarter, but as we have seen, they did not reconfigure them. While there are vestiges outside of the French Quarter of eponymous references to Spanish rule such as St. Charles Avenue for Carlos III, Carondelet Street, and Galvez Street, to name only a few, these are all outside of the French Quarter. This erasure of the Spanish spatially and culturally from the accepted narrative was aided by the assimilation of the Spanish to Francophone hegemony. Some of the more notable examples are Dominguez became Domingue, Rodriguez became Rodrigue, *banquetas* became *banquettes,* and even *Nueva Iberia* became *Nouvelle-Ibérie.* The Isleños remain a notable exception and remain identifiable people through their resistance to assimilation, living as they do in a rural part of St. Bernard Parish, southeast of New Orleans. This is ironic because in Spain the Canary Islanders are hardly considered as the "most Spanish" of people.

During Spanish rule, we see then that the colonizers indeed seem to have been creolized. The colonial enterprise was infused in Creole dynamics in new and important ways, through the negotiated relationship of metropole and colony. With the Spanish having inherited a colony that essentially was created by another country, and already with another European identity, this was not a place where the locals could be dismissed as being soulless savages. The residents in New Orleans already identified as Catholic; they already had enslaved Native Americans and Africans; and they identified as French, the country that was champion this era of the Enlightenment.

So more important than any actual traces of the French that remain in the city was the power that France continued to have through the myth of it retaining its status as the "mother country." This mythologizing disguised an agency shared by those living in New Orleans and served as a cultural commodity, still important today. This self-fashioned "Frenchness" proved successful since it influenced the governing of the colony by the Spanish Crown, overshadowed Spanish investment in the colony and inroads in the urban development of New Orleans, causing erasure of the Spanish imprint in the city's collective imaginary, just as happened later when the city became part of the United States.

Nonetheless, when we shift perspectives to the larger Caribbean Basin, it becomes clear that such "erasure" of New Orleans' historical connections to Latin America and the Caribbean has not occurred. From a pan-Caribbean perspective, New Orleans has not ceased to function as a north coast of the Caribbean economically, culturally, or iconically. The city has been referred to by scholars on the Caribbean and Latin America as a "locus of power from which US hegemony over much of Latin America has been extended" (Gruesz 470). From the eighteenth century until the burgeoning of the city of Miami, New Orleans functioned as the point of entry, a gateway, for people and goods entering the United States. Its position as a "liminal zone between the Anglo and the Latin worlds" (Gruesz 469) is an area ripe for future research with its many unanswered questions especially with the hispanization of post-Katrina New Orleans.

CHAPTER FIVE

Becoming an American City

Introduction

Dynamic changes occurred in New Orleans as it officially became part of the United States through the Louisiana Purchase. At this particular time in the city's history a confluence of opposing events came to pass having seismic repercussions for the city. For just at the moment the city was becoming an American territory, the French population doubled with the arrival of waves of refugees from the Haitian Revolution. This tension created cultural clashes where the Francophone Creole population contested the dynamics of assimilation into Anglo-America, on the one hand, as they negotiated significant aspects of the plantation society of the antebellum South on the other.

As we have already established, for centuries the circulation of ideas, culture, art, and trade passed not just east to west, from Europe to America, but north and south, from Saint-Domingue, Cuba, Veracruz, and other places south to New Orleans. Thus the arrival of the Haitian refugees capped off centuries of migration, trade, and other types of cultural exchanges. Given the great number of immigrants, their arrival transformed and brought a new way of life to the city. Before this wave of immigration, New Orleans did not have a literate population or many aspects of what we consider to be high culture. These immigrants brought newspapers, theater, and literature to New Orleans and created a new literary class of free people of color, as well as white Creoles and French immigrants. Since the refugees themselves reinforced New Orleans' tripartite racial system, consisting of whites, free people of color, and slaves, they represented the gamut of perspectives on the institution of slavery: from those of the most ardent slaveholder and those of the most radical abolitionist. Born from this amalgam are many "firsts" for African Americans, in particular, the first black newspapers, literature, and collective calls for social justice in the form of essays, manifestos, and other types of resistance to racism and the tyranny of slavery.

Vying forces, then, sought to influence and determine the course of New Orleans in the early nineteenth century. The dynamics of creolization being

what they were in the city allowed the newly arrived refugees to be assimilated into New Orleans Creoles with ease since they were Francophone and
Catholic. The traditional images that we hold of "old" New Orleans were in
fact only born at the dawn of the nineteenth century with the Haitian immigrants infusing the city with their traditions and culture. We have only to
think of Quadroon balls and the practice of *plaçage*. However, the situation
with the United States was much more fraught with challenges, especially
since President Thomas Jefferson gravely feared the presence of such a
large contingent of immigrants from a homeland where a successful slave
revolt had just occurred. From the perspective of Francophone Creoles, it
seemed as if their city had been transformed into an American colony at the
mercy of the United States government and the motor of economic change
whose *lingua franca* was English.

Historical Context of Antebellum New Orleans

At the dawn of the nineteenth century, yet again, New Orleans and the
Louisiana Territory played the role of pawn in the European arena, with
Spain returning Louisiana to the French in the secret treaty of San Ildefon-
so (1800). Napoleon, much like Louis XIV, had imperialistic ambitions in
Europe and afforded little value to this faraway colony. Going back on his
promise not to pass the territory to a third party, Napoleon negotiated the
Louisiana Purchase with the United States in 1803, before even completing
the process of taking formal possession of the colony. Once more, the city of
New Orleans was caught unawares by this sudden shift of fate.

At the beginning of the nineteenth century, the manifest destiny of the
United States and the movement west that resulted had not yet found its
way into the American imaginary. There was therefore not unanimity to
the United States buying Louisiana among these newly minted Americans.
The territory was vast and largely unknown, the implications of this purchase were anything but predetermined, and the population of the capital
city represented a French-speaking, racially diverse cohort of Creoles with
a culture often at odds with New England puritan ideals. As we will see
later in this chapter, New Orleanians of the time did not summarily dismiss
their new colonizer, as they themselves sought more freedom and liberty
promised under the American flag, although the faith in American ideals of
republicanism was often challenged in the face of forced assimilation into
Anglo-America.

It is important to remember that at the time of the Louisiana Purchase,
the population of Francophones was doubling with the waves of Domin-

guan (Haitian) immigrants arriving in New Orleans, beginning at about the time of the French Revolution and continuing through 1810. Focusing on the last wave of immigrants, Daniel Walker writes, "In total, more than 9,059 refugees entered New Orleans between May 1809 and January 1810. Of this number, 3,102 were free persons of color, 3,226 slaves, and 2,731 free whites . . . The total number of free persons of color who came in 1809 was more than the entire number present in Orleans parish (which included New Orleans) just three years earlier (2,378)" (6). In addition, immigration from France continued throughout the century that fueled ties with France commercially, through family connections, and of course symbolically. As I have stated earlier, immigrants from all parts of the globe had to assimilate to a "Creole French" melting pot culturally and linguistically, well into the nineteenth century. Throughout the century however the balance shifted, and settlers from elsewhere did not necessarily encounter Francophone contexts in their daily lives.

We will also see how ready Francophone Creoles were to fight for causes they supported, with the first call to arms for New Orleanians to fight as Americans was the Battle of New Orleans fighting against the encroachment of the British up the Mississippi River. All sectors of this tripartite Creole society bore arms in this battle. Their patriotism nonetheless was suspect enough for Andrew Jackson that at times it seems that he considered the Francophone Creole population of New Orleans a greater menace than British troops. He not only imposed martial law on the French-speaking population but refused to lift it until pressured from the court and the federal government.

The antebellum period in New Orleans saw the city become the most important port in the United States, an entrepôt for North America and the Caribbean. Just as had been the case since the city's founding, urban expansion was contested. The Faubourg Marigny was created to house this new large Francophone population. Built downriver from the French Quarter, this area, along with Faubourg Trémé, was to stand in contrast to the Faubourg Ste-Marie, or the upriver American section of the city. These primarily Francophone Faubourgs Marigny and Trémé along with the area that was now known as the "French Quarter" continued to function as the hegemonic center of Francophone Creole culture. As we have seen in the earlier chapter on the design of the French Quarter, the identity for the French-speaking Creoles that differentiated their concept of self from the American "Other" was reinforced by this notion that theirs was a space where they could live surrounded by cultural references that they named and that reminded them of their imagined French past.

However, the economic center was elsewhere. Upriver Faubourg Ste-Marie had developed into the locus of economic and political hegemonic center of the city becoming progressively more important through the ensuing decades. So Francophone Creoles needed to negotiate those very different spaces and changing loci. As we have seen elsewhere, boundaries in New Orleans are more often than not fluid, with passages between these areas. Partnerships were formed and families were made among the city's Anglophones, other newly arrived residents, and Francophones.

Accompanying the economic growth of this antebellum southern city was a growing acceptance of the southern antebellum notion of race. As we have already established, this notion of race was binary in nature—black and white. The position of free people of color in this situation quickly deteriorates. A free person of color might be a slaveholder, or the child a white, but this did not make that person white. In this system, being of African descent would only situate that person of color as black, just like a slave. Conditions for free people of color therefore were extremely uncertain and fraught with dangers since their rights were not guaranteed. Their situation got all the more precarious in the 1830s after legal restrictions were placed on their freedom. Their plight deteriorated up through the Civil War, causing an exodus of many Creoles of color from the city to more rural areas in south Louisiana where they felt safer and freer from the sorts of repression and vigilantism present in the city.

Another means of contesting the forces of American colonialism and assimilation in New Orleans was for local Francophones to engage in collective nostalgia about their identities and look back to notions of their history for assurance. It did not take long for Francophone Creoles to understand that the rights and freedoms the United States promised was at odds with the assimilation to Anglo-America it imposed on them. We see in Louisiana in the 1840s an awareness of the value of turning to the history as a way of stemming the tide of Americanization (Kress in his preface to *Louisiana*, 16). And stories, especially in the form of the historical novel, rescripted that history, and were a logical means to reacquaint contemporary readers with their past. Historical novels were especially effective because of their melding of "fact" and "fiction" to weave a tale of identity and of belonging to a distinct community with tales needing to be told. Following the Aristotelian premise that the object of art is to teach and delight, it operated as a means to recast the present through the lens of history in order to bring "new"—that is, historical—values to bear on contemporary issues. Literature functioned as an important means of nurturing self-determination and freedom from the burdens of colonialism. These cultural artifacts could evoke or bring back to life an affiliation that counters external forces of An-glo-American imperialism. For the most part, living in the French-speaking faubourgs, struggling to find balance in the changing world, this society felt itself under assault, beginning with its language now being considered "for-eign." These texts functioned as a means of resistance since they could be a place around which shared opposition to colonial legacies could be forged.

French Language after the Louisiana Purchase

Language had been a deeply contested issue in Louisiana throughout the colonial period in this hybrid culture; however, the Louisiana Purchase brought a new level of tension as an 1804 pamphlet, *Esquisse de la situation politique et civile de la Louisiane,* demonstrates. The following summary of the pamphlet is offered by Charles O'Neil in his study "French Literature in Colonial Louisiana":

> The pamphlet depicts the scene in New Orleans during the first year of American government. The author deplores the fact that a disproportionate number of recently arrived Americans are being given political posts even though most of the appointees cannot speak French. The native Louisian-ians are being told to learn English, and rumor has it that the language of the federal government is soon to become the exclusive medium of legal and political expression. The author concedes that the day may come when his generation's children will all speak English, but he inveighs against the injustice of an overnight change that would strike the French-speakers with political death.

O'Neil continues his description by stating:

> With piercing rhetoric he shames the new government by pointing out that the old absolutist government of Spain was more generous and liberal. If, he argues, the Americans are pledged to the protection of property, they have an obligation to respect the dearest property of a people, their language. Lest Louisianians continue to be made foreigners in their native land, the author begs that the free, justice-loving Americans consider favorably the petition that Louisiana's French-speakers are putting forth in their "Memorial to Congress." (28)

The "Memorial to Congress" or *"Mémoire présenté au Congrès des États-Unis d'Amérique par les habitans de la Louisiane"* represents an emotional entreaty to the United States Congress asking this body to assure that the citizens of Louisiana will continue to have the right to an elected government whose language is French. They complain of how judgments have been made that cannot be explained, much less justified, to them. This was in part due to the complicated nature of the legal system in Louisiana where there were codes from French, Spanish, and American jurisprudence. The citizens lament the lack of interest in Francophone Louisiana by the Congress, and they criticize various points relative to Louisiana's admission to the Union.

The French language was once again targeted during the Civil War by General Butler, who prohibited the use of French in public activities in the 1860s. Fifty years later the Louisiana State Board of Education suppressed the use of French in schools, punishing children caught speaking French, and the Louisiana Constitution was amended to prohibit "the use of any language other than English in the public school system."[1]

The arrival of such a large number of French-speaking immigrants from a home country that had experienced a successful slave revolution terrified the government of Thomas Jefferson, and added to the anxiety that they felt with the French language in Louisiana. Conversely, the arrival of Haitian immigrants reaffirmed the "Frenchness" of the city and reinforced a common identity between New Orleans and Dominguan Creoles that became stronger over the ensuing decades, as we will see.

Just like in the greater Caribbean Basin, there existed tension between French and English. However in nineteenth-century New Orleans, English prevailed in society, in government, and in schools. The predominance of French declined throughout the century. As we shall see in this chapter and the next, many of the authors who wrote in French in the early to mid-nineteenth century attended French-speaking schools in the city where teachers were either local Creoles or recent immigrants to New Orleans from France or Saint-Domingue. There they learned standard French from the metropole. Indeed many of these writers spent some of their youth schooled in France, especially in Paris at the Lycée Louis-le-Grand. However, English-only laws in schools marked the end of the French colonial linguistic hegemony within sociopolitical structures in Louisiana and announced the ultimate end of French literature as well. The French language with its claim to universality was displaced, becoming a "foreign language" in the curriculum of the schools, just as it had been displaced in state and local government.

In the context of literature, this displacement of French in favor of English in schools not only assured that literary production would ultimately be written in English in New Orleans, but it also guaranteed something that at the time was even more outrageous: that their society would be represented in literature exclusively by "outside" Anglophone writers. Kate Chopin, George Washington Cable, and Lafcadio Hearn came to garner wide readership and notoriety, with some of their works such as *The Awakening* ultimately enjoying canonical status. This introduction of Francophone Creole culture to a larger American audience through the works of such linguistic and cultural outsiders was unacceptable to Francophone Creoles. The literary representation of New Orleans by these authors was nothing less than an affront to French-speaking Creole attitudes, sensibilities, and cultural norms. Consequently, the Francophone Creole population of the time reviled these authors, with Cable being especially criticized.[2]

Obviously, literary works need never be "approved" by those they seek to represent, but with the absence of works written by French Creole writers, there exists no dialectic—literary or otherwise—that included voices of writers constituting an authentic cultural perspective, and whose works would therefore constitute genuine cultural artifacts of this Francophone space. Homi Bhahba posits this dilemma in his *Location of Culture*, where he theorizes about the importance of the representation, or reinscription, of such a minority perspective in cultural discourse as follows: "Terms of cultural engagement, whether antagonistic or affiliative, are produced performatively. The representation of difference must not be hastily read as the reflection of *pre-given* ethnic or cultural traits set in the fixed tablet of tradition. The social articulation of difference, from the minority perspective, is a complex, on-going negotiation that seeks to authorize cultural hybridities that emerge in moments of historical transformation. The 'right' to signify from the periphery of authorized power and privilege does not depend on the persistence of tradition; it is resourced by the power of tradition to be reinscribed through the conditions of contingency and contradictoriness that attend upon the lives of those who are 'in the minority'" (3). Francophone Creole writers indeed desired to act performatively, to reinscribe their own traditions into the emerging discourse of nineteenth-century America through their own language and in the context of their own culture. This desire was made more and more difficult to fulfill, however, because of the shifting hegemony away from the French language as English rather than French as the status of "official" language of government, education and, of course, commerce. Thus, the "social articulation of difference" disappears from the cultural landscape as the literature written in French suffers erasure.

Of course within Creole culture, questions of what might represent authentic and genuine elements of this discursive space exist within boundaries that are particularly fluid and permeable. As has already been considered in previous chapters, this should not be interpreted as meaning an absence of boundaries because New Orleans as a historically Francophone Creole space was sustained in part due to its opposition to its immediate Spanish- and English-speaking neighbors. This distinction depended on the existence of clear lines of demarcation in the collective imaginary, as relational identities suppose nonrelational ones. When the works of these English-speaking authors broaching the subject of Francophone Creole ways of life were published, it served as unwelcomed encroachment and unapproved appropriation of the distinct culture, history, and aesthetics of Francophone Creoles. As we have seen in our discussions of *créolité,* the external gaze of the "Other" underscores the innate vulnerability in being Creole because the "Other" occupies a position of privilege capable of exploiting the Creole for its own purposes as it passes negative judgment on the internal process of this baroque, disorderly culture. This American representation of Creole society could be understood then as an act that doubly marginalized Francophone Creole culture as part of the American landscape, because it both misrepresented and negatively judged this culture and its people, powered as it was by the discursive privileges of the English language and accompanying Anglophone hegemony.

Early French Creole Literary Production

Before the Louisiana Purchase, there was already some literary production, albeit small, because Francophone Creole writings had existed since the founding of New Orleans. As we have seen, the early writings consisted of travel journals written by the earliest colonists, followed by official and personal letters. By the nineteenth century, newspapers, poetry, novels, treatises, dramatic works, and so forth came into being and existed until the end of the century.[3] Basically French literature in Louisiana was born a posteriori, after the territory became part of the United States. Just as in the larger society, literary production was multicultural, multiracial, and cosmopolitan, representing the dynamics of New Orleans culture. Influences from France, from recently arrived immigrants from Saint-Domingue, and from the local Creole amalgam helped to shape a unique literature that has no equal in North America.

Themes running through these literary works include the realities of the multicultural landscape specific to New Orleans, especially treating the accompanying dynamics of assimilation and hegemony among the diverse groups that made up Creole culture. Other themes revolve around the historical events important to this community, with the year 1812 being an especially important historical touchstone. Slavery as an unjust institution, the notion of liberty, and the transnational nature of literary production of the nineteenth century in Louisiana were all of thematic import as well. The writers producing literary texts included a significant number of free men of color and some white Creole women, as well as French nationals, and refugees from Saint-Domingue, the latter's influence being especially important in the early part of the nineteenth century. The result of this robust literary output has special significance because, as we have already said, it contains some of the first works of African American literature, which were written by this community of free men of color beginning in the 1830s. Their writings included novels, poetry, and short stories, the first of which was *Le Mulâtre* by Victor Séjour written in 1837. Later in the century, the first North American newspapers and literary reviews owned by blacks were created.

In previous chapters I have examined ways in which New Orleans was an imagined space. In the realm of literature this was no less the case. From the origins of literary production in New Orleans, fact and fiction exist seamlessly, more fluidly due to Creole dynamics than elsewhere. Let us consider the make-up of the original texts from the early colonial period, some of which have been discussed in previous chapters. We have already examined the outrageous propaganda published in *Le Nouveau Mercure* to lure future colonists and investment in Louisiana. John Law clearly understood how fictional travel narratives could pose as factual, and he chose this type of narrative as a means to sell shares in his company and to attract settlers to the colony, thus enhancing his colonial enterprise. However, when these same texts are examined as literature rather than as examples of journalistic manipulation for economic gain, the interdependence of literature, history, and political propaganda emerge as important markers of the historicity of colonialism, inspired by imagined communities. Waggoner, in her introduction to *Le Plus Beau Païs du Monde: Completing the Picture of Proprietary Louisiana, 1699–1722*, states: "Law felt he could reach large segments of the population and capture their attention by publishing narrations written in the 'travel account' style. The previous travel narrations had been published in various forms, such as travel journals, diaries and commentaries on maps . . . Paul Hazard called these popular travel accounts 'a literary genre with unclear borders, practical because a writer could put anything in them from scholarly essays to museum catalogues to love stories: the travel account triumphed.' The passion for these travel accounts, and for exotic locales, is clearly seen in French literature of the eighteenth century, from Montesquieu's *Lettres persanes* to Prévost's *Histoire d'une Grecque moderne* and *Manon Lescaut*, to later works by Voltaire (*L'Ingénu, Candide, Zadig*) and Diderot's *Supplément au voyage de Bougainville*" (19–21). Law made use of material that was in vogue to create an imagined New Orleans that would attract colonists. He was perhaps the first such person who tried to profit from creating a fictionalized space that could be "sold" to outsiders for financial gain—a tradition that continues to this day.

Of all the novels mentioned above, *Manon Lescaut: L'Histoire du chevalier des Grieux et de Manon Lescaut* by Abbé Prévost left an indelible impression on the collective imagination of the French, and therefore continued to serve as a collective reference in New Orleans due to the value of the currency of French ideas in the city, for at least two hundred years. The introduction to De Villiers's history of New Orleans at the bicentennial of its founding reflects the importance of *Manon Lescaut* in the context of French colonial New Orleans. The author of the introduction was Gabriel Hanotaux, not only a member of the *Académie Française* but also president of the *Comité France-Amérique*. This scholar-activist cannot help but reference the novel as a representation of the French colonial experience. He states: "How does one not salute the delicate shadow and the fragrant ghost of our Manon Lescaut? The dubious adventure of Chevalier des Grieux is not a simple romantic invention: Manon lived" (x). The evidence that he uses to support his argument is scant and problematic, yet his conclusion is nonetheless absolute.[4]

Another text to revisit at this point is Iberville's *Gulf Journals*. Considering this journal as a literary piece reveals a sort of baroque palimpsest. Iberville describes his initial futile attempts to locate the mouth of the Mississippi River because he was wrongly following Hennepin's false *Relation*. Iberville complains that he and his men wasted thirteen hours having only *sagamité* to eat because of this forged narrative" (66–67). In other examples of early narratives, even in official government documents there is ample evidence of an interest in rescripting or reinventing certain historical moments and geographical spaces because of an interest of how naming might be viewed by the French "audience." For example, on several occasions Bienville, as we have seen, sought to rename certain areas, such as changing the name of Ile Massacre to Ile Dauphine, so as not to offend French sensibilities. When considered from a literary perspective, this desire to avoid offending the public through inappropriate language use recalls the French neoclassical aesthetic of *bienséances*, the notion that the reader should be pleased, rather than offended, by words, expressions, events necessary for empire building.

Perhaps the most striking example of the fluidity in an official narrative is found in Laussat's proclamations while in Louisiana. He first arrived ostensibly to reclaim Louisiana for France, but just a few weeks later he had to issue another proclamation—that Louisiana would instead become part of the United States. In Laussat's first official proclamation reclaiming Louisiana from the Spanish in the spring of 1803, he decries that Louisiana had been given up as a colony to Spain by calling that "one of the most shameful times," *"une des époques les plus honteuses,"* of the *ancien régime.* He explains how different the Napoleonic Empire will be as he promises citizens the love, fidelity, and courage of the empire. He goes on to say that Napoleon never lost *la mémoire* that it is French blood flowing in the veins of the former colonists. Nonetheless, just a few weeks later, Laussat found himself in a very different position relative to Louisiana because of Napoleon's ultimate selling of Louisiana to the American government. In light of this turn of events, the former proclamation reads as pure fiction when Laussat issues the second proclamation without anymore justification than saying his mission has been "changée."[5] These dueling proclamations when considered together destabilize any notion of historical veracity as they represent opaque and ultimately illegitimate "truths," resembling the earlier propaganda of the *Le Nouveau Mercure* with its having little or no reference to shared collective experience.

An overview of writing from the French and Spanish colonial periods include the following: journals of early French explorers such as Sauvole, Henri Joutel, Henri de Tonty, Pierre-Charles Le Sueur, Charlevoix, André Pénicaut, Jean de Champigny; journals of early French missionaries such as Paul Du Ru, Jacques Gravier, Jean Mermet, Gabriel Marest, François Le Maire; journals of early French colonists by, for example, Bérnard de La Harpe, Pellerin, Le Page du Pratz, Pradel, Bossu; ship captains (Vallette de Laudun); and French expatriates (Louis-Narcisse Baudry des Lozières). Early works of poetry include the *Poème en vers* by Jean François Dumont de Montigny and *La Prise du morne de Bâton Rouge* by Julian Poydras.[6]

As literature, the travel journals, or *relations*, correspond to the initial colonial process of discovery that mirrors colonization elsewhere in the Caribbean where traits of this New World are identified, documented, and thus named, with the aim according to critics of controlling the new lands. In *Lettres créoles*, Chamoiseau and Confiant argue that due to the nature of this writing as descriptive inventory this type of narrative cannot give birth to a creative writing tradition (31). This type of writing, they argue, is more of an extension of the planter mentality born of a need to "write only to fill in registers, civil or commercial, write in ledgers, or draw up texts of a judicial-police nature" (30). Thus these types of texts aim primarily to assure the European conquest of the islands. They seek to fulfill the desire of the metropole to rule over the pristine world through the process of naming and defining the parameters of their new encounters (32–33). It should not be surprising, then, that one finds very little literary production in Louisiana during both the French and the Spanish colonial rule. There needed to be a social base that was not limited to a primarily plantation society. Such a society did not exist in the earliest decades of the eighteenth century. As Mathé Allain concludes, "All in all, however, the literary balance sheet for the eighteenth-century is meager: travel relations, memoirs, histories, three poems and a few issues of a newspaper" (7). Nonetheless, it was the newspaper that helped to usher in a true literature in New Orleans.

Early Newspapers and Journals in French

The appearance of periodicals represents the starting point for nineteenth-century literary production in Louisiana and the creation of its literary culture. These texts functioned both as newspapers and as literary journals. Frans Amelinckx in "Forgotten People, Forgotten Literature: The Case of Creole Authors of Color" describe the birth of newspapers in the following way: "In Louisiana, even more than in France, the newspapers promoted a general interest in poetry, featuring, for example, the Frenchmen Béranger, Hugo, and Gautier, the local white authors Tullius Saint Céran, Oscar Dugué, and Adrien and Dominique Rouquette, and the Creoles of Color Camille Thierry, Joanni Questy, and Armand Lanusse. The Louisiana papers were, in fact, the only outlet for local literary production since all printing had to be subsidized either by the authors or by advance subscription. Although owned by white proprietors or editors, the local press readily accepted the literary production of Creoles of Color, so long as it conformed to the norms—that is, no racial or social references" (52). This echoes Benedict Anderson, who posits newspapers at the origin of community building, in his *Imagined Communities: Reflections on the Origins and Spread of Nationalism*, when he invites the reader to consider "the basic structure of two forms of imagining which first flowered in Europe in the eighteenth century: the novel and the newspaper. For these forms provided the technical means for 're-presenting' the *kind* of imagined community that is the nation" (30). The newspaper was crucial for the rise of the postrevolutionary bourgeoisie who built communities like themselves through "print-language" (74). Likewise, it was also important to the formation of an identifiable literary culture to emerge from the multicultural, multiracial, and multinational community of Creole New Orleans, where this print-language allowed for a common narrative site for the hybrid demographic that was the literati of New Orleans. In other words, newspapers became an instrument around which the population coalesced.

Ironically, the importance of newspapers for Louisiana literature, being the site where so many poems and narratives were published, is an important reason that much of the literature fell into oblivion. "The most obvious factor in the neglect of the literary production of the Creoles of Color resides in the lack of knowledge of the nineteenth-century literary mode of production and diffusion—the newspapers" (Amelinckx 57). This literature appearing in journals rather than books meant that the works did not find themselves in libraries or other collections for posterity.

The arrival of newspapers in Louisiana coincided with the influx of immigrants from Saint-Domingue. According to Nathalie Dessens, in her exhaustive study of the migration of refugees from Saint-Domingue, *From Saint-Domingue to New Orleans: Migration and Influences*, these refugees

> launched journalism in Louisiana. The 1790–1810 period was one of great dynamism, with the creation of all the main newspapers of New Orleans. In every single press venture, Saint-Domingan refugees lead the way. Louis Duclot, a refugee, founded *Le Moniteur de la Louisiane* in 1794. In 1797, one year after his arrival Jean Baptiste Lesueur Fontaine became its editor. *Le Télégraphe* was founded in early December 1803 by Claudin Beleurgey and Jean Renard, who was a printer of the city and of New Orleans Parish. J. B. Thierry and J. C. de St. Romes were responsible for launching *Le Courrier de la Louisiane*, which was published from 1807 to 1860, and Jean Leclerc founded *L'Ami des Lois*. Alexis Daudet participated in the *Louisiana Gazette*, a bilingual newspaper. Among the famous journalists were Louis Placide Canonge and Baron Jérôme Bayon de Libertas, from the Breda plantation (the very plantation where Toussaint-Louverture had been a slave), who wrote both in *L'Abeille* and *Le Courrier de la Louisiane*. (86–87)

The newspapers often published an eclectic mixture of newsworthy items, local and international, given the cosmopolitan nature of the public, while they also included literary pieces in serial form. Since these periodicals were founded by Saint-Dominguans, there is a relatively progressive attitude toward race relations represented by these journalists. "When *L'Abeille* was founded in 1827 by white refugees, the editors displayed a clear tendency toward progressive beliefs in matters of race and race relations. Several free blacks, using pen names, contributed to its columns" (Dessens 99).

This mirrors New Orleans society of the nineteenth century with its Creole cultural values and attitudes toward culture and race.

The newspaper tradition in New Orleans, begun with *Le Moniteur de la Louisiane*, was followed by over one hundred others with the last ones being *L'Abeille*, which ceased publication in 1923 after a nearly one-hundred-year stretch, and *Les Comptes Rendus de l'Athénée Louisianais*, which continued to be published until the late twentieth century (Allain 14). In the 1860s *L'Union* and later *La Tribune de la Nouvelle-Orléans* were antislavery newspapers notably owned and edited by people of color. Other newspapers and literary reviews included *Le Libéral, La Chronique, Veillées Louisianaises, L'Équité, La Renaissance Louisianaise, L'Estafette, Le Meschacébé, L'Observateur Louisianais*, and *L'Album Littéraire*.[7] Because these papers printed collaborations between white authors and authors of color, they helped garner more readership for black authors. For example, Séligny, a Creole of color, had twenty-six short stories published in *L'Abeille, Le Courrier de la Louisiane,* and *La Renaissance Louisianaise*, beginning in 1839.[8]

The revue *L'Album littéraire*, founded in 1843, was the first black literary publication in the United States (Guillaume 70). *L'Album* provided a forum to cultivate a discourse of protest by people of color, as Bell explains, "many contributors to *L'Album* used their literary skills to challenge existing social evils in nineteenth-century Louisiana" (105). This paper was especially implicated in the political engagement that stood as a protest to the eroding civil liberties for people of color in New Orleans, to the point of evoking armed combat (Michaelides 25). The newspaper was a platform to contest racism, giving voice not just to Creole free people of color, but to all people of color, enslaved and free, whom it affected. One example of this type of political discourse is a piece entitled "Horreurs du jour" that reads as follows: "But I have often asked myself this question in my moments of reflection: "Why is it that laws are not applied with the same intensity for all ranks? . . . I fear answering this question myself, but if I had the power to write the answer on the foreheads several of the most revered of august Gentlemen, you would see them on their knees asking heaven to spare them its vengeful thunder" (*L'Album littéraire: Journal des jeunes gens, amateurs de littérature,* vol. 1 78–79, cited in Michaelides 24). That these editorials could appear in the antebellum South reflects the exceptional status that New Orleans maintained into the mid-nineteenth century. But as we will see, freedom of expression for free people of color becomes more and more limited as the Civil War looms.

Besides nonfiction and essays, *L'Album* printed poems by the most influential Creoles of color in New Orleans, poems that were published in 1845 as *Les Cenelles*, the first collection of poetry in African American literature (analyzed in more detail in the next chapter).[9] This collection of poems continues in the protest tradition against the injustices found in Creole New Orleans and the growing censorship by the American government limiting the rights and privileges of free people of color, as Dessens explains: "The poems are generally related to the situation of the free people of color in Louisiana, their bitterness at racial injustice and prejudice, and their wish to see the wrongs they endured throughout their life redressed. The topics of these poems clearly point to political militancy . . . Their poems published in *Les Cenelles* and in the literary journal they had founded in 1843, *L'Album Littéraire: Journal des jeunes-gens, amateurs de littérature*, and the editorials they wrote for the journal were a clear denunciation of Louisiana society" (125). Given the limits that were imposed on people of color at this time, this pro- test needed to be veiled, however. Traditional poetic standards associated with the French Romantic movement were therefore a textual means to this end. Poets also used pseudonyms or simply did not sign their work, as Bell states: "Clearly, the 1830 law restricting reading materials, as well as the highly provocative nature of some of the pieces, persuaded a number of artists not to sign their contributions. Other writers used pseudonyms or simply initialed their works. The French-language periodical containing social commentary, poems, and short stories began as a monthly review, but at the request of subscribers, the editors produced a shortened, bimonthly edition. In one of the earliest issues, an essayist described the collection of poems and short stories as the 'first songs' of aspiring young writers; he urged his readers to 'give them wings'" (105). Considering the broad scope and weight of the 1830 law, these "wings" would have had to be tremendous to rise above it. The law reads: "Whosoever shall write, print, publish, or distribute anything having a tendency to produce discontent among the free colored population of this state, or to excite insubordination among the slaves . . . shall on conviction thereof . . . suffer imprisonment at hard labor, not less than three years, not more than twenty-one years, or death, at the discretion of the court."[10]

Literary Production in the 1830s and 1840s

The literary production of the 1830s and 1840s was, as has already been stated, quite robust both for whites and Creoles of color. There are social and political reasons for this. The social reasons related to the existence of an educated class of Creoles, white, and free people of color, who studied in New Orleans, as well as in France and elsewhere. These writers had

the economic support of their families behind them and a society that offered them the promise of a future profession that would afford them the
opportunity to write, as well. Furthermore, political reasons powered this
exchange because France at the time functioned as a beacon of nineteenth-
century republicanism. A shared sense of hope in the possibility of creating
a utopian Republic based on these principles emerges.

In New Orleans, the multiracial immigrants from Saint-Domingue were
already established in the Marigny by the 1830s and contributed in many
different ways to this dynamic republican amalgam:

> Without any doubt, the refugees' strong commitment to republicanism, a po-
> litical trend that had ensured the Saint-Domingan population of color access
> to civic equality and freedom, their active leadership in New Orleans, and
> their strong proportion within the New Orleans free population of color had
> several consequences. It reinforced their sense of community and their wish
> to improve the general situation of their class, and it most certainly fashioned
> their cultural identity.

Dessens goes on to explain the myriad of ways the refugees from the Haitian Revolution contributed to New Orleans society:

> Their presence was found in all the important ventures undertaken by free
> people of color at the time. When the *Société des Artisans* was founded by free
> artisans and war veterans of color, the initiator was a refugee, Louis Victor
> Séjour, who had fled Saint-Marc in 1794, had settled in Louisiana, and had
> been part of the free battalion of color under Savary and Daquin. The society
> also included active refugees' children, including Séjour's son, Victor Séjour,
> but also Michel Séligny and Camille Thierry. When the *Société Catholique pour
> l'Instruction des Orphelins dans l'Indigence* was founded in 1848 to administer
> the Couvent estate, many refugees of color or descendants of refugees were
> among the members of the board of directors, including Armand Lanusse,
> the school's principal, Paul Trévigne, Aristide Mary, and Rodolphe Lucien
> Desdunes. (Dessens 124–25)

The writers during the antebellum period represented an eclectic group
and included writers of fiction and nonfiction. One finds poets, dramatists,
novelists, political activists, and editors of newspapers and literary journals.
Some were educators but more often they were physicians and tradesmen.
Many—regardless of being white or a person of color—were slaveholders.
Nonetheless, at least one of these writers was among the first free men of

color to fight on the side of the Union against slavery during the Civil War, where other Creoles either chose or were forced to serve in the Confederacy. Their works were inspired both by French literature and linguistic standards, as well as local realities and considerations. This reflects another Creole amalgam where literature, while inspired by a colonial past, refuses to be limited to those colonial traditions, and appears instead as a dynamic, multidimensional construct that is comparatively speaking, unruly and perpetually baroque.[11]

The *Revue des Colonies* and Louisiana Literature

How did it happen that a young author, barely twenty years old, wrote Louisiana's first novel? More importantly how is it that the young Victor Séjour wrote his first novel on the topic of the utter tyranny and dehumanization of the institution of slavery? What might have been his lived experiences and his understanding of society and family structures that served as his literary inspiration? He was the natural child of "Juan Francisco Louis Victor Séjour Marcou, a dyer of Dominican origin, and Eloisa-Philippe Ferrand [a free woman of color] of New Orleans, the young Victor was sent to Paris, in 1836, to complete his education, where he lived for the rest of his life" (Michaelides 36). So this text mirrors many of the transnational patterns relative to New Orleans where a New Orleans native sets his tale in Saint-Domingue but gets it published while living as an expatriate in Paris. As Michaelides notes: "Far from being isolated, the Creole of Louisiana was part of a vast global network linked by a 'horizontal' axis to France and by a 'vertical' axis to the Caribbean and Mexico" (11). The privileged relationship with France gave Louisiana and New Orleans, in particular, a cultural identity that was not reduced to the confines of the new American sociopolitical-linguistic landscape and its accompanying binary racial social organization, nor was this area blended into the larger Latino Caribbean cultures. This was especially important for free people of color who expatriated to France for the desire of freedom and its ensuing educational and professional opportunities impossible at home in the American South. It was also a springboard for writers of color, such as Séjour to be published and gain notoriety abroad that enhanced their situation at home.

The transnational nature of the exchange of ideas following horizontal and vertical axes appear as pan-Caribbean phenomena. These ideas flowed from the Caribbean to Louisiana and to France. Here we see that *Le Mulâtre* was published in Paris by Cyril Bissette in his *Revue des Colonies*, whose story Bell recounts as follows: "Soon after [Séjour's] arrival in Paris, the New

Orleans writer encountered the fiery antislavery journalist Cyril Bissette. A free man of color from Martinique, Bissette had already won a legendary reputation in the French abolitionist movement. Arrested in 1822 in his home in Martinique for disseminating seditious literature, the well-to-do Bissette was stripped of his possessions, sentenced to the galleys for life, and branded with the letter *GAL* for galley slave. In France, Bissette's case became a cause célèbre. Freed from prison in 1827, the embittered exile became an impassioned enemy of slavery. In 1834, Bissette launched an abolitionist tract titled *Revue des Colonies*" (95). France at the time still allowed slavery in its colonies, with slavery not being abolished until 1848, over a decade after the publication of *Le Mulâtre*. The text, with its setting in Saint-Domingue while it was still a French colony, serves as a critique of French society as well, making this work a part of the abolitionist discourse both in France and in the United States (Michaelides 36). This serves as a transnational critique of slavery and its global implications.

By leaving New Orleans and becoming an expatriate in Paris, Séjour met Bissette, himself a Martiniquan expatriate of color. Séjour became a part of the fiercely antislavery community of writers who contributed to the *Revue des Colonies*, as Brickhouse explains:

> Over the course of its intermittent run, the *Revue* became the most radical abolitionist publication in France, the first to call for the immediate rather than gradual emancipation of slaves in the colonies. Well over a decade before Frederick Douglass launched *The North Star* to promote the abolitionist movement in the United States the *Revue* was inciting the fury of advocates of slavery throughout the Americas . . . The *Revue* became in this sense a forum for inter-American historical revisionism and anti-imperialism, a project in which a brilliantly eclectic literary consciousness worked to recruit an array of writers for its cause: the French abolitionist priest and literary historian Henri Grégoire, the eighteenth-century poet Phillis Wheatley, the nineteenth-century Haitian poet Ignace Nau, as well as Séjour, among many others. Finally, while foregrounding the inextricability of the literary history of the United States from the global economic and political forces that shaped it, the *Revue's* legacy was also in part to open a critical window onto the transnational and multilingual dimensions of a specifically African American tradition within early US literary history. (88)

Arguably, Séjour sought out Bissette because it would certainly appear that he arrived in Paris already with abolitionist leanings. It seems obvious that while still in New Orleans he was reflecting on the ideas of this provocative work. This is not surprising because as we already have seen, his father was engaged in political activism and included his son in many of his activities. There was also the circle of politically engaged free Creoles of color that made up the young Victor's literary cohort including the writer and educator Michel Séligny, who was Séjour's teacher; Joanni Questy, another educator; and Armand Lanusse, the editor of the first anthology of poetry written by Creoles of color, *Les Cenelles*.

Civil War, Reconstruction, and Francophone Creoles

The Civil War played out differently in New Orleans than in other southern cities. Among Francophone Creoles, as we have already established, there were differences of opinion regarding the morality and necessity of slavery. There were Creole whites and Creoles of color in New Orleans who supported slavery, who were slaveholders, and who fought on the side of the Confederacy. Conversely, many Creoles of color and some whites were against this institution of bondage, especially in the context of the French Enlightenment, and fought on the side of the Union. There were others still, such as the unfortunate French expatriate Garreau, who will be treated at length in the next chapter, drafted against their will to fight for the South. Garreau abhorred slavery but, along with his son, was conscripted into the Confederate army and died fighting to preserve it. Another anomaly to New Orleans and other places where Creoles of color resided in the Deep South is that, most free people of color lost wealth and property during the conflict and never recovered their middle-class social standing after the war.

In the postwar period, the voices of Creoles of color helped to craft the Constitution of 1868, considered "a remarkable document. Other state charters were cluttered with 'thou shan't abridge' evasions, with their lawyerly winks of oh-yes-you-can, provided the right loophole was found. But Louisiana's Reconstruction constitution spoke plainly of positive rights, including 'public rights.' An import from mid-nineteenth-century French republicanism . . . Another constitutional clause was also unambiguous: 'There shall be no separate school'" ("Why Louisiana Mattered," 392–93). When the ideals of Reconstruction were brought down by the growing racism of the late nineteenth century, in New Orleans the *Comité des Citoyens*, or "Citizens Committee" of Creoles of color, staged an act of civil disobedience to challenge the growing segregation and discrimination against blacks. One of the group's members, Homer Plessy, a Creole of color, had himself arrested for refusing to leave the whites-only railroad car. Taking the case to the US Supreme Court, the *Plessy v. Ferguson* case turned out as a victory for the Jim Crow South where "separate but equal" laws prevailed. The case was only overturned by the *Brown v. Board of Education* decision of 1964 that ushered in the Voting Rights Act.

This was also the time when the first newspapers owned by people of color are founded such as the *Tribune de la Nouvelle-Orléans,* owned by Dr. Louis Charles Roudanez. The *Tribune* published verse by Armand Lanusse, Joanni Questy, and Adolphe Duhart. Amelinckx explains how newspapers during Reconstruction continued to have important Francophone readership: "During the Reconstruction period and afterward, the French Creoles of Color continued their publication of creative work and their commitment to quality and justice. As a community, they remained attached to the French language and to the ideals of the French Republic of 1848. The *Weekly Louisianian,* the black Republican newspaper, published in English since 1870, added a French section in 1881 . . . Rodolphe Lucien Desdunes was the editor of the French section . . . Another English-language newspaper, the *Crusader* (1889–91), had a French section under the editorship of Paul Trévigne that published the writings of Numa Mansion, Rodolphe Desdunes, and Victor Rillieux" (54–55). Reconstruction was a time of hope and optimism about the future, a time of a new order and a reclaiming of lost civil rights.

Although New Orleans itself remained a slaving society until the end of the Civil War, and privilege and freedom were not accessible to all in New Orleans who were of African descent, there exited affective ties among many of the local Louisiana Creoles, white and black, Haitian immigrants from earlier in the nineteenth century and French expatriates seeking to live in a democratic society. This was unique in North America and therefore served to challenge the bondage and racism elsewhere on the continent. The consequences of the "Frenchness" that bound this community allowed for there to be a flow of ideas about identity, race, and justice that left an indelible mark on the United States.

While political documents such as the Constitution of 1868 have not been lost to time, the same cannot be said of other documents penned by Francophone Creoles. In the next chapter we will examine some of these works that have recently been reprinted and that give us new insights into Creole life, culture, and language in nineteenth-century New Orleans.

CHAPTER SIX

Nineteenth-Century French Creole Literature: The Final Chapter of French Colonialism

Introduction

I close this study with an analysis of literary production in New Orleans in the nineteenth century, which represents in significant ways the end of French colonialism in the city. This chapter includes an analysis of nineteenth-century works of fiction that are currently being reprinted by Editions Tintamarre written in French and originally published after the Louisiana Purchase situating them as works of American literature. In the context of postcolonial studies, however, these works emerge as important markers of contested hegemony and alterity as they give voice to perspectives and realities long forgotten.

The literature produced during that time in Louisiana had three distinct, yet related, periods mirroring its history: the earlier antebellum period of the 1830s and 1840s, the antebellum period leading up to the Civil War through the reconstruction period of the 1850s and 1860s, and the final three decades of the century. As has already been discussed, in the 1830s and 1840s free Creoles of color made significant contributions to New Orleans Creole literature, before they were systematically denied access to educational and economic opportunities in the period leading up to the Civil War; in fact, 1840 represents the "high mark of 15,072 free persons of color" in New Orleans (Walker 5). During this period, literary production was at its most vibrant, diverse state, according to some.[1] According to others, the golden age of literary production of people of color was after 1864 primarily due to their ownership of newspapers and literary reviews.[2]

This chapter does not seek to be an anthology of two hundred years of literary production in Francophone New Orleans. Instead it aims, through the analysis of key texts and literary movements, to represent sociocultural realities that were important to Creoles throughout the nineteenth century. As has been previously established, there were many social transformations that occurred during that century that corresponded to the city's Americanization, contributing to the loss of literate French-speaking Creoles because of the population's assimilation into Anglo-America.

By the end of the nineteenth century, works of literature, newspapers, and other texts written in French for a local readership disappeared with the passing of the city's last Francophone authors. Consequently, with literary production, readership, and the economy supporting works in French being unsustainable, literature written in French within this Creole culture was quickly lost, forgotten, or simply rendered unreadable due to the language barrier. Although Creole French continued to be spoken in homes, in local commerce, and among family members in and out of the city, by the dawn of the twentieth century the written word was nonetheless in English. So while the oral tradition was able to continue, albeit in a subaltern manner, in the form of stories such as *Compère Lapin*, texts in French disappeared.[3] Therefore, the French Creole literary tradition quickly fell into obscurity, and thus the literature suffered erasure from the landscape of American literary history.

Hybrid Texts

Literature written during this period is a unique product of New Orleans. Just as in the Francophone Caribbean, the literate Creole population wrote in standard French although they might have spoken both standard French and Creole. Thus Creole dialogues are found in many of the narratives. Yet the voice of the narrator appears as consistently written in standard French norms. Themes found in this literature often treat love, desire, beauty, and death, typical of the French Romantic movement, as they also treat Creole issues, including plantation life, slavery as an institution, multicultural identities, and local Louisiana history. These are Louisiana Creole themes. They have little in common with contemporary literature being produced in France.

For example, the first known play to be performed in New Orleans represents this type of hybridity:

> On February 15, 1809, the *Moniteur* announced that on February 21, the
> Théâtre de la Rue St. Pierre would present the first performance of *L'Héroïsme*
> *de Poucha-Houmma ou la fête du petit blé*, a tragedy in five acts and in verse, au-
> thored by "M. Le Blanc, an officer formerly employed by the French govern-
> ment among the Tchactas." The *Moniteur* continued: "An act of heroic fatherly
> love is the subject of this interesting work. The most respected law among the

savages is based on reciprocity; a murderer is punished by death. Cala-bé, son of Poucha-Houmma, the chief of the Houmma, killed a Choctaw while drunk. The law condemned him, but the father sacrificed his life to redeem that of his son."

Allain continues:

The author of the play, Paul Louis Le Blanc de Villeneufve, was some seventy-five years old when he wrote the tragedy. He had a long, distinguished military career in Louisiana, serving first the French and Spanish Crowns then rallying to the young American republic. When he arrived in Louisiana in 1750, at age sixteen, he heard the story of Poucha-Houmma's sacrifice, which had just taken place. Sent among the Choctaw, from 1752 to 1758, a period he describes as "the most beautiful years" of his life, Le Blanc frequently encountered Cala-bé and conversed with him about his father. Le Blanc also came to admire greatly the Indians, their courage, their dignity. He reacted strongly in the early nineteenth century when new colonists frequently expressed contempt for the Indians they encountered, degraded creatures, mired in sloth and enslaved by alcohol. Le Blanc wrote his tragedy to show these newcomers what the Indians were before the white man corrupted them. (Allain 7–8)

While the form of the play (a tragedy in five acts written in verse) and its theme (royal self-sacrifice) respect seventeenth-century neoclassical standards, it differs in significant ways from French standards. The playwright, although from France, does not seek to represent the French neoclassical notion of universal—yet nonetheless Eurocentric—truths. The author, no longer identifying with a European perspective but rather a New World perspective, seeks to educate the ignorant European immigrant in the social values prevalent throughout Native society in order to overcome the biases and prejudices of the newcomer. This newcomer embodies the forces of colonial change that are descending upon and seeking to control native peoples. The author, Paul Louis Le Blanc de Villeneufve, once a force of colonization in his youth, became transformed in this dynamic Creole space, and in the process became a Creole author and a local cultural insider. He left behind a European perspective and took on a local, Creole view of Louisiana. This change implicates his value system, his sense of self, and his sense of community, demonstrating the Creole relational rather than root identity posited by Glissant.

Alexandre Latil and His Literary Community

Insight into the literary community in nineteenth-century New Orleans can come from various texts. In addition to the information that newspapers furnished and travel narratives recounted, we can also look to the literature itself as a source of information for the cultural context in which the literature was produced. There exist works that self-consciously represent the social and cultural milieu of nineteenth-century New Orleans, where the literary community is itself represented in the literature. These works offer invaluable insights into a lost world. In particular, they offer the reader insights into the authors' relational discourse in the community of writers. These works also uncover sources of inspiration for writing present in nineteenth-century New Orleans.

For example, a small book of poetry, *Les Éphémères* (1841) by Alexandre Latil, offers rare insights into the dynamics of the literary community of the city. This work had enormous importance to Louisiana literature, as Kress explains in his piece on "Creole Literature": "Although much of [other Louisiana poets'] work is commendable, few of these poets rose to the nearly mythological stature of the well-born Alexandre Latil, whose tragic life—as a young man, he was stricken with a particularly virulent strain of leprosy—finds a powerful echo within his work, *Les Éphémères* (1841). Indeed, Latil raised Creole romanticism to a quality and expressive power that rivaled that of his French counterparts Alfred Musset, Alphonse de Lamartine, and Victor Hugo. Latil was widely known and read throughout Louisiana, where his poetry was regularly featured in the newspapers of the period." The book offers the reader insights into the contemporary community of writers and their literary production of the time. These insights are found in Latil's introduction to the collection, in the poems themselves, and in the author's notes. This volume is the most complete auto-representation of the literary community of New Orleans in the early antebellum period of the 1830s and 1840s, revealing its fundamental elements, its collective inspiration, and its shared discourse. Although Latil was a leper and lived outside of New Orleans proper, in the area around Bayou St. John, this poetry represents an ongoing dialogue with his contemporaries—writers and other intellectuals of his time. Being unable to be in physical proximity to these individuals due to his illness, poetry was the sole link he had to this community.

In the opening page of *Les Éphémères* Latil addresses his contemporaries who have encouraged his writing and the publication of his poetry, stating:

"Your support, Sirs, is the best response that you might offer to the ridiculous assertion of critics of this country, who claim that literature is languishing here, dying for lack of support and encouragement." There are two audiences implicated in this address to his readers. The first is, of course, the members of his literary community with whom he shares a love of literature and an already established relationship. The second, however, would be the world beyond this community, situated somewhere outside of the cultural boundary of Latil's literati friends. The poet's intent would be, then, to have the book function as a marker, or a cultural artifact, of his community to these "outsiders" to show that literary production does indeed exist in 1840 New Orleans.

Each of Latil's poems, or *éphémères*, begins with at least one epigraph from other poets, writers, or historical figures. These references suggest that his poetry was inspired by diverse and eclectic sources, given that the forty writers quoted included French, German, English, and Creole writers, both men and women. Latil's knowledge of French literature was extensive, judging from the twenty-three epigraphs that represent French sources. These include neoclassical French authors, such as La Rochefoucauld, Boileau, and Racine. He quotes authors of the Romanic period like Chateaubriand, Hugo, and Lamartine, who were icons of the movement. Latil also quotes more popular authors like Hégésippe Moreau and the nineteenth-century French satirist Barthélémy. The women whose epigraphs he includes range from Mme D'Hautpoul, Mme de Staël, Delphine Gay, and Marceline Desbordes-Valmore to the Queen of France Marie Leczinska. He references the Germans Grimm and Goethe, along with the English Byron and Locke. We also find six references to Creole writers: F. Calongne, C. D. Dufour, A. J. Guirot, E. A. Rouquette, Dominique Rouquette, and Cyrille-Charles Théard. Notably absent in his poems, however, were any Anglo-American writers or intellectuals. Not surprisingly, Latil's *terroir* appears as culturally separate from the rest of the United States, in spite of the fact that he himself was born an American.

Also absent from the epigraphs are Creole authors of color. The reason for this latter omission was perhaps due to Latil's being "well born" into a wealthy family of plantation owners, as Kress states. And while he has an epigraph of Lamartine, who was not only a noted poet, but also a well-known abolitionist, Latil makes it a point to distance himself from Lamartine's political leadings in a note to the twenty-first poem of *Les Éphémères*. He states, "I sincerely regret that the political opinions of M. de Lamartine did not allow me to add his name to the list of great poets" (119). So while there might be abolitionist values abounding among many recent arrivals from Saint-Domingue and France, it was not universally the case, especially among well-established Creole plantation families.

In *Les Éphémères*, the reader finds evidence of a dynamic literary community that was very aware of the latest artistic production from France. This awareness does not seem to overshadow the local situation, which remains the most inspiring for the poet. The reader finds little evidence of a desire to copy French literary production. Furthermore, the poet promotes the literary production of his people. He demonstrates pride in the beauty of the literature and the quality of the writers, rather than any hint of being an apologist for literature that might be found somehow lacking when compared to that of France.

In his first *éphémère*, *"Aux Littéraires du pays,"* Latil addresses his literary contemporaries. In a note, we learn important information about whom Latil includes in this literary community. He says: "By this title, I do not specifically mean Louisiana writers, but all those who have enriched and continue to enrich our budding literature in their most beautiful productions. Included in this title are many whose talent is generally appreciated, and who we are happy to count in our literary ranks" (113). Literally, the term *Aux Littéraires du pays* would mean "to the literary people of the country." Yet, we see that this *pays*, this country, is not simply a geographical location, but a cultural one, a product of a transnational solidarity with writers elsewhere. Since the literature was written in French, we can only assume that the community was bound by the French language it shared, especially in France.

These transnational connections to France were dynamic, representing both an east and west crossing of the Atlantic. New Orleanians kept up with current literature in France. "New Orleanians found it very easy to keep up with the latest Paris successes which were often presented in the Crescent City within a year of their French premier" (Allain 8). New Orleans writers freely traveled back and forth to France. This is evident in the second poem, *"Le Talent et l'Envie,"* dedicated to a Louisiana poet:

> I remember the day where our happy beach
> Saw your boat surge. From this shore,
> You knew how to fix all eyes on you.
> Radiant, you were coming from the beautiful land of France;
> To hear your songs everyone kept quiet:
> Virgins, wives, children, elderly people.

For two years your sweet, plaintive, agreeable and tender voice,
Charmed all our moments, and delighted to hear you,
Poet, we would clap our hands!

The scene speaks to the immediacy in poetic production relative to the public. The larger community listens to and celebrates this writing as it also engages directly with the writer. The poet enjoys a privileged position both in his role as a cosmopolitan orator and as a physical link to France. He and his poetry travel literally and figuratively between France and New Orleans. The borders between these two spaces appear as having permeable boundaries born of shared language and culture.

Boundaries for Latil are also contested because they too often obfuscate the "truth" found in literary works. For example, in the preface to *Les Éphémères* he addresses the issue of semantic boundaries that he finds problematic when discussing the distinction between classical literature and literature of the romantic period: "The author of these poems sincerely confesses that he has never truly understood this distinction that one establishes between the *classics* and the *romantics;* the line of demarcation, which one puts so much effort into tracing and at such a high price, has never been noticed by him. And the superiority that one accords so lightly to the latter seems to him illusory. He has always thought along with one of the most important writers of the day, Charles Nodier, 'that there is neither *classical* nor *romantic* in literature; but only *true* and *false, good* and *bad*'" (13). It should not be surprising to see the author problematizing literary categories and the value normally associated with works that are placed within categories. In the Creole context, as we have already established, relationships are redefined by different sets of values. These values may not mirror traditional European standards. The intermingling of local inspiration, local points of reference, and the discourses of local Creoles creates standards and aesthetics that are in many ways unique. The local nature of this artistic expression and its enthusiastic reception by the public in this poem stands in opposition to the hegemony of the metropole. In the nineteenth century, Paris was thought to be the cultural center of the Western world. This provided the literature written there with a privileged status, which does not seem to faze the literary community of mid-nineteenth-century New Orleans.

This should not be understood as indifference or a rejection of European standards, however. The following passage from the preface, in fact, would appear to say the exact opposite. Latil seems to suggest that literary creation in Louisiana, as in any French colony, would be disadvantaged due to the lack of a traditional social structure that would support the vocation of a writer. Latil continues in his preface: "As with them [the poet's compatriots], he has not had the means to acquire profound instruction, which develops aptitudes and allows for *the study of grand masters* without which there is nothing good in literature, such as Barthélemy has said. Deprived of this guidance and books, the author was only able to stumble along the route that he followed" (14). At first glance, it would appear that French standards loom as an ideal, and that the path for Creole writers is destined to be one of divergence and alterity, continuing to exist under the specter of the colonial legacy, in spite of a desire for legitimacy that informs the Creole discourse.

While historically the association of Louisiana with France has been a double-edged sword, where having a privileged relationship with France gave Louisiana and New Orleans more specifically a cultural identity that was not reduced to the confines of the new American sociopolitical-linguistic landscape and its accompanying binary racial social organization. Yet, with this connection to France also came the risk of assuming the position of a colonized second-class citizen rejected by the colonizing mother. This risk was compounded by the fact that the colonial "child" was unceremoniously abandoned by its mother country on two different occasions.

Upon further consideration, the reader sees that in fact Latil offers a twist to this relationship of colonizing subject to colonized object when he states, "[H]e has not had the means to acquire profound instruction, which develops aptitudes and allows for *the study of grand masters* [italics in the original] without which there is nothing good in literature, such as Barthélemy has said." By referencing Barthélemy, who is a popular satirist, as the authority on canonical French literature, rather than for example French literature's most renowned classical theoretician Boileau, whose epigraph Latil has already included in *Les Éphémères*, he destabilizes the literary subject, or more precisely the colonial model of literary standards. Moreover, by using italics when writing the phrase *"the study of grand masters"* he further destabilizes the French canon because the phrase functions as a quote from the satirist Barthélemy, thus changing the phrase from a simple description of literary models to a satirical critique of literature and its accompanying devices. This twist recalls Bhabha's observation, "Our task remains, however, to show how historical agency is transformed through the signifying process; how the historical event is represented in a discourse that is *somehow beyond control*" (18). The colonial discourse, according to Bhabha, is not controlled by the colonizer, but by the astute colonized who can take advantage of the position of alterity to misbehave, to contradict, and to ultimately displace.

Latil's playfulness here suggests while Creole literary production might not be up to the standards of French literature, neither does French literature live up to its own standards, thus situating Creole literature and French literature on the same transnational plane rather than hierarchically with writings from the Old World being privileged. This passage can be interpreted as a reply to the ongoing tension between France and its former colonies with France traditionally embracing a notion of its own universalism and therefore situating itself in a position of privilege. This positionality allows France to retain the role of the colonizing subject that resisted admission that the production of its colonies, current or past, could equal that of the metropole. The colonial "Other" is always considered as infantine, and must never hope to equal its colonial mother. This traditional French elitism is further destabilized as Latil ends the preface alluding to the success that poets such as the Rouquette brothers enjoyed in France, furthering the notion that Creole writers have important value.

Victor Séjour's Writings

Let us now consider the work of Victor Séjour, the author of *Le Mulâtre* (1837) introduced in the previous chapter. This work recalls Bhabha's notion that "historical agency is transformed through the signifying process" when we consider that this text is not only among the first works of African American fiction but it is also a vitriolic attack against the institution of slavery. Although this author, whose father was from Saint-Domingue and whose mother was a free woman of color from New Orleans, has recently entered the canon of African American literature, he remains largely unknown outside of that circle of specialists—especially when compared to other African Americans such as Sojourner Truth and Frederick Douglass. Séjour wrote this work while still a young man who had just immigrated to Paris from Louisiana. This was his first published work and his only social commentary against the inhumanity and injustices of slavery in his long and distinguished writing career. Set in Saint-Domingue, *Le Mulâtre's* plot is summarized as follows: the short story "features a frame narrator, a white man who functions as a sympathetic and tolerant sounding board to whom Antoine, an old man still presumably a slave and the story's embedded narrator, freely recounts a harrowing narrative of his friend Georges, a mulatto slave whose master is also his biological father. It is Georges's master-father, Alfred, against whom Georges directs retributive justice, killing him for allowing Georges's wife to be put to death for spurning Alfred's sexual advances. After poisoning Alfred's wife, Georges beheads his master with an ax and then takes his own life upon discovering that he has murdered his own father. Séjour's tragic narrative reveals that the slave, like his master, has succumbed to evil as his depravity stems from the corrupting effects of slavery" (Piacentino). Reminiscent of devices found in French historical novels, the literary themes in this historical short story represent naming, witnessing, and understanding the realities of slavery and slave societies, with historical agency being transformed through the signifying process and by the transgression of naming relationships.

Particularly important to this story is the act of naming the father, to identify an origin, even while destroying it and killing the father. Bearing witness is an aspect of the signifying process that brings one closer to establishing and understanding what truths are operating. In this story, characters need to see, to witness, with their own eyes in order to discern truths because all other indicators might be false in this corrupt and dysfunctional place. The story ends with a moral allegory, the death of the father by hand of the son who then commits suicide, a demonstration of the completely dehumanizing effects of slavery, where heroic efforts require damnation, where victims of slavery pass easily to being perpetrators of murder and other forms of tyranny.

The text suggests that biracial Creole children born from plantation society, especially through the rape of women held in slavery by their white masters, seem to go beyond the limits of language. For his entire life, the identity of Georges's father was relegated to silence, and then at the moment that the word *père* or "father" is uttered for the first time, by Alfred at the moment of his death, he only says, "*pè* . . ." as he is being decapitated. The rest of the word is uttered by Alfred's head as it rolls on the floor after the act (74). This scene recalls Bhabah's observation, "Here the transformational value of change lies in the rearticulation, or translation, of elements that are *neither the One* (unitary working class) *nor the Other* (the politics of gender) *but something else besides*, which contests the terms and territories of both" (41). The Creole identity transcends gender, class, and even race. The plantation society creates interdependency with all too often insidious, contentious, and even "unnatural" connections.

After writing this, his only work of socially engaged literature, Séjour turned to writing plays for Parisian bourgeois audiences: "Séjour enjoyed a brilliant career in France, writing more than twenty dramas that received broad acclaim on the Parisian boulevards. He was the favorite dramatist of Napoleon III and yet remained largely unknown in his native Louisiana" (Kress, "Creole Literature"). Perhaps because of his early vitriolic attack on slavery and his connections to the radicalism of the *Revue,* his ties to New Orleans were permanently severed and his legacy largely unknown there.

Other Works from the Early Nineteenth Century

Séjour was not the only New Orleanian to go to Paris and take up writing at a young age. A contemporary of Séjour was Louis-Placide Canonge, the son of a French-born lawyer who came to New Orleans via Saint-Domingue, who was educated in Paris at the Lycée Louis-le-Grand.[4] At the age of seventeen, his short story, "Fantômes," was published in *L'Abeille* in 1839. The story speaks of star-crossed Creole lovers, victims of their own insecurities and social situation. The piece had little social commentary except concerning the city of Paris. The text served as a cautionary tale about Paris harboring many dangers for young Creoles: "Paris for a young, impulsive man, or rather Paris for a young Creole, oh it is death!"[5] In comparison, Séjour's plot and themes were sophisticated and worldly beyond his teenage years.

The collection of poems *Les Cenelles* (1845), the first collection of poetry written by African American writers, represents a social commentary, albeit more subtle than *Le Mulâtre.* Since it was published in New Orleans after 1830, there were restrictions placed on the freedoms of Creole authors of color. Like *Le Mulâtre* this work should be understood as socially engaged literature protesting the limits on civil rights that were becoming more and more dangerous for free people of color. In the preface Armand Lanusse states: "Everywhere a great need for education is being felt. One begins to understand that, in whatever position fate has placed us, a good education is a shield that dulls the arrows of disdain and calumnies slung against us" (13). As Lanusse explains the protest nature of this work, he also reveals the didactic function of the anthology and the "great need to educate."

Lanusse celebrates those Creoles who are able to establish success in the arts and sciences; however, the most important audience for this work, he states, are the budding writers, implicitly referencing Creoles of color: "But those for whom we feel the most sympathy are those young men whose imagination is strongly taken by all that is great and beautiful in the career that Hugo and Dumas followed with such glory. Those who would want to fight with all the strength of our soul against the indifference of some and the wickedness of others, are the young spirits who, without having the crazy pretention of ever reaching the same heights as the great literary masters about whom we have just spoke, are however exposed to all the troubles that transcendent geniuses feel at the beginning of their literary life. Trouble which will follow them without doubt to their doors of their tomb and might even enter it" (13–14). This passage expresses the concern for future generations who are inspired to write literature in a society that offers them fewer and fewer options for education. It also acknowledges that artistic inspiration represents a powerful force in the lives of these budding artists. The fundamental solidarity of all writers of color, young and old, is posited by Armand Lanusse at the end of his preface to *Les Cenelles*, where he states: "We are publishing this collection with the aim of promoting some young poetry lovers who are not at all jealous of the success obtained by Louisiana poets on the stage and in the literary world who have had the good fortune to draw from the best Europeans sources, because these will always be subjects of emulation, but never an object of envy" (15). The tone of Lanusse's text resembles that of Latil because neither takes on the voice of apologist. Lanusse does not desire competition among writers vying for success, but instead seeks the opportunity for young artists to cultivate their craft and develop their talent. This work is the product of a time of political engagement where free authors of color treated the most important issues of the mid-century. Themes found in works of free authors of color include the legacy of the Battle of New Orleans, the founding of the Republican Party, and the abolitionist movement.

Literary Production of the 1850s and 1860s

In considering publications in the 1850s and 1860s the culture of New Orleans becomes more volatile, polarized racially and politically as the lines of demarcation between the Confederacy and the Union were more clearly drawn. In New Orleans, the racial divides were evident everywhere, and danger for all people of color grew. There existed the forced conscription of free people of color "under threat of robbery, murder, and lynching, Confederate uniforms."[6] French immigrants were also forced to fight in the Confederacy. Not surprisingly, after the war there appeared a new tendency in writings by people of color. Instead of glossing over interracial allusions, as was the case in the earlier antebellum period, now writers made explicit reference to the racial origins of the characters and the plots treated interracial issues (Amelinckx 54). Themes found in postbellum literature include the reactionary violence by planters on the eve of the Civil War, the participation of black troops in the Union army, the Battle of Port Hudson, and the fight for civil rights during Reconstruction. Creoles of color were ready to lead Louisiana in the direction of an ideal egalitarian society (Michaelides 11).

An interesting theme found in this literature critiques the newfound materialism in society, with its accompanying economic concerns, an off-shoot of the Americanization of New Orleans. This corresponds to a shift away from an interest in the arts and letters in this Francophone society. In his preface to the short story, "Monsieur Paul" (1859–1860), Joanni Questy, an influential educator and author of color, describes the culture of New Orleans and his vision for a transformation as follows: "In New Orleans, literature is only appreciated by quite a small number of aficionados. Commerce, being on almost everybody's mind, carries them without any peace of mind nor any respite, in such a whirlwind of positivism that Louisiana poets, scattered through the business crowd like imperceptible morsels, have shown their lyres to the profane and sigh for better days."[7] He desires "a new era of literary revival in Louisiana" (169) and tries to contribute to this through his writing. He challenges other writers to do the same and to draw inspiration from the world around them with its "stormy passions," "capriciousness," and "eccentric fantasies" to be found on the streets of New Orleans (167).

The story, "Monsieur Paul," is the tale of a wealthy French ex-patriot living in New Orleans in the 1850s, whose life has been full of sorrow. Under cover of darkness after having sought shelter from a sudden rain shower, he strikes up a conversation with the narrator of the story and offers his card as well as an invitation to visit his residence. The narrator takes him up on the offer, but when he arrives it is clear that Monsieur Paul did not know the narrator was a Creole of color. After a short hesitation, Monsieur Paul makes it known that he is very critical of racist attitudes in Louisiana and that he has republican leadings, holding Lamartine, Hugo, and Béranger in the highest esteem. The narrator learns that Paul must fight a duel against a former friend, of Anglo-Saxon origins. This man had seduced Paul's wife, a free woman of color and the love of Paul's life, and had taken her away along with the two children that she and Paul had together. After Paul's death as a result of the duel, the narrator learns the fate of the woman and the children, all of whom had died in miserable circumstances.

The story serves as a scathing critique of materialism, with Paul's immense wealth only bringing him heartbreak and disappointment. The text also criticizes the laws that prohibited many types of social interactions between races, including the right for legalized interracial marriage. Paul tells the narrator, "the inflexible and tyrannical law of your country does not recognize the validity of my marriage" (180). Paul is also critical of white Francophone Creoles, whom he considers, "prideful nullities of flesh and blood of which the Crescent City is overflowing" (172). The protagonist Monsieur Paul, as a recent immigrant from France, represents an important demographic in New Orleans society. Throughout the nineteenth century, New Orleans continued to be a destination for French expatriates who arrived in New Orleans in order to escape political and economic uncertainty at home. And several of the authors treated further were themselves French expatriates who, once arriving in New Orleans, took to writing and who were very involved in newspapers and produced many literary works.

The Historic Novel in Nineteenth-Century New Orleans

One of these French expatriates was Louis-Armand Garreau (1817–1865), an author, educator, and most of all political activist with strongly held republican and abolitionist ideals. He along with Léprouzé "were two of the most respected white educators within the free black community" (Bell 118). Born in Cognac, France, his life resembles in many ways the early French colonists who kept strong ties to France all the while developing roots in Louisiana. He and his young family arrived in New Orleans in 1841 and first opened a school on the corner of Rampart and Dumaine Streets. Later, his wife opened another school for girls next door (*Louisiana* 10).

Needing to return to France upon the death of his brother, he quickly finished his first novel, *Louisiana*, before his departure. This novel was inspired by the Rebellion of 1768. By 1858, he and his family returned to Louisiana to avoid imprisonment in France for his political activism against Louis-Napoleon, having published an antigovernment weekly paper and later a literary review. While in France, he also published his strongest attacks against slavery in Louisiana in *Souvenirs d'outre-mer*, whose two short stories represented slavery, planters' abuses, and marronage. His life ended as a soldier for the Confederacy, having been conscripted to fight for the South for a cause he abhorred, when he was killed in battle, just as his son had been two years earlier (*Louisiana* 15). His obituary in the black newspaper, *Tribune de la Nouvelle-Orléans*, ends saying, "no one will miss him more than the numerous friends of this man of true merit who are found among the population of color in this city" (Leroy 39).

Garreau's novel *Louisiana* (1849) treats a seminal moment of American revolutionary history that is generally ignored in this country: The rebellion by the local New Orleans' French-speaking Creole elite to Spanish colonial rule is known as the Rebellion of 1768, an event treated earlier in this study. These New Orleanians sought to establish the Republic of Louisiana driven by their desire for self-determination and sovereignty. This represents the first rebellion against a colonial power in North America.[8] Their project began well as the Louisianians caused the first Spanish governor, Ulloa, to flee from Louisiana. But when the second governor, Alejandro O'Reilly, arrived with twenty-three ships in 1769, their cause was lost. The leaders were executed at what is now Frenchmen Street.

The author portrays the trauma of French Creoles who are abandoned by France, when Louisiana is ceded to Spain, and then who are silenced and marginalized, lost amid the colonial hegemony that sought to control them. Gayarré's depiction of the reaction in Louisiana to the news of becoming a Spanish colony is as follows: "It was not enough that the colony was divided and that one part was given over to England, it was also yet necessary that the portion that remained with France was made to swear allegiance to a foreign sovereign! There were no more French in the former Louisiana; there were only England and Spain."[9] The novel presents no reconciliation of this dilemma, and there is no healing of the pain caused by the loss of France in New Orleans.

Garreau was neither the first nor the last author to write a text inspired by this revolt. According to Kress, in his preface to *Louisiana*, the first work treating the subject was the play, *The Martyr Patriots; or, Louisiana in 1769, an Historical Tragedy, in Five Acts* (1836), by T. Wharton Collens, followed by *Les Martyrs de la Louisiane* (1839), a play by Auguste Lussan; *France et Espagne, ou la Louisiane en 1768 et 1769* (1850), a novel by Louis Placide Canonge; *La Chemise Sanglante ou la Louisiane répulicaine* (1851) and "Lafrénière" (1894), a short story by François Tujaque (22).

Among these writers an awareness of the value of turning to the history of Louisiana for literary inspiration becomes evident, as a way to stem the tide of Americanization (*Louisiana* 16). The historical novel was a logical means to reacquaint contemporary New Orleans readers with their history. Garreau argues the importance of the historic novels as follows: "There are few people who read history, fewer still their own region's history. There are however facts, events of such importance that they should have public notoriety. . . . So yes, to make these names, these events known by all, why not give history a less austere form? Why not, in a word, dramatize history; put it in action, so to speak? The historic novel was too much slandered . . . It has its purpose, in my mind—but only as far as the characters of the story are true and the facts attributed to them authentic" (*Louisiana* 24). The historical novel's interest for the contemporary reader resides in their lessons be they moral, political, or social. History performs an important function as a didactic medium with relevance to the readers implicated in this history.

We have already seen this in Séjour's historical novel *Le Mulâtre*, where situating issues of current importance in a historical narrative allows a re-contextualization of the past to inform collective attitudes about the present. This is true in *Louisiana*, beginning with its very title. Kress, in his introduction to *Louisiana*, interprets the title this way: "This title reflects rather the ultimate fate of the French colony. In the end, modern American Louisiana was born from the failed attempt to form a Franco-Louisiana republic. The consequences of this failure—consequences that resonate in the name of the novel itself—led unfailingly to the Americanization of what had been French and Francophone Louisiana" (25). The historical novel's reinterpretation of history has implied sociopolitical implications since lessons of the past are presented to a contemporary reader in such a way as to make a comparison with their lives inevitable.

As we saw in the previous chapter, historic novels became popular in nineteenth-century Louisiana, and authors strove to establish a French Creole order, or more accurately a reordering of historical events blending the imagined and the historical, the *terroir* of Louisiana with an imaginary elsewhere, establishing a literary history during a time of cultural and linguistic assimilation into Anglo-America. Literary works took on political significance as they functioned to unite a people against cultural and linguistic assimilation.

In *Louisiana*, the story of the young protagonist is intertwined with the story of the territory of *La Louisiane* itself. Anyone living in nineteenth-century Louisiana, for example, would not have failed to notice the title is "Louisiana" and not "Louisiane." There appears, then, tension between the English title and the novel written in the French language. The young girl Louisiana has a special relationship with Bienville, a character in the novel, "Louisiana is speaking about her uncle Bienville and explains her relation to him, 'Sweet old man, he always indulged me in the tender way of the best fathers! It is he who gave me my name Louisiana. This name reminds him of the colony that he founded, led with such care, such perseverance, and love!'" (29). The narrator develops this comparison further saying, "At the age of 86, he [Bienville] only had one emotion that kept him alive: his love for his two Louisianas. The first one he considered his daughter, the other which he had made the personification of the first" (30). Here the distinction between young girl and colonial territory is blurred, seemingly secondary to the abiding love felt by Bienville for both entities. In the novel, the narrator roundly criticizes the king, blaming him for giving up Louisiana because he preferred his "shameful debauchery" to governing the colony. The narrator suggests that the king's right-hand man, the Duke of Choiseul, agreed to a meeting between King Louis XV and the Louisiana envoy Milhet, who had gone to France as a representative of New Orleanians. Milhet, accompanied by Bienville, had hoped to have an audience with the king in order to persuade him to take back the Louisiana Territory from the Spanish. In the novel it was the king himself who refused the meeting (50). History suggests otherwise, that it was Choiseul himself who refused to recommend this audience with the king. (*Louisiana* 20). It would appear as though Garreau's own republican biases might be represented in this passage, as well as elsewhere in the novel.

The passage where the Creoles decide to revolt represents a specific moment of self-fashioning the Louisiana identity. One of the rebellion's leaders states, "[I]f Louis XV does not want us to be French, since we do not want to be Spanish, well Sir, we will be . . . Louisianians, and we will have no master" (53). The moment is a clarifying moment for the characters. They were willing to obey France, to be loyal subjects of the French crown, and to not excessively test the role that the metropole played in their determination. It was, however, France who broke that bond, that social order. And once that order was broken, a new order emerged. Just as the Creole identity had melded to "France" and negotiated that existence under the rubric of "Frenchness" so was it that once France was out of the picture as a mother country to the colony, the settlers immediately adapted a more authentic name, that of being a Lousianian.

The Lousianians did not shift in their position through this change in name; it appears that they simply changed their label and claimed what was already true, that their collective identity was rooted in Louisiana rather than in Europe. They were therefore already independent. This novel along with other written about this Rebellion of 1768 then act as a memorial to the fallen and to the gallant efforts of this group of American revolutionaries since a physical memorial did not exist. It was a story whose aim it was to commit this story to a collective memory, "to make these names, these events known by all."

Writings in the Last Decades of the Nineteenth Century

Additional historical novels and short stories written by Louisiana authors include *Le Vieux Salomon, Saint Denis, Calista, La Nouvelle Atala, Habitation St-Ybars,* and the *Quaderoon Tretralogy.* These other works might not follow the strict definition that Garreau had for the historical novel and its aim to teach history to the masses. They do, however, share the quality of the historical novel in their representing a past time in a way that would speak to contemporary audiences, appealing to their literary, cultural, and linguistic sensibilities.

Le Vieux Salomon was written by another French émigré author, Charles Testut (1819–1892), who came to Louisiana around 1843 after the earthquake in Point-à-Pitre, Guadeloupe, destroyed that city. Besides being an author, he was a physician and a publisher, having bought *La Chronique,* a weekly newspaper, a few years after his moving to New Orleans. He later founded other papers. Among all the writers, he was the most outspoken Marxist as well. His most well known work is *Le Vieux Salomon,* written in 1858 and published in 1871 in *L'Équité,* a Marxist newspaper he founded. This makes the work the first Marxist novel written in America, as the description of the book by Éditions Tintamarre states: "Testut's Marxist critique of slavery, an institution that reduces human beings to the state of goods that can be bought and sold, offers a distilled vision of an unjust society in which even those who produce the goods become the property of a wealthy and immoral few."[10] Wishing to create a utopian society, the author in the preface directly addresses readers, calling them to have courage: "Courage, brothers! . . . Courage and patience! Physical slavery was brought down, the proletariat, economic slavery, will also be when the time comes, and these two scourges [that] once destroyed True Liberty will be born from the bosom of the order, between equality and fraternity in the second stable in a second Bethlehem" (9). This text, published during the optimism of Reconstruction, sought to promote the ongoing eliminating of social and economic inequity.

Rather than focusing on political events, the plot of this historical novel represents an epic story of the strength, love, and spiritual connections that help shape destiny of a family that takes them from Guadeloupe to Louisiana. In the preface, Testut claims to have been the scribe for this remarkable story: "Salomon, poor old black man that I met and admired, you are watching me from on high . . . Courageous Casimir and noble Rose with whom I've shed tears! Nights that I have dedicated to recount your five-year ordeal, more agitated than the waves from a turbulent sea, are for me ineffable memories, and you can read the pages where I have mixed tears for your pain and delirium for your joys" (10). His protagonists, free people of color Casimir and Rose, live on the edge of freedom as they are slaves, maroons, and wanderers at various times in the novel. They manage to survive many dangers through their own efforts and the efforts of those around them regardless of race. However they drew the most strength from their spiritual guide Salomon. The settings of the novel detail architectural, urban, and natural spaces, as well as voodoo practices, all of which make this novel a valuable cultural artifact and historical link between New Orleans and the Caribbean.

Testut also wrote two other works of historical fiction. *Saint-Denis* is the story of the founder of the French post of Natchitoches, a settlement made to serve as a French boundary with Spanish territory and to promote trade with the Spanish possessions in New Mexico. In *Saint-Denis* the metaphor of the agitated sea is important as it represents a clash of social elements inherent in this cultural contact zone of Natchitoches pervasive throughout the story: "There are here men of all nations, it is a kind of agitated sea with each wave pushing in the opposite direction" (54). But all of these men needed to come around the table to eat dinner: "However the mealtime hour has sounded. There is no sumptuous table, resplendent white tablecloth, porcelain or crystal . . . Some salted meat, a little game and a biscuit that was not prepared the night before, that is sure! But no matter . . . these are the men of courage, and courage has its happiness in material misery! Also, they sing, without remorse, as any without cares, sometimes an old refrain from Europe, at other times, the monotone and slow stanzas like the rhyme of nomad people. Among them there are children of France, Canada, and the forests of the New World . . . The future and the past of Louisiana . . . The fathers of future dominators, and the primitive possessors whose races must be snuffed out, from one day to the next, under the intelligent domination of genius and conquest" (20). Both past and present blend at this gathering and the process of Creolization results in a new world order.

Testut's other historical novel is *Calista*, the story of a German princess's escape from tyranny of the court of the Czar Alexis of Russian, arriving in Louisiana where she made a new life. Just as in *Saint-Denis*, the irony found in the description of the history of Louisiana and its newfound glory built on its very modest roots and on the yoke of slavery recalls Testut's Marxist leanings:

When one harkens back, in one's mind, to this period so near to us that they have some men whose fathers saw it, one wonders how, in these rapid years, these swamps were covered with numerous beautiful houses; these little markets exposed to the elements changed into vast covered markets with a thousand columns with all the products of the land, waters, and forests, teeming in an immense space . . . How all the pleasures and comforts of life are abundant there, where the least would act ruthlessly; how this new city that hardly used to see any women, and a few adventure seekers more or less worthy of respect is populated today with the most beautiful creature in the world . . .

> How this river-king, before carrier of little pirogues is covered today with in-
> numerable ships, moving in the air, flags from every nation in the world!

The narrative continues by casting the destiny of Louisiana in the following
manner:

> And yet how many years were lost during these fast years, each changing of
> the flag made Louisiana take a step backwards in its march toward progress.
> Each change of nationality prevented this love of country, so fertile in great
> things, to take root in hearts. Governed by absolutism and by the metro-
> pole, Louisiana was ill at ease; but when, by being a slave state, she became
> mistress of herself; when she was no longer only one star in the flag of liberty,
> she advanced majestically, great in progress. The fertile and generous land
> paid a hundred times over the labor of men; everywhere business expanded
> affluence, the arts, civilization and the sweet things in life. (192)

In *Calisto* and *Saint-Denis* the reader is faced with a tension between the
abundance and progress that is represented in the New World, opposed
to the continued hegemony enjoyed by Europeans and slaveholders in this
New World. Any enthusiasm for Louisiana needs to be qualified for this
Marxist immigrant.

Adrien-Emmanuel Rouquette (1813–1887) a Francophone white Creole
born in New Orleans, made important contributions to Creole literature.
In his youth his family moved to Bayou St. John after the bankruptcy and
suicide of his father, and later they relocated farther away from New Orleans, to the north shore of Lake Pontartrain where he had many Choctaw
friends. His education was eclectic with his studying in Kentucky and New
Jersey and then in France in Nantes, Rennes, and Paris. While trained
in law but never practicing it, his literary works were known in France,
where he lived on three different occasions, as well as in the United States.
He and his brother were referenced in *Les Éphémères* by Alexandre Latil.
Furthermore in middle age he became a Catholic priest and insisted on living among the Choctaw Indians, where he spent the last two decades of his
life. His best-known work of fiction, *La Nouvelle Atala,* is a depiction of the
Choctaw Nation and its negotiating a coexistence with Creole society. The
text can also be read as a mystical work delving into the divine to be found
in nature.

The title suggests that the novel was inspired by Chateaubriand's early
nineteenth-century work *Atala.* However, Rouquette allows for a tension
between the earlier novel and his own by seeming to vaunt Chateaubriand

as one of the great writers of all time and nonetheless criticizing him at other points. This is perhaps inspired by the misrepresentation of Louisiana and its denigrating Native American society found in *Atala*. In spite of Rouquette's having gained fame as a writer in France, of all the authors treated in this current volume, he is the most overtly critical of the pretentiousness found in French culture and with the literati. In the preface, Rouquette explains: "Whatever the fate of *La Nouvelle Atala* might be, in the great circles of literary refinement, before the Supreme Learned Assembly whose seat is in Paris or elsewhere, it is always certain to find its place in the sun of the native desert. The uncultivated flower will lose its petals in the same solitude where it blooms. And no one will go there to desecrate its repose, far from the turmoil of inhospitable cities, and far from the deceptive brilliance of a disenchanted civilization" (30–31). Just like Latil, Lanusse, and others, Creole writers from Louisiana addressed the colonial hegemony and the privilege that France enjoyed in letters. They engaged in debate around the subject and created literary traditions that were both inspired by and distinct from their French counterparts.

Rouquette anticipates the erasure of his work from literary history, as he sketches a self-fashioned exile. In the novel's first page, the narrator takes up the question of exile more directly, allowing that one might then be free to find a fitting place in the world: "Exile has always been the home country of abandoned misfortune and misunderstood genius; exile has given hospitality to the unfortunate, the persecuted, the outcast. The foreign land for the exiled is as nice and impartial as the most distant history. Expatriation becomes then a duty, when honor is no longer glory, nor humanity a virtue. The wings of vapor are thus not too rapid to take the victim away from ostracism to other more welcoming shores, so that they be placed beyond the cape of storms" (33). The right to change one's homeland is among the very first rights of an individual, being "incontestable and imprescriptible" (73). In the context of this native Louisianian author, the direction of exile does not directly refer to Europe, or Louisiana, but rather it was an exile from civilization itself. The outcasts, such as the main character, Atala, and her servant, whose role is reminiscent of the post–Civil War reality for former slaves, find themselves—independently—in the same forest living among the same native people. They are exiles finding refuge.

The name of the protagonist was Atala, given to the girl because of her parents' *grande admiration* for Chateaubriand and his novel (34). This is reminiscent of the role Manon Lescaut has played in Francophone Louisiana lore. The self-fashioning and fluid identity in this Creole space allows the girl Atala to choose to live in nature among the Choctaw nation early in the novel; the dénouement of the story reveals that she is biologically the daughter of the character of Hopoyouksa, a Breton from one of the area's most important families. Not surprisingly, he emigrated from France to escape the materialism, depravity, and bourgeois values of France. He chose to become a *sauvage* and live outside of the "literary and political contagion, outside of blind instincts and crazy theories of this great impious century, which calls itself the *century of the Enlightenment*" (89). Atala's mother was a Choctaw woman. The story ends at the moment of Atala's death, when she understands who she is and how she has been living among her biological family after all. Atala's initial exile then allowed her to discover her true identity.

The tale of Atala implicates the role of poetry to represent truth and the role of the poet who occupies a seminal position at the dawn of civilization, "civilizing newborn societies" (48). Once in the forest, this young woman begins to express herself poetically, to speak in a divine tongue, and to live her destiny of being born a poet. For the author, poets are born not made, and the greats such as Plato and even Chataubriand were only prosists not poets (47). Thus the author does not attempt to reconcile the dichotomy of civilization versus savagery, good versus evil, France versus Louisiana, as he both lauds and criticizes Chateaubriand. One effect of this ambiguity, then, serves to problematize French literature as an undisputed model for Creole writing.

Alfred Mercier, Witness of His Times

A contemporary of Rouquette was Alfred Mercier, born on the west bank of the Mississippi River just outside of New Orleans in 1816. This important figure in Louisiana literature and an activist in French New Orleans lived through the antebellum period, the Civil War, and the postwar period, dying in 1894. He was educated in Paris at the Lycée Louis-le-Grand, lived as an adult in Italy and Paris, married a French woman, and received the French Legion of Honor. Publishing most of his works after the Civil War in the 1870s, he founded *l'Athénée louisianais* in 1876 to promote French language and scholarly production in New Orleans. Mercier, a white Creole, was also a physician.

His best-known work is the historical novel *L'Habitation Saint-Ybars ou Maîtres et Esclaves en Louisiane (récit social)* in 1881. This social commentary on plantation life and slavery was set at the end of the antebellum period and spanned the Civil War and the postwar period. It presented a nuanced yet ultimately mordant attack on slavery and plantation society, with its dehumanizing slaveholders and slaves alike. This novel stands as the most complete attack on slavery written by a native Creole and not a French immigrant to Louisiana.

The novel also explores family dynamics, including the role of domestic slaves in the family structure, especially that of female domestic slaves who were arguably more maternal than mothers of the white children. Addressed in this novel are the depths of sexual exploitation of women across the racial spectrum, and their ensuing subversion of the system especially in the case of free women of color. The novel depicts episodes of sexual and psychological abuse, adultery, and violence. At the same time, the work speaks of the physical beauty of this fertile land and the triumph over adversity of even the most disenfranchised.

Although set on a plantation, the family members and other characters of the novel represent a multicultural, multinational, and multiracial group. The family was descended from Canadian immigrants who arrived in 1749 (69). However, at the end of the story the last direct descendant of this line raises serious doubt about the supposed purity and the social standing of their family, which he refers to as a product of the collective imagination. This position in fact implicates all privileged white Creole families: "You make it a crime for Blanchette to have had a slave for a mother. You forget, dear friends, that our ancestors also were slaves. Yes, we all live under the same blessed sky of America, descendants of the French, English, Spanish, Italian, Portuguese, Swiss, Swedish, etc., making all of us the grandchildren of the wretched who spent long centuries with their heads held down by the weight of servitude. . . . And do not believe, dear cousins, that it is necessary to go back very far in history to see our ancestors wearing colliers with the names of their masters, like the ones we put on our dogs. Decency does not permit me to tell you how the lords treated our female ancestors, at the age when they were fresh and beautiful. Are we, you and me, really less respectable, less free for this? No, without a doubt" (216–17). This accusation addresses the myth of whiteness in New Orleans society in the late nineteenth century, as it also criticizes the historical abuses associated with white privilege there.

In the plantation house there were two slaves identified as offspring of St-Ybars men. Slaves that were considered as having skin that was too fair had lower social status among other slaves. These same slaves would criticize the St-Ybars children who lost their ability to converse in Creole. The transnational connections the drive the plot connect the family to Spain and Russia, in addition to France and Saint-Domingue. France serves as a place of refuge for confused adolescents. Conversely, there was a negative

critique of how journalists wrote about Louisiana as being a place of canni-
bals and voodoo practitioners. These stereotypes stand in sharp contrast to
the refinement of the St-Ybars children. The family patriarch was a Renaissance man who enjoyed the poetry of Homer, Virgil, Dante, Milton, Byron,
Lamartine, and Hugo.

The novel describes postwar race relations in the following way: "Whites
want to take back their former supremacy in affairs of state. The free people
of color and the blacks, advised by their allies from the North, dispute that.
The result is violent animosities, bloody fights, battles in which the highest
number killed always are blacks. In a word, we risk having a new civil war
that is complicated by a social war" (201). The reader is not surprised, then,
that the book ends with the family having completely deteriorated. They
suffered financial ruin, a diaspora of all but one of the surviving St-Ybars
children, and a series of suicides. This foreshadows Mercier's last work,
Johnelle, which is a study in the unraveling fabric of Creole society. In *St-
Ybars* the extended family is presented as morally bankrupt, although not
completely without compassion. The plantation is also in ruins. Life is to be
found by emigrating to Europe (268).

Johnelle was more contemporary in nature yet no less of a social commentary. Written in 1891 just before his death, it represents a completely
dysfunctional French-speaking Creole society. The novel depicts the disin-
tegration of the family structure, the bankrupt morals of society, especially
of mothers who chose to end their pregnancies in order to preserve their
own handsome figures, and the society's complete assimilation into Anglo-
America. In this book the author writes a story that describes the end of a
society, the death of a people.

George Dessommes was a protégé of Mercier, as well as a poet and novelist. Born in New Orleans in 1855, his family expatriated to France during
the Civil War, giving him opportunity to study at the Lycée Louis-le-Grand,
before returning to New Orleans in 1870.[11] His profession was in the cotton
and textile industry, and it appears to have been the reason for his various
moves away from New Orleans during his adulthood, especially his moving to Mississippi and Montreal. He died in Hollywood in 1929, not having
published anything in the last thirty-five years of his life (Heckenbach 16).

As a young adult, Dessommes was well known in New Orleans literary circles of the 1870s. He was a poet, who published in the journal *Le
Carillon,* and an important voice in the literary community of New Orleans,
through his affiliation with Mercier's *L'Athénée louisianais.* Themes treated
in his poems include love, desire, and glory, as well as specifically New
Orleans themes such as a day on Canal Street, a raging storm, and the

Americanization of New Orleans. The first poem and the last poem he published offer a telling contrast and represent the realities of being a Francophone Creole writer from New Orleans in the late nineteenth century. His first poem, "Ma Première Chanson," written in 1873, situates the poet as a born raconteur who must sing because he was a born songwriter. He sketches an entire life of singing, from the inspiration of his youth, through the challenges of living in a land that has just been defeated in war, to dying happy after having lived a fully realized life of poetry. His last poem, "A la Mémoire du Docteur Mercier," written in 1894, commemorated the death of his dear friend and mentor, who represented a natural-born writer, and perhaps more importantly a leader in the preservation of Francophone Creole language and culture in New Orleans. Rather than painting the picture of a life full of joy and fulfillment as an artist, the poet depicts the life of Mercier as a long, determined struggle full of lost illusions and lost hope. This poem was the last piece that Dessommes ever published, although he was still relatively young.

Dessommes's one novel was *Tante Cydette*, and it appeared in series form in 1888. The story revolves around the designs of a Creole family matriarch, Tante Cydette, who desires to marry her wealthy niece Ermence to a newly arrived Frenchman, Henry de Fallex, at the emotional and psychological expense of her other niece Louise from the poorer branch of the extended family who loved de Fallex. Louise's life was truly grim as she lived in squalor, caring for her dying widowed mother and three younger siblings. The reason for this misery is that her father, a physician, "was carried away by his artistic temperament, having neglected his profession for literature, which the public never forgives in this positivist society" (50). The story offers no depiction of the robust literary life of New Orleans that Latil describes in his poems. Instead in *Tante Cydette* following a literary path leads to misery. The book recalls the social commentary of "Monsieur Paul." Ermence's father has no time for her, even on the day of her marriage, because of his incessant preoccupation with business. Concern for material wealth and commercial success overcomes basic love of a father for his daughter.

Tante Cydette willingly destroys lives of her extended family to promote her own interest. Lost is a sense of her being a part of a larger community. Instead her self-interest appears interlaced with her desire to arrange a marriage to enhance the social status of her immediate family. As soon as de Fallex arrives in New Orleans, he causes a stir, capturing the imagination of Tante Cydette and many others. "One cannot imagine the prestige that the individual who has come from far away has with us, from Europe, or from anywhere!" (54). The foreigner conjures the imagination no matter his origins, his profession, or his character. He becomes a fetish, and prey for all the women looking to make a good marriage for their daughters—or nieces, in this case. Cydette wants to win. The wishes of others are completely secondary to her strategic desire to win the prize of a marriage to this rare commodity of a Frenchman of apparent wealth. This dynamic mirrors the relationship between mothers who are oblivious to their children in Mercier's *Johnelle,* published three years later. If we interpret Louise as a metaphor for Louisiana, the effect of Tante Cydette's actions serves to destroy Louisiana itself, simply for the sake of appearances, a concern for an arbitrary status and a desire for victory over others.

Sidonie de la Houssaye

A final notable author of this period was Sidonie de la Houssaye (1820–1894), who spent most of her life in rural St. Mary Parish, part of the Acadian area, in the town of Franklin. Given that living off of literary writing was nearly impossible during this time period, it is remarkable that de la Houssaye supported her family as a writer, especially during the difficult postbellum period. Her best-known work is the historical tetralogy *Les Quarteronnes de la Nouvelle-Orléans,* set in antebellum New Orleans, and as the title implies, represents the world of *plaçées* in Creole society.

De la Houssaye managed to have a career as a writer because she actively sought a readership outside of Francophone Creole society, and attempted, with mixed results, to ally herself with George Washington Cable, who bought one of her stories, "Voyage de ma grand-mère" (*Les Quarteronnes de la Nouvelle-Orléans I* 27). The cost of this strategy relative to her relationship with her community was high and "[a]t the end of the 1880s, Sidonie de la Houssaye provokes a general outcry from her fellow countrymen of Franklin through a letter that became public, against her will, where she accuses her countrymen of being racist and misers" (*Les Quarteronnes de la Nouvelle-Orléans I* 10). This in addition to her collaboration with Cable, who was generally despised for his condescending, stereotypical portraits of Creoles, reached a feverous level in 1894–1895 with the publication of *Octavia, la quarteronne* near the time of her death (*Les Quarteronnes de la Nouvelle-Orléans I* 10).

Given that the relationship with Cable did not yield audiences of readers in the North for de la Houssaye, and that the local population was outraged by her works, how did she cultivate a readership? It was perhaps because after the Civil War, New Orleans started to promote itself as a destination for the sex trade, an idea that this book fosters (*Les Quarteronnes*

∂e la Nouvelle-Orléans I 15). De la Houssaye claimed historical authenticity of the manuscripts. In the introduction to the novels, the author professes to have found her grandmother's trunk full of old papers and letters in 1878, and continues: "Finally in the middle of some treasures that I had just discovered, in the middle of old mite-eaten manuscripts, I felt a scroll attached with a ribbon—it was blue actually—carrying the inscription: '*Les Quarteronnes ∂e la Nouvelle-Orléans,* from 1800–1830.' I let out a cry because it truly was a treasure that I had just discovered" (41). She concludes the introduction to the novel, saying: "Since it is thanks to my grandmother that I am writing this story, I will allow her tell the story of the life of these women" (42).

In spite of the fact that this author is perhaps the most researched among scholars of Francophone Louisiana literature today, since she never resided in New Orleans, her books do not represent a textured picture of the city itself. References to specific locations in the city are also generally lacking, especially in comparison to other Creole novels on New Orleans. However, she presents rich descriptions of the tripartite racial structure of Creole society distinct of the antebellum period, one that was so distinct from the rest of the United States.

However, when de la Houssaye still harbored the hopes of cultivating a northern readership with the help of Cable, the plots of her novels followed a more stereotypical storyline objectifying the women of color. In the series' first two works, *Octavia* and *Violetta,* the *plaçées,* were exoticized tropes of white men's sexual desire with the power to completely destroy the men who are under their spell. When the hoped-for American readership did not materialize, de la Houssaye's *Gina* and *Dahlia* presented the *plaçées* in a much more realistic, nuanced light, one that could be understood by her Creole readers familiar with their local history and family heritage. Families were multiracial, and emotional attachments crossed color lines.[12]

(Re)Scripting the Imaginary

Nineteenth-century New Orleans literature gives voice to the Francophone Creoles of New Orleans as these texts allow for an understanding of the fluidity and plurality of Francophone perspectives in the decades after New Orleans became an American city. These works, largely erased from North American literary history, challenge notions of race, literary standards, and received views of history. French Creole literature and newspapers of New Orleans represented the ongoing creolization of New Orleans during the nineteenth century resulting from continual immigration, the Civil War, and the ever-present threat of assimilation into Anglo-America. These literary texts, then, allowed for the patterns of displacement and migration inherent in the immigrant experience to coalesce in the shared French language and experiences of being Francophone experiences. Not overdetermined by French models and styles, these writers sought to create an original literature that represented their Creole world, and these writers seem generally unconcerned with being judged through French literary standards. The historical novel in particular was a textual space of self-fashioning to rewrite Creole New Orleans history. This literature also evidenced a triangulation between Louisiana, the Caribbean (especially Haiti), and France, with connections to the Caribbean very often having more import in these writings. Arguably, the most valuable aspect that a rereading of these texts offers is a new understanding of attitudes of race and issues relating to slavery in nineteenth-century New Orleans, with progressive attitudes toward civil rights shared by free people of color and white authors in this community. The in-betweenness of the space of New Orleans allowed for slippages, self-fashioning, and originality that is unique in North America.

CONCLUSION

As this book contends, New Orleans emerges as an "imagined" community, one that blends a French colonial imprint with Creole Caribbean dynamics. The migration of Acadians to Louisiana at the time New Orleans became a Spanish dominion and the arrival of refugees from the Haitian Revolution at the time when the city became an American territory reinforced its Francophone identity. As we have seen, in the contested process of establishing itself as an urban space in the antebellum South, the culture of New Orleans became a liability for New Orleans elite after the Louisiana Purchase. The tripartite system of race in New Orleans society remained incompatible with the "black and white" binary of the surrounding slaving society. The multihued complexion of its people and cultural slippages that produced its society associated with and operated through a supposed monolithic "French" presence within the context of Anglo-America. Since being Creole suggested African descent, referencing the society as French allowed for a less racially charged and contested social order.

This affinity with France positioned New Orleans outside of the dominant American narrative and its Anglo-Saxon and Protestant hegemony. As we have seen, for all that New Orleanians have assimilated into American sociopolitical and linguistic norms, New Orleans has not been refashioned enough culturally to fit into this discrete national story; its positionality in a cultural contact zone will not allow it. As we have explored, never in New Orleans colonial history did a colonial power become so established in the city that it imposed policies that effectively disenfranchised its residents from enjoying significant agency and self-determination. Locals remained in positions to be able to "talk back" to those who tried to control them and contest policies that did not suit local realities. Rather than operating as univocal, however, this expression emerges as polyphonic, representing often-competing voices, thus providing fertile ground for creolization.

As we have posited in this study, the multicultural population has been historically adept at inventing itself as a type of "commodity." Today we can understand how the tourist industry represents an extension of this particular historical pattern at play for three hundred years. The present study has detailed how New Orleans since its founding by Bienville has been built in large part upon myth, desire, and willing or unwilling interdependence among people of different origins. Selling New Orleans, as we have established, has happened since John Law. Moreover, depending on which side of the Atlantic one is positioned, in 1803 Louisiana was either a "Purchase" or a "Sale," as the French call it.[1] Marketing New Orleans as an exotic locale has made it a commodity from the earliest years of French colonialism. Throughout colonial periods local identity emerged from the collective New World relation that built upon cultural slippages, mythologizing, and tendencies toward self-fashioning. Through the centuries identifying as "French" has added value to the Creole space.

The unique type of "Frenchness" found in New Orleans took centuries to coalesce. "Frenchness" in this context then consists of patterns of evoking the past to inform the present in the hopes of sustaining local hegemony. This reference functions as an umbrella term that provides inclusiveness binding this multicultural, multiracial place and its peoples. However, the reference should not be considered completely stable and unchanging through time; we only have to think about the fluidity associated with race and race relations in New Orleans to see how specific historical periods informed the meaning of the term. Surviving through both accommodation and resistance, "Frenchness" operates as a fluid reference with permeable boundaries. This dynamic allows for cultural fusion with minimal conflict because when markers of change or of difference are accommodated and assimilated into "Frenchness," the process occurs covertly. In other words, the process sustaining New Orleans as a French space represents ongoing creolization spanning the last three centuries.

The blending of "Frenchness," globalization, and commodification has engendered ties to France and *la Francophonie* that are operative and important today. Imagined connections with France engendered real connections and reclaimed lost ones. In this postcolonial time, New Orleans successfully retains a foothold in the transnational Francophone world. As such, New Orleans remains today part of immigration pathways for French-speaking Europeans, Africans, and others from the Americas and the Caribbean. This occurs because Francophones identify with this place, recognizing connections to their own histories and cultures. Thus, the economy of Francophone cultures continues to implicate the Crescent City especially in the areas of tourism, the arts, and education.

The mid-twentieth century reified some of these dynamics. For example, Francophone connections were recast in the 1960s when Louisiana officially became a bilingual state of the United States. Today it would be hard to imagine regions with large non-English-speaking populations, such as California or Florida, becoming officially bilingual states. However in the 1960s a time of the civil rights movement and social upheaval, this movement was led by whites, with the white Cajun population successfully lobbying for this law. Early on Creoles of color were not included in this political movement, so questions of race and ensuing racial discrimination were not implicated in this ruling.

In the last decades of the twentieth century, Cajun and Creole cultures have become nationally and internationally prominent. The cultural renaissance in southwest Louisiana (Acadiana) has foregrounded Louisiana's French heritage in popular culture and in the global economy.[2] From cultural commodities such as music festivals that featured Cajun and zydeco music, to the Cajun chefs like Paul Prudhomme, to the films like *The Big Easy* and *The Princess and the Frog,* we see a new representation of two traditionally distinct geographical and cultural regions in south Louisiana. As we have discussed, New Orleans was founded nearly fifty years before the first Acadians arrived in Louisiana. The French administrators who documented their arrival did not consider those Acadians to be French. They settled outside of New Orleans by choice, wanting to protect their distinct culture and allow family groups to take root after their ten-year diaspora. However, with the rise of popularity of Cajun and Creole cultures in popular culture in the late twentieth century, New Orleans experienced another cultural slippage, one that melded New Orleans and southwest Louisiana into one "French" culture largely for the purposes of tourism. For cultural insiders to the region, however, the distinction between the "city" and "Cajun Country" remains clear, with differences relating to language, food, music, and many other popular traditions.

The process of creolization began a new chapter with Katrina making landfall along the Gulf Coast in August 2005. Soon after the storm a banner emerged as the icon for recovery efforts: An oversized golden fleur-de-lys on a light blue background with the words "Recover, Rebuild, Rebirth." This iconic banner, omnipresent in the city for several years after Katrina, was the refashioned emblem of the Bourbon dynasty. The remaking of New Orleans built on its French foundation, recalling its French past in order to imagine its refashioned future. As we have seen, this is the same pattern that has played out repeatedly; versions of the Bourbon flag have been a symbol of New Orleans throughout its history. Echoing the 1760s, New Orleans Creoles flew the Bourbon flag at a moment of hispanization with arrival of Latin Americans as the workforce for rebuilding efforts. In this post-Katrina era with the New Orleans diaspora and the remaking of the city, cultural fusion continues both inside and outside of this urban space. Social equilibrium has shifted; residents have been displaced; new migrations to the city have occurred. Creolization has begun a new chapter in the twenty-first century.

After Katrina many were asking the questions about why to "save" New Orleans, why New Orleans "matters." In his excellent response to this questioning, Lawrence Powell, in his 2012 article "Why Louisiana Mattered," began his answer by saying, "What happened here refused to stay put. Key developments in Louisiana history rippled across American law, culture, and politics. Indeed their influence did more than reflect national trends. They started them" (390). We only have to think about how jazz was born in New Orleans only later to become the most renowned American musical genre to illustrate Powell's point.

In the context of race relations, as we have detailed, the community of free people of color in New Orleans challenged American notions of race before the Civil War. Then in the period of Reconstruction, their voices helped to craft the Constitution of 1868. Later during post-Reconstruction this community continued to contest racism and segregation when Homer Plessy, a New Orleans Creole, who along with the *Comité des citoyens*, brought the cause of racial equity to the Supreme Court in the landmark case of *Plessy vs. Ferguson*. The affective ties that held together the French-speaking Creole community at the time could not outweigh the hegemony of racial segregation in the southern United States, but it was strong enough to endure as a maker of resistance to institutional racial segregation and social injustice.

Powell reflects on the importance of this case and other moments in Louisiana history as follows: "I don't want to overstate Louisiana's national significance. . . . [T]he highest court in the land might well have reached 'separate but equal' even without the prod of the *Plessy* case. But these epic events would have had other vectors. The timing would have been different, and our textbooks impoverished of a great quotient of the human drama that makes history compellingly relevant. I like to think it was because Louisiana was exceptional. After all, new distributaries don't always originate inside the mainstream. Sometimes they form outside it. That's what the instances when Louisiana's complex racial and political history intersected with American history seem to bear out" (401). This complex racial and political history can be seen as a model for a sustained multicultural population that shares a common sense of identity—an identity that refused to be lost to the American melting pot.

If we project the lessons of history onto the future, it might very well be that the lessons of Hurricane Katrina and post-Katrina New Orleans might become cautionary tales for twenty-first-century America. We may find that the experience of Katrina will have remained etched in our collective memory when we face the next disaster bringing catastrophic change to our country. For in the wake of the destruction, displacement, death, and general chaos of Katrina and its aftermath, New Orleans has managed to survive. Creole New Orleanians reclaimed their city and remade as they could. Today we find a resilient and vibrant culture with its people demonstrating the courage to rebuild their city in their own way, inspired by a shared sense of a privileged relationship with France and a particular kind of "Frenchness." These same traits have propelled the city throughout its history, through hurricanes, epidemics, fires, and wars.

As unlikely as it may seem, the world has "French" New Orleans . . . still.

NOTES

Preface

1. See Errol Barron's *New Orleans Observed: Drawings and Observations of America's Most Foreign City* and Richard Megraw's *Confronting Modernity: Art and Society in Louisiana*, 3.

2. Other cities in south Louisiana did not follow the same process of urbanization as New Orleans. Baton Rouge was a military outpost during the French period, Natchitoches was settled before New Orleans but functioned more as a buffer against the Spanish, and Lafayette, or Vermilionville as it was first called, was settled by Acadians a century after New Orleans was founded.

Introduction

1. The meanings of this term relative to New Orleans and the French Caribbean are explored later in this introduction and at greater length in chapter 3. This term remains capitalized throughout this study.

2. See the Website for the French Consulate in New Orleans for examples of this privileged relationship: http://www.consulfrance-nouvelleorleans.org/.

3. While this is not the only version of French colonialism in North America, it remains the framework for twenty-first-century histories such as Havard and Vidal's *Histoire de l'Amérique française* (2008).

4. Other original expressions found in New Orleans include lagniappe, banquette, geaux (such as Geaux Saints), and even Vieux Carré (referring to the French Quarter).

5. Meaning *"That's just not French."*

6. The Quinipissas, living in the area that became New Orleans, were part of the Bayougoula Nation; the Natchez Nation was upriver from New Orleans, but when the Natchez Revolt occurred in 1729, it had an important impact on early New Orleans since colonists who survived the uprising migrated back to New Orleans.

7. Much of this discussion regarding race and demographics in early New Orleans is drawn from the seminal work by Shannon Dawdy, *Building the Devil's Empire: French Colonial New Orleans* (Chicago: University of Chicago Press, 2008). I am very much indebted to her meticulous research of the period. This particular quote is from page 163.

8. See J. Michael Dash's "The Postwar Routes of Caribbean Creolization," in *Creolization in Cultural Creativity*, 235.

9. See Mary Louise Pratt's "Arts of the Contact Zone."

172

Chapter 1

1. Recent works on the history of the French colonial enterprise include Lawrence Powell's *The Accidental City: Improvising New Orleans*, Richard Campanella's *Bienville's Dilemma: A Historical Geography of New Orleans*, Shannon Dawdy's *Building the Devil's Empire: French Colonial New Orleans*, Jennifer Spear's *Race, Sex, and Social Order in Early New Orleans*, and Ned Sublette's *The World That Made New Orleans*.

2. See *Iberville's Gulf Journals*, 75 n. 122.

3. By the time of the Louisiana Purchase, French territory only included lands west of the Mississippi River and New Orleans.

4. See M. Vallette de Laudun's *Journal d'un voyage à la Louisiane, fait en 1720*.

5. For further description of the trappers, see Powell's chapter 1, "An Impossible River"; C13 C 2 Fo. 4 Bob. 66.

6. This island was later named Dauphin Island.

7. This experience mirrors in many ways the exploration of the mouth of the Mississippi by Cabeza de Vaca over 150 years earlier.

8. The name the Spanish gave to the Mississippi River. Iberville was in possession of a recent Spanish map that helped guide him. See Powell, *The Accidental City: Improvising New Orleans*, 11.

9. Jerry Micelle, "From Law Court to Local Government," 419–20, quoted in Dawdy, *Building the Devil's Empire*, 197.

10. *Sagamité* is "a term used to describe a number of dishes with a corn (not rice) base, ranging from hasty pudding to broths" (see Greenwald's note in *A Company Man*, 73 n. 121.

11. *Mémoires sur la Louisiane ou le Mississippi 1732*, 128.

12. See Reinhartz, "Establishing a Transatlantic Graphic Dialogue, 1492–1800."

13. In 1699 Bienville was startled to find "an English frigate, the *Carolina Galley*, heading straight into French Louisiana on a mission of colonization. Bienville famously bluffed the English captain, Louis Bond, into believing that the French would forcibly expel them from the region; the departure of the vessel gave English Turn [*Détour des Anglais*], the last great meander of the Mississippi, its name" (*Time and Place in New Orleans: Past Geographies in the Present Day*, 21).

14. Val de Terre, ANF-AC, C13 A6, fol. 352. B10. Written sometime before December 1722. See *Correspondance à l'arrivée en provenance de la Louisiane*. From the Historic New Orleans Collection.

15. This same practice of delineation and exclusion is seen in the French records of the Acadians as they arrived in Louisiana. They were not referred to as French. The conclusion of this study addresses the paradox of how Louisiana's Cajuns have been a key factor in sustaining the notion of New Orleans as a French space.

16. This resistance on the part of the French to engage in a negotiated discourse in its

colonies builds on Edouard Glissant's notion of Relation that will be treated in chapter 3 in the context of *la créolité.*

17. *Raynal, Tome VI*, 107.

18. We will treat Le Page du Pratz's design for a slave encampment later in this chapter when we study the history of Louisiana that he penned.

19. This initial absence of the French takes on significance in the next chapter, which analyzes the urban design of the city informed by Pauger's initial plan and how this design represented an attempt to transpose a French imprint, and thus old world "order," in this colonial space that otherwise was considered "savage."

20. This is a verse in the Book of Psalms, 104:15: "Touch ye not my anointed."

21. See C13 A 21 fol. 295. Bobine 28. 26 juin 1736, C 13 A 21 fol. 299. Sans date and C 13 A 22 fol. 170 Bobine 29. June 1, 1737, in the Historic New Orleans Collection.

22. See Part 3 of Pradel's correspondence for the situation of Widow Pradel.

Chapter 2

1. In this chapter we are focusing on the urban grid as posited by Pauger during the French colonial period, and do not focus on the secondary streets that exist today and which were established well into the city's American period.

2. See Marjorie Bourdelais, *La Nouvelle-Orléans: Croissance démographique, intégrations urbaine et sociale.*

3. The important competing sites for the privilege of being the capital of Louisiana were Pensacola, Mobile, Dauphin Island, Biloxi, English Turn, Manchac, Bayou St. John at Lake Pontchartrain, and Natchez.

4. It should also not be surprising that many living in New Orleans before Pauger's plan was implemented were not pleased with having to follow a planned settlement process, and rebuild accordingly. Even after the plan was established Pauger had to take some residents to court for not following it (De Villiers, 91–92). All of this added to his unfulfilled desire to return to France.

5. Although Dumaine was renamed Calle de los Almacenes for a time during the Spanish period, the original French name was restored in 1803 (Hall-Quest, 22).

6. See Lewis's treatment of French history from 1715 to 1804.

7. For a study of the Cult of St. Ann in North American, see Mary Dunn's "'A Devotion Which . . . Distinguishes this People from all Others'—The Cult of Saint Anne and the Making of the Colonial Community in Seventeenth-Century New France."

8. There were, however, instances where the placement of St. Louis Street was one street upriver from where it is on the maps of 1759, 1762, and 1764.

9. See Gregory's study of Place Vendôme through history, *Paris Deluxe: Place Vendôme.*

10. See the *Vieux Carré Survey* of the Historic New Orleans Collection.

Chapter 3

1. In comparing creolization in the French, Spanish, and English colonies, one important distinction is that in the French colonies there existed different categorizations for racial mixing, that is, *métissage*, in the construction of societies whereas in the Spanish colonies and British colonies there was more of a focus on distinction and separation of the races, as the Spanish code of *limpieza de sangre*, or pure blood, indicates that measures the amount of purity, that is, whiteness and christianity, or "impurity," that is, non-European, non-Christian, in an individual's lineage.

There are also Francophone Creole societies found in the Asia Pacific, such as in Reunion and Mauritius, which were born of the same creolization processes.

2. See the seminal work *Haiti Unbound: A Spiralist Challenge to the Postcolonial Canon* by Kaiama Glover, which serves as a response to the current hegemony that Martinique enjoys in the area of Caribbean Creole literary studies.

3. For more insights into Caribbean theoretical traditions, see *Autofiction and Advocacy in the Francophone Caribbean* by Renée Larrier.

4. For one of the few texts treating New Orleans in the context of Creole theory, see Nick Spitzer's *"Monde Créole:* The Cultural World of French Louisiana Creoles and the Creolization of World Cultures" in *Creolization as Cultural Creativity.*

5. Recent works on Creole language of Louisiana include *French and Creole in Louisiana* by Albert Valdman, editor (New York: Plenum, 1997), *Dictonary of Louisiana Creole* by Valdman et al. (Bloomington: Indiana University Press, 1998), and *If I Could Turn My Tongue Like That: The Creole Language of Pointe Coupee Parish, Louisiana* by Thomas Klingler (Baton Rouge: Louisiana State University Press, 2003), as cited by Desmond in his introduction to *Louisiana Folktales.*

6. During the French colonial period there were meticulous census records reflecting the attitude of the French to record in an encyclopedic manner the demographics of their colonies as they also recorded its flora and fauna. There have been many studies of the census records during this period. See, for example, Spear's *Race, Sex, and Social Order in Early New Orleans*, 94–99.

7. For example, in Caillot's *Relation* he refers to all women from Louisiana as Creoles. This *Relation* was written in 1730.

8. For more insights into this caste system, see Spear's thoughtful analysis in *Race, Sex, and Social Order in Early New Orleans.*

9. http://www.neworleansonline.com/neworleans/multicultural/multiculturalhistory/creole.html (accessed January 4, 2013). This is a Website of the New Orleans Tourist Marketing Corporation.

Chapter 4

1. The French Quarter has Spanish street plaques that one might assume date from the Spanish period. They are however a mid-twentieth-century phenomenon, a donation from Spain for the bicentennial of Louisiana passing to Spanish dominion. See "Gift from Spain: New Tiles for Jackson Square."

2. Gayarré 124; quoted in Kress, Introduction to *Louisiana*, 19.

3. Acadia refers to what are now the Maritime Provinces in eastern Canada.

4. See C 13 A 45 fol. 2 et 21. Bobine 54. 30 avril 1765, C 13 A 45 fol. 56, Bobine 54. 14 mai 1765 at the Historic New Orleans Collection.

5. In spite of the Acadians' French heritage and language, the correspondence shows that the group was not considered as French by French administrators. This is another example of the "grammar of exclusion" treated earlier.

6. C 13 A 45 fol. 6. Bobine 54. 8 mars 1766.

7. Dawdy offers the following counterpoint: "The size of the free colored population of New Orleans in the late French period has been seriously underestimated because their status represented either a dangerous or an unimportant distinction to Louisiana administrators creating the 1760 censuses . . . It also qualifies a common argument that subsequent Spanish policies created the city's large population of free people of color by encouraging manumissions. While manumissions certainly accelerated, Spanish policies also helped create this new social group simply by 'coloring' people who were already there and already free" (178).

8. A later governor, Esteban Miro, married into one of the most important families in New Orleans, the MacCarty family, and another Spanish colonist married the widow of Joseph Milhet, one of the rebels of 1768 who was executed by O'Reilly. See Montero de Pedro, *Españoles en Nueva Orleans y Luisiana*, 23–24.

Chapter 5

1. See http://www.codofil.org/english/lafrenchhistory.html (accessed July 1, 2012).

2. See Allain's observation about Adrien Rouquette's critique of Cable, "The French Literature of Louisiana," 10.

3. There were a few other authors who continued to write at the dawn of the twentieth century, but they were so few in number as to not represent a coherent movement or literary community.

4. For an explanation of how Prévost might have arrived at his descriptions of Louisiana landscape, see Gaines's "A Dream Colony: Geosocial (Mis)Representations of Louisiana in French Literature 1682–1805."

5. *Proclamation au nom de la République Française, 6 Germinal, An XI de la République Fran-*

çaise and *Proclamation au nom de la République Française, 8 Frimaire an XII de la République Française et 30 Novembre 1803* by Laussat.

6. For the most complete list of texts written during the French and Spanish colonial periods in Louisiana, see Allain's "The French Literature of Louisiana" in *The Louisiana Purchase Bicentennial Series in Louisiana History: Louisiana Literature and Literary Figures.*

7. For the most complete information to date, see both the Bibliothèque Tintamarre, oeuvres louisianaises en ligne, http://www.centenary.edu/french/louisiane.html, sponsored by Century College, and Louisiana State University's Creole Echoes site, http://www.lib.lsu.edu/special/exhibits/e-exhibits/creole/homepage/index.html (accessed May 17, 2012).

8. Quoted in Chris Michaelides's introduction to *Paroles d'honneur: Écrits de Créoles de Couleur Néo-Orléanais,* page 34, a compilation of the earliest writings of New Orleans' Creoles of color.

9. The first African American published poets, however, were Jupiter Hammon and Phillis Wheatley, both slaves whose work was published individually, whereas in this case New Orleans had an important cohort of Creoles of color who published collectively, certainly owing to the fact that they were free.

10. Act passed at the Second Session of the Ninth Legislature of the State of Louisiana, 1830, 97, quoted in Amelinckx in "Forgotten People," 52.

11. See Glissant's *Poetics of Relation,* 79.

Chapter 6

1. See Clint Bruce, "Les Feuilletons du *Courrier de la Louisiane*: les années Jérôme Bayon (1843–1849)" in http://www.centenary.edu/french/courrier/index.html.

2. See Amelinckx, "Forgotten People, Forgotten Literature," 54.

3. It would seem that Desdunes's *Nos Hommes et Notre Histoire* having been published in 1911 suggests that French remained more important to Creoles of color than to the white segment of the population.

4. See http://www.lib.lsu.edu/special/exhibits/e-exhibits/creole/People/people.html (accessed on June 15, 2012).

5. Canonge's "Fantômes" in *Contes et Récits de la Louisiane Créole,* Tome II, p. 12.

6. Reference to Charles Berthélemy Roussève's *The Negro in Louisiana: Aspects of His History and Literature* (New Orleans: Xavier University Press, 1937), 93, quoted in Michaelides's note on 232.

7. Questy's "Monsieur Paul" appears in Michaelides's *Paroles d'Honneur,* and this quote is from page 167.

8. For a more historical study of this event please refer to chapter 4 in this text.

9. Gayarré 124, quoted in Kress in his introduction to the novel, 19.

10. See http://www.centenary.edu/editions/levieuxsalomon_en.html (accessed August 11, 2014).

11. For detailed information on the life of Dessommes, see the introduction to *Tante Cydette* by Ida Eve Heckenbach.

12. See Christian Hommel's introduction to *Les Quarteronnes de la Nouvelle-Orléans: Gina*.

Conclusion

1. In French, the Louisiana Purchase is referred to as *La Vente de la Louisiane* to mean the selling of the territory to the Americans.

2. Two of the most highly regarded scholars in this area are Barry J. Ancelet and Carl Brasseaux. For an introduction to Cajun culture and the cultural renaissance in southwest Louisiana, see Ancelet, Brasseaux et al., *Cajun Country*. See also Guenin-Lelle's "The Birth of Cajun Poetry: An Analysis of *Cris sur le bayou: Naissance d'une poésie acadienne en Louisiane*" and "The Role of Music Festivals in the Cultural Renaissance of Southwest Louisiana in the Late Twentieth Century."

BIBLIOGRAPHY

Adélaïde-Merlande, Jacques. *Delgrès ou la Guadeloupe en 1802.* Paris: Éditions Karthala, 1986. Print.

Allain, Mathé. "The French Literature of Louisiana." *The Louisiana Purchase Bicentennial Series in Louisiana History: Louisiana Literature and Literary Figures.* Edited by Mathé Allain. Vol. 17. Lafayette: Center for Louisiana Studies, 2004. Print.

Amelinckx, Frans C. "Forgotten People, Forgotten Literature: The Case of Creole Authors of Color." *The Louisiana Purchase Bicentennial Series in Louisiana History: Louisiana Literature and Literary Figures.* Edited by Mathé Allain. Vol. 17. Lafayette: Center for Louisiana Studies, 2004. Print.

Ancelet, Barry Jean, Jay Edwards, and Glen Pitre. *Cajun Country.* Jackson: University Press of Mississippi, 1991. Print.

Anderson, Benedict. *Imagined Communities: Reflections on the Origin and Spread of Nationalism.* London: Verso, 1983. Print.

Asbury, Herbert. *The French Quarter: An Informal History of New Orleans Underworld.* Garden City, NY: Garden City Publishing Co., 1938. Print.

Augarde, Jacques. "Un Écrivain Mauricien: Malcolm de Chazal." *Les Écrivains de la Négritude et de la Créolité. Actes du Troisième Colloque International Francophone du Canton de Payrac (Lot) Organisé par l'Association des Écrivains de Langue Française.* Paris: Sepeg International, 1993. Print.

Badiane, Mamadou. "Négritude, Antillanité et Créolité ou de l'éclatement de l'identité fixe." *French Review* 85.5 (2012): 837–47. Print.

Baillardel, A., and A. Prioult, eds. *Le Chevalier de Pradel, Vie d'un colon français en Louisiane au XVIIIe siècle d'après sa correspondance et celle de sa famille.* Paris: Maisonneuve Frères, 1928. Print.

Baron, Robert, and Ana Cara, eds. *Creolization as Cultural Creativity.* Jackson: University Press of Mississippi, 2011. Print.

Barron, Errol. *New Orleans Observed: Drawings and Observations of America's Most Foreign City.* New Orleans: Tulane School of Architecture, Walsworth Publishing Company, 2011. Print.

Batigne, Stéphane. "Esprits du fleuve." *Québec: Espace et Sentiment.* Edited by Stéphane Batigne. Paris: Éditions Autrement, 2001. Print.

Bebel-Gisler, Dany. *Le Défi culturel guadeloupéen: devenir ce que nous sommes.* Paris: Éditions caribéennes, 1989. Print.

Bebel-Gisler, Dany, and Laënnec Hurbon. *Cultures et pouvoir dans la Caraïbe: langue créole, vaudou, sectes religieuses en Guadeloupe et en Haïti.* Paris: Éditions Harmattan, 1987. Print.

Beers, Henry Putney. *French and Spanish Records of Louisiana: A Bibliographical Guide to Archive and Manuscript Sources.* Baton Rouge: Louisiana State University Press, 1989. Print.

Bell, Caryn Cossé. Introduction. *Rappelez-vous concitoyens!* By Pierre-Aristide Desdunes. Shreveport: Les Cahiers du Tintamarre, 2010. 8–87. Print.

———. *Revolution, Romanticism, and the Afro-Creole Protest Tradition in Louisiana 1718–1868.* Baton Rouge: Louisiana State University Press, 1997. Print.

Bernabé, Jean, Patrick Chamoiseau, and Raphaël Confiant. *Éloge à la créolité.* Paris: Éditions Gallimard, 1989. Print.

Bertrand, Henry. "Jean Albany, chanter réunionnais de la Créolité." *Les Écrivains de la Négritude et de la Créolité. Actes du Troisième Colloque International Francophone du Canton de Payrac (Lot) Organisé par l'Association des Écrivains de Langue Française.* Paris: Sepeg International, 1993. Print.

Bhabha, Homi K. *The Location of Culture.* London: Routledge, 2007. Print.

Bibliothèque Tintamarre oeuvres louisianaises en ligne. Web. June 15, 2012. http://www.centenary.edu/french/louisiane.html.

Blaise, J., L. Farrugia, Cl. Trebos, and S. Zobda-Quitman. *Culture et politique en Guadeloupe et Martinique.* Paris: Éditions Karthala, 1981. Print.

Bond, Bradley G., ed. *French Colonial Louisiana and the Atlantic World.* Baton Rouge: Louisiana State University Press, 2005. Print.

Boullier, David-Renaud. *Essai philosophique sur l'âme des bêtes, où l'on traite de son existence et de sa nature, et où l'on mêle par occasion diverses réflexions sur la nature de la liberté, sur celle de nos sensations, sur l'union de l'âme et du corps, sur l'immortalité de l'âme et où l'on réfute diverses objections de Mr Bayle.* Amsterdam: F. Changuion, 1728. Print.

Bourdelais, Marjorie. *La Nouvelle-Orléans: Croissance démographique, intégrations urbaine et sociale (1803–1860).* Bern: Peter Lang, 2012. Print.

Branche, Jerome, ed. *Race, Colonialism, and Social Transformation in Latin America and the Caribbean.* Gainesville: University Press of Florida, 2008. Print.

Brasseaux, Carl A. "The Administration of Slave Regulations in French Louisiana, 1724–1766." *Louisiana History: The Journal of the Louisiana Historical Association* 21, no. 2 (1980): 139–58. Print.

———. "Confusion, Conflict, and Currency: An Introduction to the Rebellion of 1768." *Louisiana History: The Journal of the Louisiana Historical Association* 18, no. 2 (1977): 161–69. Print.

———. "The Moral Climate of French Colonial Louisiana, 1699–1763." *Louisiana History: The Journal of the Louisiana Historical Association* 27, no. 1 (1986): 27–41. Print.

Brasseaux, Carl A., and Glenn R. Conrad, eds. *The Road to Louisiana: The Saint Domingue Refugees 1792–1809.* Lafayette: Center for Louisiana Studies, 1992. Print.

Brasseaux, Carl A., and Richard E. Chandler. "The Britain Incident, 1769–1770: Anglo-Hispanic Tensions in the Western Gulf." *Southwestern Historical Quarterly* 87, no. 4 (1984): 357–70. Print.

Brichant, Colette Dubois. *La France au Cours des Ages: Grands jours et vie quotidienne.* New York: McGraw Hill, 1973. Print.

Brickhouse, Anna. *Transamerican Literary Relations and the Nineteenth-Century Public Sphere.* Cambridge: Cambridge University Press, 2004. Print.

Britton, Celia. *Edouard Glissant and Postcolonial Theory.* Charlottesville: University Press of Virginia, 1999. Print.

Bruce, Clint. "Les Feuilletons du *Courrier de la Louisiane*: les années Jérôme Bayon (1843–1849)." Bibliothèque Tintamarre. Web. May 20, 2014. http://www.centenary.edu/french/courrier/index.html.

Bryan, Violet Harrington. *The Myth of New Orleans in Literature: Dialogues of Race and Gender.* Knoxville: University of Tennessee Press, 1993. Print.

Buisseret, David. "Urbanization in the Old World and in the New." *Transatlantic History.* Edited by Steven G. Reinhardt and Dennis Reinhartz. College Station: Texas A & M University Press, 2006. Print.

Buman, Nathan A. "Historigraphical Examinations of the 1811 Slave Insurrection." *Louisiana History: The Journal of the Louisiana Historical Association* 53, no. 3 (2012): 318–37. Print.

Caillot, Marc-Antoine. "Relation du Voyage de la Louisiane ou Nouvelle France fait par le Sr. Caillot en l'année 1730." Ms. 2005.11. Historic New Orleans Collection. Print.

———. *A Company Man: The Remarkable French-Atlantic Voyage of a Clerk for the Company of the Indies.* Edited by Erin M. Greenwald. Translated by Teri F. Chalmers. New Orleans: Historic New Orleans Collection, 2013. Print.

Campanella, Richard. *Bienville's Dilemma: A Historical Geography of New Orleans.* Lafayette: Center for Louisiana Studies, 2008. Print.

———. "Geography of a Food, or Georgraphy of a Word? The Curious Cultural Diffusion of *Sagamité*." *Louisiana History: The Journal of the Louisiana Historical Association* 54, no. 4 (2013): 465–76. Print.

———. *Time and Place in New Orleans: Past Geographies in the Present Day.* Gretna, LA: Pelican Publishing Co., 2002. Print.

Chamoiseau, Patrick, and Raphaël Confiant. *Lettres créoles.* Paris: Folio, 1999. Print.

Charlevoix, Pierre-François-Xavier de. *Journal d'un voyage fait par ordre du roi dans l'Amérique septentrionale.* 3 vols. Letters of January 10, 1722, and January 26, 1722. Paris: Rollin, 1744. Print.

Charters, Samuel. *A Trumpet around the Corner: The Story of New Orleans Jazz.* Jackson: University Press of Mississippi, 2008. Print.

Chase, John Churchill. *Frenchmen, Desire, Good Children, and Other Streets of New Orleans.* New York: Collier Books, 1979. Print.

Chateaubriand, François-René de. *Le Nouvel Atala/René.* Paris: Éditions Flammarion, 1964. Print.

Chaudenson, Robert. *La Créolisation: Théorie, Applications, Implications.* Paris: Harmattan, 2003. Print.

———. *Creolization of Language and Culture.* London: Routledge, 2001. Print.

———. *Des Iles, des hommes, des langues.* Paris: Éditions Harmattan, 1992. Print.

Chaudenson, Robert, and Didier de Robillard. *Langue, économie et développement.* Vol. 1. Aix-Marseille: Institut d'études créoles et francophones, 1989. Print.

Choppin, Jules. *Fables et Rêveries.* Shreveport: Les Cahiers du Tintamarre, 2007. Print.

Clark, Emily. *Masterless Mistresses: The New Orleans Ursulines and the Development of a New World Society, 1727–1834.* Chapel Hill: University of North Carolina Press, 2007. Print.

Clark, Emily, ed. *Voices from an Early American Convent: Marie Madeleine Hachard and the New Orleans Ursulines, 1727–1760.* Baton Rouge: Louisiana State University Press, 2007. Print.

Confiant, Raphaël. *Commandeur du sucre.* Paris: Éditions Écriture, 1994. Print.

———. *Les Maîtres de la parole créole.* Paris: Éditions Gallimard, 1995 Print.

Contes et Récits de la Louisiane créole. Vol. 1. Edited by Ashley Owens. Shreveport: Les Cahiers du Tintamarre, 2006. Print.

Contes et Récits de la Louisiane créole. Vol. 2. Edited by Mary Ham. Shreveport: Les Cahiers du Tintamarre, 2008. Print.

Cooper, Frederick, and Ann Laura Stoler, eds. *Tensions of Empire: Colonial Cultures in a Bourgeois World.* Berkeley: University of California Press, 1997. Print.

Correspondance à l'arrivée en provenance de la Louisiane. ANF-AC, C_{13}. Historic New Orleans Collection. Microform.

Council for the Development of French in Louisiana. Web. July 15, 2013. http://www.codofil.org/english/lafrenchhistory.html.

Creole Echoes. Web. June 15, 2012. http://www.lib.lsu.edu/special/exhibits/e-exhibits/creole/People/people.html.

Daley, T. A. "Victor Sejour." *Phylon* 4, no. 1 (1943): 5–16. Print.

Dash, J. Michael. "The Postwar Routes of Caribbean Creolization." *Creolization as Cultural Creativity.* Edited by Robert Baron and Ana C. Cara. Jackson: University Press of Mississippi, 2011. Print.

Dawdy, Shannon Lee. *Building the Devil's Empire: French Colonial New Orleans.* Chicago: University of Chicago Press, 2008. Print.

Dayan, Joan. "Women, History and the Gods: Reflections on Mayotte Capécia and Marie Chauvet." *An Introduction to Caribbean Francophone Writing: Guadeloupe and Martinique.* Edited by Sam Haigh. Oxford: Berg, 1999. Print.

De la Houssaye, Sidonie. *Amis et Fortune: Roman louisianais.* Shreveport: Les Cahiers du Tintamarre, 2010. Print.

——. *Contes d'une grand-mère louisianaise.* Shreveport: Éditions Tintamarre, 2007. Print.

——. *Les Quarteronnes de la Nouvelle-Orléans I: Octavia la Quarteronne suivi par Violetta la Quarteronne.* Shreveport: Éditions Tintamarre, 2006. Print.

——. *Les Quarteronnes de la Nouvelle-Orléans II: Gina la Quarteronne.* Shreveport: Éditions Tintamarre, 2009. Print.

Deleris, Ferdinand. "La Femme dans l'Œuvre Poétique et Théâtrale de Jacques Rabemananjara." *Les Écrivains de la Négritude et de la Créolité. Actes du Troisième Colloque International Francophone du Canton de Payrac (Lot) Organisé par l'Association des Écrivains de Langue Française.* Paris: Sepeg International, 1993. Print.

Derbigny, Pierre. *Mémoire à consulter sur la Réclamation de la Batture, située en face du Faubourg Sainte-Marie de la Nouvelle-Orléans.* Nouvelle-Orléans: Chez Jean Renard, Imprimeur de la Ville et Paroisse d'Orléans, 1807. Print.

Desdunes, Pierre-Aristide. *Nos hommes et notre histoire: Notices biographiques accompagnées de réflexions personnelles et de souvenirs personnels.* Montreal: Arbour and Dupont, 1911. Print.

——. *Rappelez-vous concitoyens!* Shreveport: Les Cahiers du Tintamarre, 2010. Print.

Desmond, Russell. Introduction. *Louisiana Folktales: Lapin, Bouki, and Other Creole Stories in French Dialect and English Translation.* Edited by Alcée Fortier. Lafayette: University of Louisiana at Lafayette Press, 2011. Print.

Dessens, Nathalie. *From Saint-Domingue to New Orleans: Migration and Influences.* Gainesville: University Press of Florida, 2007. Print.

Dessommes, George. *Tante Cydette: Nouvelle Louisianaise.* Gretna, LA: Classiques Pélican, 2001. Print.

——. *Vendanges.* Edited by Margaret Mahoney. Shreveport: Les Cahiers du Tintamarre, 2007. Print.

De Ville, Winston. *Gulf Coast Colonials: A Compendium of French Families in Early Eighteenth Century Louisiana.* Baltimore: Clearfield Co., 1999. Print.

——. *The New Orleans French 1720–1733.* Baltimore: Clearfield Co., 1994. Print.

De Villiers du Terrage, Marc. *Les Dernières Années de la Louisiane Française: Le Chevalier de Kerlérec d'Abbadie-Aubry, Laussat.* Paris: Librairie Orientale et Américaine, 1905. Print.

——. *Histoire de la Fondation de la Nouvelle-Orléans (1717–1722).* Paris: Presses de l'Imprimerie Nationale, 1917. Print.

Din, Gilbert C., and John E. Harkins. *The New Orleans Cabildo: Colonial Louisiana's First City Government 1769–1803.* Baton Rouge: Louisiana State University Press, 1996. Print.

Dominguez, Virginia. *White by Definition: Social Classification in Creole Louisiana.* New Brunswick, NJ: Rutgers University Press, 1986. Print.

Dubois, Laurent. *A Colony of Citizens: Revolution and Slave Emancipation in the French Caribbean, 1787–1804.* Chapel Hill: University of North Carolina Press, 2004. Print.

Dunn, Mary. "'A Devotion Which . . . Distinguishes this People from all Others'—The Cult of Saint Anne and the Making of the Colonial Community in Seventeenth-Century New France." *Québec Studies* 51 (2011): 3–19. Print.

Durand, Marc. *Histoire du Québec.* Paris: Éditions Imago, 2002. Print.

Dzero, Irinia. "Meanings of Hybritity in Aimé Césaire's *Discours sur le colonialisme.*" *French Review* 85, no. 1 (2011): 102–14. Print.

Ewell, Barbara, and Pamela Glenn Menke, eds. *Southern Local Color: Stories of Region, Race and Gender.* Athens: University of Georgia Press, 2002. Print.

Faber, Eberhard. "The Passion of the Prefect: Pierre Clément De Laussat, 1803 New Orleans, and the Bonapartist Louisiana That Never Was." *Louisiana History: The Journal of the Louisiana Historical Association* 54, no. 3 (2013): 261–91. Print.

Fortier, Alcée. "French Literature in Louisiana." *Transactions and Proceedings of the Modern Language Association of America* 2 (1886): 31–60. Print.

Freiberg, Edna B. *Bayou St. John in Colonial Louisiana 1699–1803.* New Orleans: Harvey Press, 1980. Print.

French Consulate in New Orleans. Web. June 4, 2014. http://www.consulfrance-nou velleorleans.org/.

Gaines, James F. "A Dream Colony: Geosocial (Mis)Representations of Louisiana in French Literature 1682–1805." *Regional Dimensions* 6 (1988): 1–25. Print.

Gallo, Max. *Louis XIV: L'Hiver du Grand Roi.* Paris: XO Éditions, 2007. Print.

Galloway, Patricia K. *La Salle and His Legacy: Frenchmen and Indians in the Lower Mississippi Valley.* Jackson: University Press of Mississippi, 1982. Print.

Garraway, Doris. *The Libertine Colony: Creolization in the Early French Caribbean.* Durham, NC: Duke University Press, 2005. Print.

Garreau, Louis-Armand. *Bras Coupé et autres récits louisianais.* Shreveport: Éditions Tintamarre, 2007. Print.

———. *Louisiana.* Shreveport: Éditions Tintamarre, 2003. Print.

Gaston, Jessie Ruth. "The Case of Voodoo in New Orleans." *Africanisms in American Culture.* Edited by Joseph E. Holloway. Bloomington: Indiana University Press, 2005. Print.

Gayarré, Charles. *History of Louisiana Volume II.* Gretna, LA: Pelican Publishing Co., 1974. Print.

Gehman, Mary. *The Free People of Color of New Orleans: An Introduction.* New Orleans: Margaret Media, 1994. Print.

———. *Women and New Orleans.* New Orleans: Margaret Media, 1988. Print.

"Gift from Spain: New Tiles for Jackson Square." Web. January 10, 2015. http://www .wdsu.com/news/local-news/new-orleans/Gift-from-Spain-New-tile-signs-for-Jack son-Square/19725326.

Gilman, Daniel Coit, et al., eds. *The New International Encyclopedia.* Vol. 5. New York: Dodd, Mead and Company, 1905. Print.

Gilroy, Paul. "Cosmopolitanism Contested." *Postcolonial Melancholia.* New York: Columbia University Press, 2005. Print.

Giraud, Marcel. *A History of French Louisiana.* Translated by Joseph C. Lambert. Vol. 1. Baton Rouge: Louisiana State University Press, 1990. Print.

——. *A History of French Louisiana.* Translated by Brian Pearce. Vol. 2. Baton Rouge: Louisiana State University Press, 1993. Print.

——. *A History of French Louisiana.* Translated by Brian Pearce. Vol. 5. Baton Rouge: Louisiana State University Press, 1991. Print.

——*Histoire de la Louisiane française.* Vol. 4. Paris: Presses de France, 1974. Print.

Glissant, Édouard. *Caribbean Discourse: Selected Essays.* Translated by J. Michael Dash. Charlottesville: University Press of Virginia, 1989. Print.

——. *Le Discours antillais.* Paris: Gallimard, 1997. Print.

——. *Introduction à une poétique du divers.* Paris: Éditions Gallimard, 2001. Print.

——. *Pays rêvé, pays réel.* Paris: Éditions Gallimard, 2000. Print.

——. *Poetics of Relation.* Translated by Betsy Wing. Ann Arbor: University of Michigan Press, 1997. Print.

Glover, Kaiama L. *Haiti Unbound: A Spiralist Challenge to the Postcolonial Canon.* Liverpool: Liverpool University Press, 2010. Print.

Gosson, Renée. "Cultural and Environmental Assimilation in Martinique: An Interview with Raphaël Confiant." *Caribbean Literature and the Environment: Between Nature and Culture.* Edited by Elizabeth DeLoughrey, Renée Gosson, and George Handley. Charlottesville: University of Virginia Press, 2005. Print.

Gregory, Alexis. *Paris Deluxe: Place Vendôme.* New York: Rizzoli, 1997. Print.

Gruesz, Kirsten Silva. "The Gulf of Mexico System and the 'Latinness' of New Orleans." *Hemispheric American Literary History* 18, no. 3 (2006): 468–95. Print.

Guenin-Lelle, Dianne. "The Birth of Cajun Poetry: An Analysis of *Cris sur le bayou: Naissance d'une poésie acadienne en Louisiane.*" *The Louisiana Purchase Bicentennial Series in Louisiana History: Louisiana Literature and Literary Figures.* Edited by Mathé Allain. Vol. 17. Lafayette: Center for Louisiana Studies, 2004. Print.

Guenin-Lelle, Dianne, and Alison Harris. "The Role of Music Festivals in the Cultural Renaissance of Southwest Louisiana in the Late Twentieth Century." *Louisiana History* 50, no. 4 (2009): 461–72.

Guillaume, Alfred, Jr. "Love, Death, and Faith in the New Orleans Poets of Color." *The Louisiana Purchase Bicentennial Series in Louisiana History: Louisiana Literature and Literary Figures.* Edited by Mathé Allain. Vol. 17. Lafayette: Center for Louisiana Studies, 2004. Print.

Haigh, Sam, ed. *An Introduction to Caribbean Francophone Writing: Guadeloupe and Martinique.* Oxford: Berg, 1999. Print.

Hall, Gwendolyn Midlo. *Africans in Colonial Louisiana: The Development of Afro-Creole Cul-*

ture in the Eighteenth Century. Baton Rouge: Louisiana State University Press, 1992. Print.

———. "Epilogue: Historical Memory, Consciousness, and Conscience in the New Millennium." *French Colonial Louisiana and the Atlantic World*. Edited by Bradley G. Bond. Baton Rouge: Louisiana State University Press, 2005. 291–310. Print.

Hall-Quest, Olga. *Old New Orleans, the Creole City: Its Role in American History, 1718–1803*. New York: E. P. Dutton & Co., 1968. Print.

Hanger, Kimberly S. *Bounded Lives, Bounded Places: Free Black Society in Colonial New Orleans, 1769–1803*. Durham, NC: Duke University Press, 1997. Print.

Hanotaux, Gabriel. Introduction. *Histoire de la Fondation de la Nouvelle-Orléans (1717–1722)*. By Marc de Villiers du Terrage. Paris: Presses de l'Imprimerie Nationale, 1917. vii–xii. Print.

Hava, J. G. *Emigration espagnole en Louisiane*. Nouvelle-Orléans: Imprimerie Cosmopolite, 1881. Print.

Havard, Gilles, and Cécile Vidal. *Histoire de l'Amérique française*. Paris: Éditions Flammarion, 2008. Print.

Heckenbach, Ida Eve. Introduction. *Tante Cydette: Nouvelle Louisianaise*. By George Dessommes. Gretna, LA: Classiques Pélican, 2001. Print.

Hennepin, Louis. *Description de la Louisiane, nouvellement découverte*. Paris: Chez Amable Auroy, 1688. Print.

Hersch, Charles. *Subversive Sounds: Race and the Birth of Jazz in New Orleans*. Chicago: University of Chicago Press, 2007. Print.

Hirsch, Arnold R., and Joseph Logsdon, eds. *Creole New Orleans: Race and Americanization*. Baton Rouge: Louisiana State University Press, 1992. Print.

Hommel, Christian. Introduction. *Les Quarteronnes de la Nouvelle-Orléans I: Octavia la Quarteronne suivi par Violetta la Quarteronne*. By Sidonie de la Houssaye. Shreveport: Éditions Tintamarre, 2006. 7–39. Print.

———. Introduction. *Les Quarteronnes de la Nouvelle-Orléans II: Gina la Quarteronne*. By Sidonie de la Houssaye. Shreveport: Éditions Tintamarre, 2009. 7–9. Print.

Iberville, Pierre le Moyne, sieur d'. *Iberville's Gulf Journals*. Edited and translated by Richebourg Gaillard McWilliams. Tuscaloosa: University of Alabama Press, 1981. Print.

Ingersoll, Thomas N. *Mammon and Manon in Early New Orleans: The First Slave Society in the Deep South, 1718–1819*. Knoxville: University of Tennessee Press, 1999. Print.

Jackson, Joy J. *New Orleans in the Gilded Age: Politics and Urban Progress 1880–1896*. Lafayette: Louisiana Historical Association, 1969. Print.

Jaham, Marie-Reine de. "Je suis Créole." *Les Écrivains de la Négritude et de la Créolité. Actes du Troisième Colloque International Francophone du Canton de Payrac (Lot) Organisé par l'Association des Écrivains de Langue Française*. Paris: Sepeg International, 1993. Print.

Jouanny, Robert. "De la Négritude à la Créolité: Un Autre Retour au Pays Natal." *Les*

Écrivains de la Négritude et de la Créolité. Actes du Troisième Colloque International Franco-phone du Canton de Payrac (Lot) Organisé par l'Association des Écrivains de Langue Française. Paris: Sepeg International, 1993. Print.

Joubert, Jean-Louis. "Rêves d'Afrique, Songes d'Asie." *Les Écrivains de la Négritude et de la Créolité. Actes du Troisième Colloque International Francophone du Canton de Payrac (Lot) Organisé par l'Association des Écrivains de Langue Française.* Paris: Sepeg International, 1993. Print.

Kane, Harnett T. *Queen New Orleans: City by the River.* New York: Bonanza Books, 1949. Print.

Kein, Sybil, ed. *Creole: The History and Legacy of Louisiana's Free People of Color.* Baton Rouge: Louisiana State University Press, 2000. Print.

King, Grace. *Jean-Baptiste Le Moyne Sieur de Bienville.* New York: Dodd, Mead, 1893. Print.

Klingler, Thomas. *If I Could Turn My Tongue Like That: The Creole Language of Pointe Coupée Parish, Louisiana.* Baton Rouge: Louisiana State University Press, 2003. Print.

Kress, Dana. "Creole Literature." *KnowLA Encyclopedia of Louisiana.* Edited by David Johnson. Louisiana Endowment for the Humanities. September 14, 2011. Web. http://www.www.knowla.org/entry.php?rec=1176.

———. Introduction. *Louisiana.* By Louis-Armand Garreau. Shreveport: Éditions Tinta-marre, 2003. 9–25. Print.

Langlois, Gilles-Antoine. *Des villes pour la Louisiane française, Théorie et pratique de l'urbanis-tique coloniale au 18e siècle.* Paris: Éditions Harmattan, 2003. Print.

Lanusse, Armand. *Les Cenelles.* Edited by Mia D. Reamer. Shreveport: Les Cahiers du Tintamarre, 2003. Print.

Larrier, Renée. *Autofiction and Advocacy in the Francophone Caribbean.* Gainesville: University Press of Florida, 2006. Print.

Latil, Alexandre. *Les Éphémères.* Edited by Kelsey A. Bellamy. Shreveport: Les Cahiers du Tintamarre, 2003. Print.

Laussat, Pierre-Clément de. *Proclamation au nom de la République Française, 6 Germinal, An XI de la République Française.* Nouvelle-Orléans: n.p., 1802. Microform.

———. *Proclamation au nom de la République Française, 8 Frimaire an XII de la République Française et 30 Novembre 1803.* Nouvelle-Orléans: n.p., 1803. Microform.

Lavoie, Bernard. "Un Américain de France, du sud de la Louisiane." *The Louisiana Purchase Bicentennial Series in Louisiana History: Louisiana Literature and Literary Figures.* Edited by Mathé Allain. Vol. 17. Lafayette: Center for Louisiana Studies, 2004. Print.

Lemmon, Alfred E., John T. Magill, and Jason R. Wiese, eds. *Charting New Orleans: Five Hundred Years of Maps. Historic New Orleans Collection.* New Orleans: Historic New Orleans Collection, 2003. Print.

Le Page du Pratz, Antoine Simon. *History of Louisiana or of the Western Parts of Virginia and*

Carolina: Containing a Description of the Countries that lie on Both Sides of the River Missis-sippi. Books 1–4. London: T. Becket, 1774. Print.

Leroy, Fabrice. Introduction. *Bras Coupé et autres récits louisianais.* By Louis-Armand Garreau. Shreveport: Éditions Tintamarre, 2007. 7–39. Print.

Lewis, Gwynne. *France 1715–1804: Power and the People.* Harlow, England: Pearson Education, 2004. Print.

Livingston, Edouard. *Rapport fait à l'Assemblée Générale de l'État de la Louisiane, sur le projet d'un Code Pénal, pour le dit État.* Nouvelle-Orléans: Benjamin Levy, 1822. Print.

Long, Carolyn Morrow. *A New Orleans Voudou Priestess: The Legend and Reality of Marie Laveau.* Gainesville: University Press of Florida, 2006. Print.

Louisiana Citizens. *Mémoire présenté au Congrès des États-Unis d'Amérique par les habitans de la Louisiane.* Nouvelle-Orléans: De l'imprimerie du Moniteur, 1804. Print.

Lowrey, Walter M. "The Engineers and the Mississippi." *Louisiana History: The Journal of the Louisiana Historical Association* 5, no. 3 (1964): 233–55. Print.

Maduell, Charles R., Jr. *The Census Tables for the French Colony of Louisiana from 1699–1732.* Baltimore: Clearfield Co., 2008. Print.

Mann, Rob. "French Colonial Archaeology." *Archaeology of Louisiana.* Edited by Mark A. Rees. Baton Rouge: Louisiana State University Press, 2010. Print.

March, Christian. *Le Discours des mères martiniquaises. Diglossie et créolité: un point de vue sociologique.* Paris: Éditions Harmattan, 1996. Print.

Margry, Pierre. *Découvertes et établissements des Français dans l'ouest et dans le sud de l'Amérique Septentrionale (1614–1754).* Vol. 1–3. Paris: D. Jouaust, 1876. Print.

Marlin-Godier, Micheline. *Fort-de-France la ville et la municipalité de 1884 à 1914.* Petit-Bourg, Guadeloupe: Ibis Rouge Éditions, 2000. Print.

Martin, Désirée. *Les Veilles d'une soeur.* Edited by May Waggoner. Shreveport: Éditions Tintamarre, 2008. Print.

Martin, François Xavier. *The History of Louisiana.* Gretna, LA: Firebird Press, 2000. Print.

McKinney, Louise. *New Orleans: A Cultural History.* Oxford: Oxford University Press, 2006. Print.

McManners, John. *Church and Society in Eighteenth-Century France.* 2 vols. Oxford: Oxford University Press, 1998. Print.

Megraw, Richard. *Confronting Modernity: Art and Society in Louisiana.* Jackson: University Press of Mississippi, 2008. Print.

Mercier, Alfred. *Le Fou de Palerme, suivi de L'Artiste amoureux, Nouvelles siciliennes.* Edited by Carrie A. Lombardino. Shreveport: Les Cahiers du Tintamarre, 2006. Print.

——. *L'Habitation Saint-Ybars ou Maîtres et Esclaves en Louisiane (récit social).* Edited by D. A. Kress. Shreveport: Les Cahiers du Tintamarre, 2003. Print.

——. *Hénoch Jédéjias.* Edited by Joëlle Roy, May Rush Gwin Waggoner, and Rachael Williams-Mejri. Shreveport: Les Cahiers du Tintamarre, 2009. Print.

——. *Johnelle.* Edited by Christine Elizabeth Downes. Shreveport: Les Cahiers du Tintamarre, 2008. Print.

——. *Lidia.* Edited by Jenni M. Loer. Shreveport: Les Cahiers du Tintamarre, 2003. Print.

Michaelides, Chris, ed. *Paroles d'honneur: Écrits de Créoles de couleur néo-orléanais (1837–1872).* Shreveport: Éditions Tintamarre, 2004. Print.

Miller, DeMond Shondell, and Jason David Rivera. *Hurricane Katrina and the Redefinition of Landscape.* Landham, MD: Lexington Books, 2009. Print.

Miller, Edward L. *New Orleans and the Texas Revolution.* College Station: Texas A & M University Press, 2004. Print.

Montero de Pedro, José. *Españoles en Nueva Orleans y Luisiana.* Madrid: Ediciones Cultura Hispanica del Centro Iberoamericano de Cooperación, 1979. Print.

——. *The Spanish in New Orleans and Louisiana.* Translated by Richard E. Chandler. Gretna, LA: Pelican Publishing Co., 2000. Print.

Montlezun, Baron de. *Voyage fait dans les Années 1816–1817 de New York à la Nouvelle-Orléans, et de l'Orénoque au Mississipi, par les Petites et Grandes Antilles, contenant des détails absolument nouveaux sur ces contrées; des portraits de personages influent dans les États-Unis, et des anecdotes sur les réfugiés qui y sont établis.* 2 vols. Paris: Librairie de Gide fils, 1818. Print.

Moore, John Hebron. "The Cypress Lumber Industry of the Lower Mississippi Valley during the Colonial Period." *Louisiana History: The Journal of the Louisiana Historical Association* 24, no. 1 (1983): 25–47. Print.

Morel, Lise. "In Praise of Creoleness." *An Introduction to Caribbean Francophone Writing: Guadeloupe and Martinique.* Edited by Sam Haigh. Oxford: Berg, 1999. Print.

Morris, Christopher. "Impenetrable but Easy: The French Transformation of the Lower Mississippi Valley and the Founding of New Orleans." *Transforming New Orleans and Its Environs.* Edited by Craig E. Colten. Pittsburgh: University of Pittsburgh Press, 2000. Print.

Mouhout, Jean-François. "The Emigration of the Acadians from France to Louisiana: A New Perspective." *Louisiana History: The Journal of the Louisiana Historical Association* 53, no. 2 (2012): 133–67. Print.

Murdoch, H. Adlai. "Creole Counterdiscourses and French Departmental Hegemony: Reclaiming 'Here' from 'There.'" *Race, Colonialism, and Social Transformation in Latin America and the Caribbean.* Edited by Jerome Branche. Gainesville: University Press of Florida, 2008. Print.

Murrell, Nathaniel Samuel. *Afro-Caribbean Religions: An Introduction to Their Historical, Cultural and Sacred Traditions.* Philadelphia: Temple University Press, 2010. Print.

New Orleans Tourist Marketing Corporation. Web. January 4, 2013. http://www.neworleansonline.com/neworleans/multicultural/multiculturalhistory/creole.

Nolan, Charles. *Cathedral-Basilica of St. Louis King of France*. Strasbourg: Éditions du Signe, 2009. Print.

O'Neil, Charles Edwards. "French Literature in Colonial Louisiana." *The Louisiana Purchase Bicentennial Series in Louisiana History: Louisiana Literature and Literary Figures*. Edited by Mathé Allain. Vol. 17. Lafayette: Center for Louisiana Studies, 2004. Print.

——. "The French Regency and the Colonial Engineers: Street Names of Early New Orleans." *Louisiana History: The Journal of the Louisiana Historical Association* 39, no. 2 (1998): 207–14. Print.

Ong, Aihwa. *Flexible Citizenship: The Cultural Logistics of Transnationality*. Durham, NC: Duke University Press, 1999. Print.

Paz, Manuel de. "Canarias y América: Aspectos de una vinculación histórica." *Anuario Americanista Europeo* 4–5 (2006–2007): 197–211. Print.

Pellerin, Gérard. Lettre. Bibliothèque de l'Arsenal, Paris. Ms. 4497, fol. 54. Print.

Perret, J. John. "Sidonie de la Houssaye's Quadroon Tetralogy: 'Les Quarteronnes de la Nouvelle Orléans.'" *The Louisiana Purchase Bicentennial Series in Louisiana History: Louisiana Literature and Literary Figures*. Edited by Mathé Allain. Vol. 17. Lafayette: Center for Louisiana Studies, 2004. Print.

Pfaff, Françoise. *Conversations with Maryse Condé*. Lincoln: University of Nebraska Press, 1997. Print.

Piacentino, Ed. "Seeds of Rebellion in Plantation Fiction: Victor Séjour's 'The Mulatto.'" *Southern Spaces: An Interdisciplinary Journal about Regions, Places, and Cultures of the US South and Their Global Connections*. August 28, 2007. Web. March 7, 2012. http://www.southernspaces.org/2007/seeds-rebellion-plantation-fiction-victor-s%C3%A9jours-mulatto.

Powell, Lawrence N. *The Accidental City: Improvising New Orleans*. Cambridge, MA: Harvard University Press, 2013. Print.

——. "Why Louisiana Mattered." *Louisiana History: The Journal of the Louisiana Historical Association* 53, no. 4 (2012): 389–401. Print.

Poydras, Julien. *The Right of the Public to the Batture of New Orleans or Port of St. Mary*. Washington: A. & C. Way, 1809. Print.

Prabhu, Anjali. "Interrogating Hybridity: Subaltern Agency and Totality in Postcolonial Theory." *Diacritics* 35, no. 2 (2005): 76–92. Print.

Praeger, Michèle. *The Imaginary Caribbean and Caribbean Imaginary*. Lincoln: University of Nebraska Press, 2003. Print.

Pratt, Mary Louise. "Arts of the Contact Zone." *MLA Profession* (1991): 33–40. Print.

Prévost, Abbé. *Manon Lescaut: L'Histoire du chevalier des Grieux et de Manon Lescaut*. Paris: Classsiques de Poche, 2005. Print.

Questy, Joanni. "Monsieur Paul." *Paroles d'honneur: Écrits de Créoles de couleur néo-orléanais*

(1837–1872). Edited by Chris Michaelides. Shreveport: Éditions Tintamarre, 2004. Print.

Raeburn, Bruce Boyd. *New Orleans Style and the Writing of American Jazz History*. Ann Arbor: University of Michigan Press, 2009. Print.

Raynal, Guillaume-Thomas, Abbé. *Histoire philosophique et politique des établissements et du commerce des Européens dans les deux Indes*. 10 vols. Genève: Chez Jean-Léonard Pellet, 1780. Print.

——. *A Philosophical and Political History of the Settlements and Trade of the Europeans in the East and West Indies*. Translated by J. O. Justamond. 10 vols. London: W. Strahan, 1783. Print.

Rees, Mark, ed. *Archaeology of Louisiana*. Baton Rouge: Louisiana State University Press, 2010. Print.

Reinecke, George. "Alfred Mercier, French Novelist of New Orleans." *The Louisiana Purchase Bicentennial Series in Louisiana History: Louisiana Literature and Literary Figures*. Edited by Mathé Allain. Vol. 17. Lafayette: Center for Louisiana Studies, 2004. Print.

Reinhartz, Dennis. "Establishing a Transatlantic Graphic Dialogue, 1492–1800." *Transatlantic History*. Edited by Steven G. Reinhardt and Dennis Reinhartz. College Station: Texas A & M University Press, 2006. Print.

Relation de l'incendie qu'a éprouvé la ville de la Nouvelle-Orléans, le 21 mars 1788. N.p.: Imprimerie Royale, 1788. Print.

Ripley, George, and Charles A. Dana, eds. *The New American Encyclopedia: A Popular Dictionary of General Knowledge*. Vol. 3. New York: Appleton and Company, 1858. Print.

Ritchie, Catherine, ed. *Histoire de France*. Paris: Larousse, 2005. Print.

Rouquette, Adrien-Emmanuel. *La Nouvelle Atala*. Edited by Elizabeth B. Landry. Shreveport: Éditions Tintamarre, 2003. Print.

Rousey, Dennis C. *Policing the Southern City: New Orleans, 1805–1889*. Baton Rouge: Louisiana State University Press, 1996. Print.

Saint-Prot, Charles. "Les Chemins de l'Identité." *Les Écrivains de la Négritude et de la Créolité. Actes du Troisième Colloque International Francophone du Canton de Payrac (Lot) Organisé par l'Association des Écrivains de Langue Française*. Paris: Sepeg International, 1993. Print.

Saxon, Lyle. *Fabulous New Orleans*. New York: D. Appleton-Century Company, 1939. Print.

——. *Gumbo Ya-Ya: A Collection of Louisiana Folk Tales*. New York: Bonanza Books, 1945. Print.

Schafer, Judith Kelleher. *Brothels, Depravity, and Abandoned Women: Illegal Sex in Antebellum New Orleans*. Baton Rouge: Louisiana State University Press, 2009. Print.

Schneider, Frank. *Gawd, I Love New Orleans*. New Orleans: FLAPS Publisher, 1997. Print.

Scott, James C. *Seeing Like a State: How Certain Schemes to Improve the Human Condition Have Failed.* New Haven, CT: Yale University Press, 1998. Print.

Séjour, Victor. "Le Mulâtre." *Paroles d'honneur: Écrits de Créoles de couleur néo-orléanais (1837–1872).* Edited by Chris Michaelides. Shreveport: Éditions Tintamarre, 2004. Print.

Sillery, Barbara. "The Hidden Nation: The Houmas Speak." *Mardi Gras, Gumbo, and Zydeco: Readings in Louisiana Culture.* Edited by Marcia Gaudet and James C. McDonald. Jackson: University Press of Mississippi, 2003. Print.

Spear, Jennifer M. *Race, Sex, and Social Order in Early New Orleans.* Baltimore: Johns Hopkins University Press, 2009. Print.

Spitzer, Nick. "*Monde Créole:* The Cultural World of French Louisiana Creoles and the Creolization of World Cultures." *Creolization as Cultural Creativity.* Edited by Robert Baron and Ana C. Cara. Jackson: University Press of Mississippi, 2011. Print.

Starr, S. Frederick. *New Orleans Unmasqued.* New Orleans: Édition Dedeaux, 1985. Print.

Stoddard, Amos. *Sketches, Historical and Descriptive of Louisiana.* Baton Rouge: Claitor's Publishing Division, 1974. Print.

Sublette, Ned. *The World That Made New Orleans: From Spanish Silver to Congo Square.* Chicago: Lawrence Hill Books, 2008. Print.

Testut, Charles. *Calisto.* Edited by Elizabeth C. Lyles. Shreveport: Les Cahiers du Tintamarre, 2009. Print.

——. *Le Vieux Salomon: Une famille d'esclaves au XIXe siècle.* Shreveport: Les Cahiers du Tintamarre, 2003. Print.

——. *Saint-Denis.* Edited by Courtney Herzog. Shreveport: Les Cahiers du Tintamarre, 2003. Print.

Thierry, Camille. *Les Vagabondes: Poésies Américaines.* Edited by Frans C. Amelinckx and May Rush Gwin Waggoner. Shreveport: Éditions Tintamarre, 2004. Print.

Thompson, Shirley Elizabeth. *Exiles at Home: The Struggle to Become American in Creole New Orleans.* Cambridge, MA: Harvard University Press, 2009. Print.

Toledano, Roulhac, and Mary Louise Christovich. *New Orleans Architecture: Faubourg Tremé to the Bayou Road.* Vol. 6. Gretna, LA: Pelican Publishing Co., 2003.

Tolzmann, Don Heinrich, ed. *Louisiana's German Heritage: Louis Voss' Introductory History.* Bowie, MD: Heritage Books, 1994. Print.

Tonti, Henri de. *Relations de la Louisiane et du fleuve Mississippi.* Amsterdam: Bernard, 1720. Microform.

Toussaint, François-Vincent. *Eclaircissement sur les Mœurs.* Amsterdam: Chez Marc-Michel Rey, 1762. Print.

Tucker, Susan, ed. *New Orleans Cuisine: Fourteen Signature Dishes and Their Histories.* Jackson: University Press of Mississippi, 2009. Print.

Tujague, François. *Chroniques louisianaises.* Shreveport: Les Cahiers du Tintamarre, 2003. Print.

Upton, Dell. "Grid as Design Method: The Spatial Imagination in Early New Orleans." *Architecture, Design Methods, Inca Structures: Festschrift for Jean-Pierre Protezen*. Edited by Johanna Dehlinger and Hans Dehlinger. Kassel: Kassel University Press, 2009. Print.

Usner, Daniel H., Jr. "Between Creoles and Yankees: The Discursive Representation of Colonial Louisiana in American History." *French Colonial Louisiana and the Atlantic World*. Edited by Bradley G. Bond. Baton Rouge: Louisiana State University Press, 2005. Print.

———. *Indians, Settlers, and Slaves in a Frontier Exchange Economy*. Chapel Hill: University of North Carolina Press, 1992. Print.

Valdman, Albert, ed. *French and Creole in Louisiana*. New York: Plenum, 1997. Print.

Valdman, Albert, et al. *Dictionary of Louisiana French: As Spoken in Cajun, Creole, and American Indian Communities*. Jackson: University Press of Mississippi, 2010. Print.

Vallette de Laudun, M. *Journal d'un voyage à la Louisiane, fait en 1720 par M.***, capitaine de vaisseau du Roi*. La Haye: Chez Musier fils & Fournier, 1768. Print.

Van Kien, Thai. "Georges Pompidou, Pham Duy Khiêm, Léopold Senghor." *Les Écrivains de la Négritude et de la Créolité. Actes du Troisième Colloque International Francophone du Canton de Payrac (Lot) Organisé par l'Association des Écrivains de Langue Française*. Paris: Sepeg International, 1993. Print.

Vernet, Julien. "Citizen Laussat and the St. Julien Case: Royalists and Revolutionaries in Early Nineteenth-Century Louisiana." *Louisiana History: The Journal of the Louisiana Historical Association* 51, no. 2 (2010): 195–204. Print.

Viatte, Auguste. *Histoire Littéraire de l'Amérique Française des Origines à 1950*. Paris: Presses Universitaires de France, 1954. Print.

Vieux Carré Survey. Historic New Orleans Collection. 1966. Print.

Waggoner, May Rush Gwin, ed. *Le Plus Beau Païs du monde: Completing the Picture of Propriety Louisiana 1699–1722*. Lafayette: Center for Louisiana Studies, 2005. Print.

Walker, Daniel E. *No More, No More: Slavery and Cultural Resistance in Havana and New Orleans*. Minneapolis: University of Minnesota Press, 2004. Print.

Watts, Edward. *In This Remote Country: French Colonial Culture in the Anglo-American Imagination, 1780–1860*. Chapel Hill: University of North Carolina Press, 2006. Print.

Weeks, Charles A. *Paths to a Middle Ground: The Diplomacy of Natchez, Boukfouka, Nogales, and San Fernando de las Barrancas, 1791–1795*. Tuscaloosa: University of Alabama Press, 2010. Print.

Wilson, Samuel Jr. "Louisiana Drawings by Alexandre De Batz." *Journal of the Society of Architectural Historians* 22, no. 2 (1963): 75–89. Print.

———. "The Plantation of the Company of the Indies." *Louisiana History: The Journal of the Louisiana Historical Association* 31, no. 2 (1990): 161–91. Print.

Wiston-Glynn, A. W. *John Law of Lauriston, Financier and Statesman*. Edinburgh: E. Saunders & Co., 1909. Print.

Zimra, Clarisse. "Daughters of Mayotte, Sons of Frantz: The Unrequited Self in Caribbean Literature." *An Introduction to Caribbean Francophone Writing: Guadeloupe and Martinique.* Edited by Sam Haigh. Oxford: Berg, 1999. Print.

INDEX

CPSIA information can be obtained
at www.ICGtesting.com
Printed in the USA
LVHW021514061118
596179LV00004B/731/P

9 781496 820303